After-School Theatre Programs
for At-Risk Teenagers

After-School Theatre Programs for At-Risk Teenagers

PHILIP ZWERLING

McFarland & Company, Inc., Publishers
Jefferson, North Carolina, and London

LIBRARY OF CONGRESS CATALOGUING-IN-PUBLICATION DATA

Zwerling, Philip.
    After-school theatre programs for at-risk teenagers / Philip
Zwerling.
      p.   cm.
    Includes bibliographical references and index.

    ISBN-13: 978-0-7864-3187-8
    softcover : 50# alkaline paper ∞

    1. Problem youth—Services for—United States. 2. Juvenile
delinquency—Prevention. 3. After-school programs—United
States. I. Title.
HV1421.Z84 2008
362.7083—dc22   2007040365

British Library cataloguing data are available

Cover photograph ©2008 PhotoSpin

Manufactured in the United States of America

McFarland & Company, Inc., Publishers
  Box 611, Jefferson, North Carolina 28640
    www.mcfarlandpub.com

For Susie

Table of Contents

Preface

I DIDN'T WANT TO WRITE THIS BOOK. I hoped to search it out on a library shelf or stumble upon it on a bookstore table where I could pick it up and use it. But there was no book like this until now. There were books and articles and Websites, of course, on community theatre, full of marvelous projects for teenagers, senior citizens, prisoners, abused women, etc. They contained tantalizing anecdotes of people grasping insights in drama and using those "aha" moments to turn their lives around. But no one had the cold hard facts, the numbers and percentages, the experimental data to convince the skeptical that this creative art worked better than all the jail cells, cops on the beat and drug therapies in which our society had already foolishly invested billions of dollars.

This book represents four years of my research, observation, and participation in the field of community-based theatre where people are every day doing incredible and largely unheralded work. In the end I had to write the book I had hoped to find, praying that perhaps a few more souls, a few legislators, a few educators, police chiefs, funding agencies and philanthropists might suggest spending a few more dollars to make theatre and save lives.

I left the ministry in 1993 after 20 years of serving churches, and I went back to school to study first playwriting and then theatre. When people heard of this vocational segue, the response I heard again and again was, "Oh, that's a natural, after all church is a kind of theatre and being a minister is a kind of acting." When I first got this reaction I was insulted. For me, theatre and acting represented fantasy and illusion and mere entertainment and I thought that what I had been doing as a minister had been true and real and life changing. Slowly I began to realize that theatre can have just as great an impact for good in the world, both on individual lives and on our society as a whole, as any church.

As a minister, I sat by the bed of elderly people as they died; I presided at solemn and life-changing events like weddings (straight and gay) and funerals; I visited people in hospitals and in prison; I entered war zones in Central America; I defied my own government to shelter refugees in my home and in my church. More recently, as a theatre scholar and practitioner, I saw disaffected and rebellious teenagers from our poorest urban areas act out their deepest fears and most hidden hopes, their conflicts and insecurities, on stages private and public and come away changed for the better.

In a long-ago directing class with the late Dr. Bob Egan at the University of California, Santa Barbara, I first heard the name Augusto Boal and I set off on a years-long exploration of the history, theory, and, finally, the efficacy of community-based theatre.

Writing is a lonely job but making theatre is communal. Many people helped me along the way: my mentor Dr. Robert Potter and his colleagues at UCSB, Dr. Catherine Cole, Dr. Simon Williams, Dr. Thomas Scheff, and Dr. Shane Jimerson; the practitioners who shared their wisdom and experiences: Augusto Boal, Doug Paterson, Brent Blair, Mady Schutzman, Yolanda Broyles-Gonzalez, Nancy Davis, Jose Santana, and Leigh Curran; the folks who sat still for interviews and the teenagers who shared their unflagging enthusiasm—many of them are listed in the bibliography. Special thanks to Kathleen Nunn, an undergraduate at Ursinus College who served as my research assistant (and many thanks to Ursinus for funding that role) for the appendix listing of over 100 after-school theatre programs working with teenagers across the country, a list gathered here for the first time. Finally but most importantly, thanks to my wife Susan, who let me complain and whine and then bucked me up and got me back to work.

CHAPTER 1

A Boy Like Johnny

I STILL RECALL THE LIGHTS FLASHING silently in the night sky that October as my friends and I, all seven- and eight-year-olds, craned our necks for a peak at the tiny, round machine orbiting our earth. For my generation, those twinkling lights of the little *Sputnik* satellite rang alarm bells in every American home and school. This 1957 Soviet success added a space race to the decade-old Cold War competition and led to finger-pointing at home and pointed questions in Congress about how the Russians had surpassed us technologically and whether the United States would be left behind in the race for supremacy. But the issue I remember best and the indictment directed straight at me and my little friends came in Rudolf Flesch's book of the same year: *Why Johnny Can't Read*. Mike Davidow's later *Why Johnny Can't Read and Ivan Can* made the charge clear. It turned out that it was all our fault; that we kids had failed, failed our schoolwork, our upward striving parents of the "Greatest Generation" who had won their war, and failed our country.

A hundred thousand Russian eight-year-olds caught us wasting our time reading comic books and watching television cartoons and, doing their patriotic duty, read better, thought harder, and aimed higher than all the little Johnnys my age. History, they say, repeats and today I see another American society in trouble, blaming its young people and once again the charge is misdirected. But raising the issue can again help us find a solution.

Sputnik led directly to the formation of NASA and the race to the moon. Revamped American schools stressed science and math, academic

3

rigor, and accelerated learning. In the end, the United States landed the only men on the moon and the Soviet Union imploded 20 years after that "giant leap for mankind." Today, without a space race, arms race, or knowledge race the U.S. public school system slides into crisis and, with youth violence at epidemic levels, corollary questions must be asked: why can't today's Johnny stay in school, off drugs, and out of jail?

My generation hid under our school desks in fear of incoming Russian ICBMs, but today's youth "duck and cover" to escape teen bullies wielding shotguns in places normally tranquil, retreats like Littleton, Paducah, and Pearl. This sort of domestic terrorism takes far more American lives each year than al-Qaeda and the Taliban combined. But without an identifiable foreign foe challenging us for global dominance, no one seems to recognize today's domestic danger, the loss of a generation of teenagers to the newest public health menace identified by the U.S. surgeon general: youth violence.

In 2005, 17,000 Americans were murdered within our country's borders. Lawrence Sherman, criminologist at the University of Pennsylvania asks: "Why aren't we talking about these deaths and how they could be prevented? Why isn't the reality of daily terrorism on the streets of our cities worth as much attention as the possibility of international terrorism?"[1]

In the next chapter I'll detail the danger and lay out more of the frightening statistics, but first I want you to see the human face of the problem. This time it's not just Johnny. It might Juan, or Carlos, Rena, LaQuandra, or Shaquille. Whether they can read or not, they are still potential victims of beatings and shootings and sometimes they're the perpetrators as well. As Philadelphia deputy police commissioner Richard Ross puts it: "Kids not old enough to drive are sustaining gunshot wounds [and carrying guns]."[2] My 1950's Long Island, New York, Levittown-like subdivision was entirely white and a homogenous mass of intact nuclear middle-class families. School bullies struggled to stake out their territory with their fists rather than automatic weapons. Today's at-risk teens may be white, Latino, Asian, or black and there may be no adult at home most, or all, of the time. Worse today, "kids" according to Jeffrey Roth, associate director at the Jerry Lee Center of Criminology, "get used to growing up in an environment where [shootings] happen a lot and then they don't think twice about doing that."[3]

Three years ago, when I stepped off the perfectly tranquil, groomed, and sun-splashed campus of the University of California, Santa Barbara, as a graduate student in theatre, and into the narrow, noisy and graffiti-decorated streets of next-door Isla Vista, or later traveled down the coast into the Oxnard and Venice ghettos, the teens hanging out on the corners and the iron bars on the windows of the homes made it clear I wasn't in Kansas, or Long Island, anymore. I didn't know what I was getting into but I thought I had some ideas that might help. And in some ways I was right, even as I discovered how much I had to learn. I'd like you to see what I saw and feel what I felt because only when you understand the problem can we move on to a solution. And just as our country successfully answered the challenge of *Sputnik*, so can we also solve the problem of youth violence and get American teens back on track. This isn't a story about "ain't it awful," though it is awful, but a story of how we can succeed for a new generation just as we have in the past.

This Johnny whom I got to know and like, Juan really, lives in Isla Vista. Of course, his name's not really Juan, but he is real and this is a real story. When I first met him, Juan was 17, a small, wiry kid, with sandy colored hair, fine bones, and a little soul patch of a beard beneath his lower lip. He stood about 5' 6" and seemed just a shade brighter and slightly more mature than his peers. Always neatly dressed in worn clothes, quiet, and self-contained, he tended to fade into the background. He spoke both English and Spanish fluently but had few memories of his native Mexico. Without close friends, Juan usually walked into the Teen Center alone. It took a while to get to know him. I was still getting to know him when they took him away to jail.

Squeezed between the lush campus of the University of California and the Pacific Ocean, Isla Vista houses 20,000 other people besides Juan, 60 percent of them college students, most of them Anglo and most from privileged backgrounds. The rest are working-class Latinos with little hope they'll ever enroll in the university they see each day. Almost everyone rents. Rents are high and both populations have to pack tenants into every available space to get by. Supposedly the most densely settled community west of the Mississippi, Isla Vista is home to 58 people per acre. The average household annual income is just $23,800, compared to a state average of $64,700.[4]

Older and married, I didn't hang out with the university's undergraduates very much, but I got to know the streets of Isla Vista pretty well when it came time for me to make the move from teen theatre director to dissertation researcher midway through my first year with the program. Our campus Human Subjects Board required me to get signed consent forms from all of the parents of the teens I would be working with. I'd thought "human subjects" and "informed consent" were terms used for drug trials and experimental surgeries and confined to the sciences rather than research in the humanities. However, because I was going to be asking children about school attendance, fighting, drug use and sex, I was first trained and then tested in the legal protections for these human subjects and my questionnaires and release forms all had to be approved by the board.

The upside was that I got into the homes of all the teens I would be following through the year. I translated the forms into Spanish and used my fluency with the language to track down and speak with the parents. All lived in rented units that were small, packed with kids, and invariably clean and well kept. I gave up on daytime visits since I never found anyone at home until the workday was done. Although I was a stranger and an Anglo, all of the parents were happy to speak to me and all signed the releases. They hoped the theatre program would be an educational enrichment for their kids. Each apartment complex was exclusively Latino. Next door or down the block were the student apartments, often run down, vandalized, and always noisy.

The college kids drink and party. On weekends music blares from open apartment windows while hundreds congregate in the streets below, socializing, showing off, and cruising. Special occasions are marked with the ritual burning of couches dragged off porches and into the streets. Each semester a drunken student dies after a fall from the nearby cliffs onto the rocks below or fails to return from an ill-advised midnight swim. In 2001, UCSB freshman David Attias, son of a prominent television director, mentally disturbed and racing his car down an Isla Vista street, careened through an evening party crowd and killed four students.

The Latino teens attend area public schools, work at menial jobs, or are unemployed. They skateboard, hang out, and sometimes run with gangs. One evening I asked some of the kids how many gangs there were in the Isla Vista area (also including Goleta and Santa Barbara) and they came up with a total of 18 with colorful names like Hoe Train and South Side Ladies (girl gangs), Goleta Trece (taggers of the ubiquitous G13 graffiti), Los Locos, Tres Puntos, 3MC, and the Picasso Gang (not artists but teens who claim Picasso Street as their turf). Juan lives on Sabado Tarde Street, or Saturday Afternoon Street, where parties are frequent. Scrapes between the college students and Latino teens are common with allegations of racism and violence made by each against the other.

One Isla Vista homeowner, identified as Mrs. Gallery, described her hometown to the *Santa Barbara News-Press*:

More than half the people who live here are between the ages of 18 and 23 and they have no one to answer to. They don't have to answer to the University, because the University has made it clear that anything that happens off-campus is none of their business. They don't have to answer to their parents because they are not around. They don't have to answer to adult neighbors because there are none. The only people they have to answer to are the cops and that's only when things have gone way too far.[5]

In June 2002 the Santa Barbara Grand Jury called Isla Vista "a community in neglect" and cited problems of crime, congestion, overcrowding, poor lighting, and blight.[6]

When middle-class homeowners in Goleta voted to incorporate as a new city in 2002, they neatly gerrymandered the city limits around the Isla Vista community to exclude a population they described as "uninformed," "lazy," "easily manipulated," "bloc voters," and "uncommitted to the community welfare."[7]

Juan lives there, sharing an apartment with an older brother. I soon learn that they don't get along and that Juan's mom moved out a year earlier to stay with her boyfriend. Juan has a grandmother and other family in Mexico. He came here as a young child and is a U.S. citizen. Whenever he and his brother hit a rough patch, his brother throws him out and then Juan looks for a friend to stay with or sleeps on the streets. Sometimes he goes to school and sometimes he doesn't. He doesn't see much percentage in it. One day he got suspended for speaking Spanish while working in the school cafeteria in violation of English-only rules. He speaks English just fine but sees no reason to limit himself to just one language.

Juan drops in on our theatre group meetings at the Teen Center. It's an ugly one-story stucco edifice, a little tumble down, in the center of Isla Vista. The director has given me free use of a small meeting room to get started, and I've modeled our program on an older and successful City at Peace group in nearby Santa Barbara, recruiting university undergraduates to help play acting games and discussions of community and personal problems with the hope of shaping these issues into a public performance at the end of the year.

When we outgrow the little room, we move into the central recreation room one evening a week and try to create a little private space with movable dividers. Nearby are cast-off couches, a television, an old stereo, and a wall of newly acquired computers on which teens are supposed to be trained from a special grant program. There's a director and his aide, both male and Latino, and a white female Americorps volunteer who becomes more and more angry about the sexism she perceives in the center staff as the year progresses. She leaves at the end of the first year.

I'm the naif here. A theatre ethnography course requires us to write a grant proposal. I figure rather than just write up some proposal as an academic exercise, it would be better to write a real proposal and submit it to a real grantor and get real money in addition to a grade. I hope I can score a film projector or some hardware for Santa Barbara's City at Peace but the folks there surprise me by asking me to propose funding for a new Isla Vista program. No good deed goes unpunished and, sure enough, the university awards me a grant, the undergraduates volunteer to help and then disappear, and before I know it I'm running a teen program in Isla Vista, without any experience, any training, or any help. Foolishly, I decide it's a great place to try out the forum theatre techniques of Augusto Boal I've been studying in class. But I'll write more about that in chapter 8.

Boys and girls from the neighborhood come into the center after school for tutoring and to hang out. Most of the kids, ages 12 to 18, know each other and include batches of siblings. The director steers them to my new program on Thursday nights and I meet Juan and 20 other teens, all but one Latino. I studied Spanish for many years but their streetwise slang often eludes me.

Violence is a given for teens in Isla Vista. Shopkeepers chase the skateboarders off the sidewalks. Parents get drunk at home, college students get drunk on the streets, and shouting and fighting follow. The teens explain to me that school fights are "like weddings," that is, community occasions that bring everyone together to watch what is an important social event. Gossip is the fuel for the flare-ups and every teen has a story of carrying tales "he said this about you..." and "she told me this about her..." so that the swirl of rivalries and petty slights keep everyone on guard and maneuvers the teens into having to fight to save face with their peers.

Violence is built into the culture as well. When I think about trying a little of Jacob Moreno's sociometry just for fun, where teens must silently arrange themselves in order of height, feelings, or birth dates, it's the more experienced Americorps volunteer who tells me I can't ask the boys to publicly reveal the month and day of their nativity since birthdays are the time for "friends" to gather and beat up the birthday boy. For me, the work is a continual lesson in cultural differences.

Violence isn't just a male issue either. Little Maria, 14, slender and petite, with a squeaky voice, shares stories of ongoing fights at home; physical altercations with her father in which they trade obscenities and blows.

Perhaps because of this, Maria is always one of the first girls to resort to hitting in a disagreement among the teens. The girls fight with girls; the boys with boys, and, although I never see a boy actually strike a girl, I certainly see the boys try to physically intimidate the girls, menacing them with their size, bulk, and swagger.

And the violence enters from outside the group. When we dramatize the real life problems they face, the most frequently mentioned problem after family is police brutality and harassment. Nearly all the teens have stories of being hassled by the Isla Vista police, a problem they uniformly ascribe to their youth and ethnicity. Juan has a legal driver's license but gets pulled over by the police all the time. According to Juan, his evening strolls in I.V. are regularly interrupted by police on bikes or in cars asking to see his identification and questioning him about drugs, frisking him, and warning him to stay out of trouble, for no other reason, to his mind, than being Mexican and a teenager.

The violence endemic in their lives shapes the teens emotionally and behaviorally. As one of our theatre games, I introduce the "trust exercise" where one person stands in the middle of the circle and then lets themself fall backward or to the side, trusting that their friends will catch them before they hit the floor. These kids, however, think it's hilarious to let people actually fall and we have to abandon the exercise before someone gets hurt. Many of our "cooperation" games literally fell flat with teens who are more interested in showing each other up than in working together. Their ethos seems to be "do unto others" before they do something bad unto you.

It should come as no surprise then that halfway through our first year the director closes down the Teen Center for a week. There have been three fights in a single weekend on the center grounds. Several kids had to be taken to the hospital. The culprits escaped and it was unclear if they were locals or interlopers. One fight had led to another and there always seemed to be someone looking to even the score. The director approaches me: Did I, he wonders, think it possible that our theatre games and role-playing, often loud and physical, "have gotten the kids hopped up." No, I tell him; if anything our program is designed as a safety valve for feelings and energy, a place to experiment with nonviolent solutions to everyday problems. In fact, for these teens violence is too often a way to add spice and excitement to a very limited and limiting world. We've been trying to show them some alternative strategies.

Theirs is a world limited in ways I haven't even imagined. We play the game "Have you ever...?" a variation of "musical chairs." One person standing in the center of the circle asks "Have you ever...?" and fills in the blank describing any activity you might guess people have done like driving a car, skateboarding, etc. Then everyone who has done that activity must get up and seek a new chair while the person in the center, who is "it," takes theirs. One night a university student working with me stands in the middle of our circle and calls out: "Have you ever gone surfing?" Although we are gathered less than a half-mile from the ocean and popular surfing beaches, not one of the teens rises from their chair even as all of the college students get up. For working-class Latinos, the Anglo surfing culture is simply outside of, though right next to, their little world.

I see all of these contradictions, limitations and possibilities converge in Juan. One night as we sat in our circle, Sara writes furiously in her notebook. Other teens peek at her work. One asks: "What's that?" "Poetry," says Sara. "Can we hear it?" another wants to know. So Sara reads her free verse. I have to say it's god-awful poetry filled with trite images of teen angst and lots of whining about parents and school. Of course, the other teens love it. "Have you got more?" She has lots more and keeps reading to a rapt audience that would not have listened for two minutes to "good" poetry read by their teacher at school. When Sara has exhausted her material, Juan jumps up: "I'll get my poetry. I've been writing for a long time. I'll be right back." I didn't know Juan wrote poetry. I wouldn't have guessed he even knew what it was. But, sure enough, 20 minutes later Juan is back with sheaves of unbound paper on which he has penciled in longhand his thoughts and feelings. A boy I had never seen read a book or mention an author had been privately writing for months. The group sits as quietly as I had ever seen them and listens as Juan reads his work. Again, I wouldn't call it good poetry but I would call it personal, powerful, and heartfelt.

As Juan reads, one of his older friends, an Asian boy of college age, sticks his head in the room and catches Juan's eye. Juan waves him off this time. He's busy. This is important to him. But many nights in the past I have seen the same signal entice Juan to get up, head for the door and exit into the night. I'd tried a few times to invite these friends in but they always refused. Juan has to go with them when they show up. I always ask him to stay and question him about what they do together without ever getting a straight answer. I don't honestly know what they do but I suspect it's not good. My own guess is that Juan hooks college kids up with drugs from his side of the barrio, but I have no proof for these suspicions.

In January we take the Isla Vista teens to a gathering with the Santa Barbara City at Peace teens at the Casa de Maria Retreat Center. As we drive through Montecito and its streets lined with multimillion dollar homes, Eduardo exclaims with surprise: "So this is where the rich people live." Javier tells me he's been looking forward to the retreat because it means "I get away from my family for the weekend." The retreat is difficult because the Santa Barbara group is older, more heavily female, and Anglo and the two groups clash frequently. However, the Isla Vista teens have a great time playing on the beautiful grounds of the old estate and swimming contentedly, much to my surprise, in the unheated outdoor pool on a cool winter day.

Less appetizing for me are the violent, homophobic, sexist and racist song lyrics I listen to on the way home. I let the boys use my CD player to play discs that they have burned of their favorite rap songs. One line I jot down later is representative: "shut the fuck up nigger bitch." When I raise objections to the words, they tell me this is the music they like and that they don't necessarily agree with sentiments of the singer. But the lyrics seem to fit comfortably into their world and the personal stories they've told me.

Adapting an idea from Santa Barbara City at Peace where he also works with teens, Tim, a 25-year-old graduate of the university's theatre program brings in a video camera and the kids take renewed interest in our theatrical dramatizations when they have the opportunity to see their recorded efforts played back for them on the old Teen Center television. For a little while they become the stars. One evening we ask them to create their own television commercials because we think that having seen commercials all their lives this may be an exercise they can relate to. A group of the boys come up with a rather obscene video about a pill taken to enhance penis size but a group of girls answers effectively with an ad for "Detection" a product designed to "end erection" and another about "Patrol" for when "you can't control." Sex is a source of interest and intrigue but some of these kids know firsthand what it's like to have too many babies in the family or have friends who left school after getting pregnant.

Even more effective, from my point of view, is the game we play the next week. We ask the teens what dreams they have for their futures. They name things like "going to college," "graduating high school," and Juan's "finding work as a mechanic." We ask them to first stand in a circle and then to lie down with their feet touching and their heads pointing outward like the spokes of a wheel. We ask them to each take an orange as a physical representation of their dreams and put it at the top of their heads. We invite them to stand up and ask them how they expect to reach their dreams now represented as the oranges on the floor. The oranges are physically out of reach as they stand within the circle. The kids give up quickly and decide they can't reach their dreams after all. We challenge them to think about it some more. Finally, someone gets the idea that if they all hold one person at a time and that person leans all the way out they can retrieve their orange. It only works if everyone cooperates and at last everyone has their orange and, perhaps, a new inspiration about how to reach their dreams.

Our City at Peace teens participate in the theatre games that are physical ("Knots," "Kitty Wants a Corner," "Jailbreak," "Killer," etc.) enthusiastically, gorge themselves on pizza, and, more reluctantly dramatize their personal issues. Lack of privacy, kids arriving late and leaving early, and a tendency to form cliques and trade obscene remarks in Spanish, regularly disrupt the group work.

We structure each meeting in a similar manner: (1) one or two theatre games; (2) a check-in where everyone shares good and bad personal experiences of the previous week; (3) determining and then reviewing the ground rules; (4) dramatizing a problem, or tackling listening exercises, or conflict resolution exercises; (5) eat pizza; (6) play more games or dramatics; and (7) close the evening in a circle.

Ground rules, or agreements, generated by the teens themselves include:

1. no put-downs
2. no drugs
3. no fighting
4. confidentiality
5. right to pass
6. right not to come
7. respect each other
8. no interruptions
9. tell the truth
10. if you leave, you can't return that same evening
11. shared authority

They usually break at least three of the rules each night but, for the most part, keep coming back each week.

We go to see live theatre shows with diminishing success. Everyone seems to enjoy seeing Teatro de Esperanza, in which much of the dialogue is in Spanish, perform on the UCSB campus, but the kids grow noisily disruptive when I take them to see Leilani Chan's one-woman show presenting Hawaiian culture, which is foreign to them, and finally none want to attend a production of *The Diviners*, put on by the Santa Barbara Youth Theatre at the Center Stage Theatre. I guess we produce enough drama in-house ourselves.

Their own dramatizations deal with intriguing experiences: Edgardo was accused, unjustly he maintains, of stealing food from his school cafeteria; Martina "beats up a white girl" at school and is suspended; Maria has physical fights with her father that are always fodder for our stage; the local turf battles that pit teens identified as "gangsters" against those known as "skaters"; Juan's trouble at school for speaking Spanish while working in the high school cafeteria; and a boy who is accused of looking down a girl's blouse. Juan also has an ongoing problem that hangs over us: his brother has informed him that he is to be kicked out of his home on his approaching 18th birthday. What happens then is anyone's guess.

The group's role is to brainstorm possible solutions to these real-life scenarios and then dramatize the problem and its possible solutions as well. At first, most of the offered "solutions" are violent in nature. Why not just beat up the "gangsters" or blow up the school cafeteria? But after rejecting these as impractical, though fun, the young people often came up with creative options.

For example, one evening some of the girls bring up the behavior of boys at their high school, where the guys hang out and make sexual comments and rude noises as the girls walk by. We ask for volunteers to dramatize the situation and four or five of the boys immediately jump up and take their position at one end of the room. As the three girls walk by them, ostensibly on their way to class, the boys, needing no dialogue coaching or ideas for this one, begin making all manner of animal noises while offering sexual come-ons and innuendoes in Spanish.

When the rowdy demonstration ends, the participants share their reactions: as expected the girls are unhappy with the boys' behavior, which the boys justify as all in good, if not clean, fun. Ideas for resolving the conflict are then solicited from the group at large.

None of the suggestions seems right, even the ones about beating someone up, until someone suggests "change places." Of course! Now we have the girls hang out at the end of the room and instruct the boys to walk by them. The girls have difficulty being as outspoken and obnoxious as the boys at first but soon overcome this initial inhibition and throw themselves into the roles. The boys struggle to walk by without returning the comments in kind. After a bit, we get each group to play the scene within the strictures of their opposing set of sexual stereotypes. The girls boisterously offer catcalls and various anatomical descriptions of the individual boys. The boys walk by, trying mightily not to respond, or even listen, heads down, faces beet red.

You can imagine the debriefing that follows: the girls unanimously affirm: "that's the way it is, hoped you like a taste of your own medicine." The boys are sheepish and alternately combative, angry at the girls, and ill at ease with their own disempowerment and embarrassment.

Could this be a real learning experience, maybe even a catharsis resulting in a behavioral change? Using mimesis, the imitation of an action, that is, imitating the actions of the boys on the school playground, we had, as the Greek philosopher Plato feared in such undertakings, stirred up all kinds of emotions: anger, fear, shame, sexual longing, etc. and discharged them. Plato wanted to ban playwrights from his idealized Republic for putting make-believe onstage and agitating an audience. But, as his student, Aristotle, countered Plato and defended mimesis, we had attained new knowledge and a catharsis. The knowledge the boys gained was what it felt like to be ogled and put down in public. That new knowledge was not simply intellectual, I saw that it was felt in the body as well as known in the mind, if we are to make that mind/body bifurcation. The result that night was a spontaneous insight and the expression of suppressed emotional responses. The acting out of emotions lead to a form of emotional cleansing.

Would the playground be a different place the next day because of this dramatization? I don't know. Had the conditions been created for changes to occur? Clearly, yes.

In the spring I begin my studies observing similar after-school theatre programs in Oxnard and Venice and Tim assumes responsibility for the Isla Vista group. When I drop by a month later, I get to see the new skits they're working on and hear about their plans for a public performance. Maria, Sara, Edgardo and the others are still there. I don't see Juan, though, and when I ask, I'm told he's in jail awaiting trial for burglary. No one seems to know if he really did it, whether it's drug related, or if his brother really threw him out. If he's not guilty of this crime, Juan may well have been guilty of something else. All I know is that he was a nice kid who wrote poetry and had a lot of potential.

Why start a book about solutions and hope with a story of a sad ending? Partly because it's true and partly because right now sad endings predominate for a lot of our young people. And partly because I realized that everything I've done and written is for Juan, and ten thousand kids like him. If he'd stayed in the program, if he'd written more poetry and dealt less drugs, if his brother had let him stay in their home, if any one of a thousand things had been different, Juan would be a creative, contributing member of society. Now he's in jail and his life is not likely to get better. As I'll detail in the next chapter, jail time usually leads not to rehabilitation but to more jail time. In later chapters you'll meet lots of other Johnnys and Juans who are clearly benefiting from after-school theatre programs that keep them in school and out of trouble. In the end, Juan's loss is a signal in the sky to our society just like that old *Sputnik*; because it's our loss too. And, perhaps, like *Sputnik*, our present failures in saving our youth can shame us into a new race to save our teens, a race that can be won not by NASA, but by a hundred different after-school theatre programs already struggling, struggling for funding, volunteers, and support, all across our country.

CHAPTER 2

Why Johnny Can't Stay in School, Off Drugs, or Out of Jail

YOU'VE MET JOHNNY AND YOU'VE SEEN HIS LIFE. He's real, he's unique, and yet he's just a statistic in a much bigger, sadder, and scarier picture. Youth violence, violence committed by young people and violence directed at them, bedevils America. Though many programs have been developed and billions of dollars have already been expended, success eludes us, threatening our citizens' safety and our society's future. One emerging possibility with unexplored potential is the imaginative art of theatre. After years of study, I have become convinced that modest, inexpensive, after-school theatre programs, housed in schools, churches, and youth centers, staffed by volunteers, and multiplied across the country, can stem the tide of youth violence. But before I describe in detail how and why theatre works, how the very process of making theatre defuses violent antipathies, frustrations, prejudices, and fears, and leads to personal growth and maturity, let us examine the extent of the growing problem and, in cataloging a long chain of ineffective responses, see the common threads of coercion and punishment that have doomed our efforts to date.

Once labeled "juvenile delinquents," "disadvantaged" and "inner-city youth," the perpetrators and victims of youth violence, ages 13 to 19, are now labeled "at-risk teenagers." This relatively new term dates from 1983 and was coined to reflect a broad category of youth who are "at risk of not reaching a goal that ordinarily would have been attainable" such as academic success and high school graduation.[1] The term is valuable in bringing together the myriad of challenges to their health and well-being that our teenagers face today, and valuable also because it describes only a potential and not a fixed category: these kids are "at risk" right now but they don't have to remain "at risk" one day longer.

Specifically, these are the teenagers we see in foster homes, continuation schools, group homes, the probation system, and juvenile detention centers and who have typically had problems with drug abuse, school truancy, gang membership, and the criminal justice system. They generally, though not always, come from lower-income homes, have experienced sexual and/or physical abuse, and are in danger of dropping out of school or going to prison.

Our nation, for all of its affluence, has the highest rate of youth violence in the world. Although violent crime is down by one-third in the United States since its historic peak in 1993, youth violence remained at "epidemic" proportions in 2001.[2] For example, in the year 2000 the rate of violent crimes against individuals increased 17 percent over the previous year in California's schools according to the State Department of Education.[3] Violent crime overall ticked upward in 2005 for the first time in a decade.

Much teen violence is never reported to authorities. "Police arrest nearly two million juveniles each year.... Self report studies indicate that if citizens and police detected and apprehended all adolescents committing delinquent acts, very few juveniles, probably less than 10% would escape being labeled delinquents."[4] In one study of 847 boys and girls 13 to 16 years old, 88 percent of those interviewed confessed to at least one offense for which they could have been adjudicated delinquents. However, only 9 percent of their offenses were detected by police and only 2 percent of them suffered legal consequences.[5]

Many teenagers are indeed caught, however, and 368 youths per 100,000 in the population, more than one teen in every 300, are locked up. Dr. Aaron Kipnis, author of *Angry Young Men* and president of the Fatherhood Coalition, was himself once classified as a juvenile delinquent. His story is personal in its particulars but representative of the challenges facing tens of thousands of young people. From age four to nine Kipnis shuttled between half a dozen foster homes and from ages 11 to 23 he was continuously on probation or on parole. Kipnis spent seven of his teen years in jail or on the streets of Los Angeles and San Francisco. He slept in abandoned buildings, stole from shops, abused drugs, and prostituted his body. He fought off rape, was twice beaten by gay bashers and attempted suicide three times as a teenager. The unusual part of his story is that he turned his life around, returned to school, and earned a Ph.D. Having survived the streets, he knows whereof he writes and the situation he describes is grave: "Today American boys suffer higher rates of homicide, suicide, incarceration, functional illiteracy, school failure, child poverty, gang involvement, gun carrying, drug abuse, violent victimization, male prostitution, sexual assault, AIDS, and homelessness than youth in any other Western industrialized nation."[6]

As Kipnis makes plain, at-risk youth face a litany of problems: drug and alcohol abuse, early sexual activity, sexual abuse, dropping out of school, physical abuse, violence at school, suicide, poverty, and homelessness. Let us look at the dimensions of each of these problems, at how they intersect, and at their cumulative negative impact on youth.

Teenage drug and alcohol abuse is rampant. Forty-five percent of teens admit to illicit drug use while 37 percent of male teens admit to having had 4 or 5 alcoholic drinks on at least one occasion in the previous month.[7] According to a survey by the National Center on Addiction and Substance Abuse, "61% of U.S. high school teens and 40% of middle school age kids say drugs are used, kept, and sold in their schools."[8] Drug and alcohol abuse lead directly to additional risky behavior when the teens took to the road: "a new survey [by the California Institute of Transportation] of southern California teens found that more than 70% had been involved in drunk driving, drag racing, or other reckless behavior behind the wheel."[9]

Not surprisingly, such dangerous activities continue into early adulthood. The National Institute on Alcohol Abuse and Alcoholism's Task Force on College Drinking reported that "alcohol consumption by college students contributes to 600,000 assaults, 500,000 injuries, and 70,000 sexual assaults every year ... 400,000 students between the ages of 18 and 24 reported having unprotected sex while under the influence."[10]

The onset of teen sexual activity is occurring at an earlier age than in the past. From 1985 to 1987 10 percent of girls and 27 percent of boys admitted to having sex before the age of 15. By 1992 percentages of teens sexually active by age 15 was 58 percent for black males, 19 percent for white males, and 27 percent for Hispanic males. For girls, the percentages were 39 percent for blacks and 25 percent for whites and Hispanics.[11] As a consequence, pregnancy rates increased as did the incidences of sexually transmitted diseases. The pregnancy rate in California was 9 percent for Hispanic teenage girls, 6 percent for blacks and 2 percent for whites.[12] Some of this sexual activity is forced upon teens by adults and "one in four girls and one in six boys is sexually abused."[13]

As alcohol and drug abuse underlie some sexual assaults and unprotected consensual sexual activity, leading to increased rates of unplanned pregnancy and sexually transmitted diseases, these behaviors likewise impact school drop-out rates, poverty, and violence and then recycle into a further round of substance abuse, unprotected sexual activity, and school and employment failure. But these losses are not racially or economically neutral. Black, Latino, and poor teens bear the disproportionate burden of failure.

The high school drop-out rate nationally in 2005 for all races was 30 percent, but was 35 percent for black students, 53 percent for Hispanics and 63 percent for economically disadvantaged youth. Fifty-six percent of entering high school students in the Los Angeles Unified School District, second largest in the country and just down the freeway from the three after-school theatre programs I studied for this book, failed to graduate; in Detroit, the figure was a staggering 79 percent failure rate.[14] Incredibly, by age 18 "more African American males are in jail than are in school."[15]

Violence committed against teens, rather than by teens, also grows. The numbers are frightening. One million children suffer moderate physical abuse in their homes each year; 160,000 are seriously injured and 1,000 die each year from parental abuse and neglect.[16] Not only the absolute numbers but the very rate at which children are abused doubled between 1986 and 1993 alone.[17]

Too many children live alone and in poverty. Twenty percent of children live below the poverty line and 150,000 young people are homeless in America.[18] Forty-four percent of school-age kids do not live with both biological parents.[19] According to the Nation magazine, 2,833 children drop out of school each and every day, 11 million lack health care coverage, and 14 million children who do attend school sit in buildings in dire need of repair.[20] The schools themselves are often scenes of violence: in 1997 alone, 180,000 school fights led to arrests, and there were 120,000 thefts and 110,000 incidents of vandalism in schools that also led to arrests.[21] In fact, teen arrests for serious offenses were up 50 percent from 1980 to 1994.[22]

Violence begins at a young age. Fully one-third of U.S. school kids in grades 6 to 10 have bullied other children or been bullied according to the Journal of the American Medical Association.[23] Education takes a back seat to survival in many schools and "just to live, to duck the bullet ... is the daily goal of numerous youth in the U.S. inner cities," according to the urban studies report of Milbray McLaughlin.[24]

But it would be a mistake to think that such violence is confined to inner-city schools. Recent fatal school shootings in rural and suburban areas including Pearl, Mississippi; Paducah, Kentucky; Jonesboro, Arkansas; Springfield, Oregon; and Littleton, Colorado, speak to an epidemic of violence nationally that cuts across geographical differences.

Most often that violence is directed inward. According to the 2001 surgeon general's report, the suicide rate among young people has tripled from 1995 to 2000.[25] In fact, the National Institute of Health reports that "suicide claims more teen lives each year than all other natural causes combined."[26] But you have to wonder what it means when the institute considers suicide a "natural cause" of death.

Teens are angry and they have access to drugs and weapons. According to a "Year 2000" survey of 10,000 teens, 26 percent of them have used or carried a weapon.[27] In the same year, the Joseph and Edna Josephson Institute on Ethics surveyed 8,600 high school teenagers and found that 15 percent had gone to school drunk in the past year; 68 percent had hit someone because they were angry in the past year; and 46 percent had hit people on at least two occasions in the previous year. Fifty percent said they could get a gun if they wanted one.[28]

We know that handguns kill 13 children on average every day in the United States and although adolescents constitute 14 percent of the population, they make up 30 percent of all victims of violent crime.[29] In fact, homicide is the second leading cause of death among 15–24 year olds nationally[30] and the number one cause of death for adolescents in New York City.[31] In Los Angeles County alone, 3 of every 100 black youths now age 15 will be a murder victim before reaching age 45.

Sociologists and psychologists have correlated the many and varied risk factors teenagers face and there are no surprises. In *Preventing Youth Violence*, Raymond Flannery writes, "the sociological factors that are traditionally linked to youth violence are poverty, inadequate schooling, domestic violence, discrimination, substance abuse, easily available weapons [and] gangs."[32]

All of the experts seem to agree that poverty is a growing risk factor for youth. While the national child poverty rate was 14.4 percent in 1973, it had grown to include 20.5 percent of America's children by 1995.[33] The connection seems rather direct: in her study of the juvenile justice system, Valerie Polakow writes that "90% of people arrested are either unemployed, underemployed, or living below the poverty line."[34] Medical experts have long warned that poverty exposes children to physical health risks like tuberculosis, lead poisoning, and asthma, but homicide must be added to this list of health risks: 25,000 children were murdered in the United States from 1985 to 1994.[35]

Patricia Timberg developed a checklist of factors influencing delinquency:

1. lack of social bonding to the family, the school, or the community
2. loss of sense of power, security, and confidence
3. low expectations from significant others
4. membership in an ethnic and cultural minority in a low socioeconomic group
5. family management problems with negative communication styles
6. learning disabilities, emotional disturbances, and socially maladjusted behavior
7. child abuse and neglect
8. academic failure and lack of commitment to the school experience due to a lack of relevancy and meaning in the educational curriculum
9. antisocial behavior
10. substance abuse[36]

Timberg points out that the more of these risk factors that exist in the life of any individual young person, the higher their risk of delinquency. Dr. James Garbarino, author of books like *Lost Boys* and *Children in Danger*, makes a similar point, stressing the "central importance of risk accumulation,"[37] arguing that young people may be able to handle one or two risk factors but tend to be swamped as further risk factors overwhelm them.[38]

As we have seen, specific risk factors do appear to interact, some as introductions to others. In their study published by the American Psychological Association, Martha Burt et al. find that "there is ample evidence that antisocial, sexual, and drug using behaviors tend to correlate.... There is also some evidence that antisocial behavior tends to precede substance abuse."[39] In his 2001 report on youth violence, the surgeon general lists 20 risk factors for youth violence across the individual domain (substance abuse, simply being male, exposure to television violence, etc.), family (poverty, parental abuse, neglect, etc.), school (poor attitude) and peers (antisocial peers) and divides them as early onset (ages 6 to 11) and late onset (ages 12–14).[40] The surgeon general then correlates their destructive effect based upon the age at which they appear in children's lives.[41]

Interestingly, risk factors shift in importance as children develop: for ages 6 to 11 substance abuse is a large factor and antisocial peers a small one, but those factors are reversed in importance for youngsters ages 12 to

14. The surgeon general's report concludes: "Risk factors do not operate in isolation—the more risk factors a child or young person is exposed to the greater the likelihood that he or she will become violent."[42]

Applying these same risk factors to the general population of young people, "the U. S. Department of Health and Human Services reported ... that only 45% of 15 year olds, 31% of 16 year olds, 24% of 17 year olds and 16% of 18 year olds are 'risk free.'"[43] These figures indicate that the vast majority of American teens may be classified as "at risk." For their part, Lee Manning and Leroy Baruth in their study of teens at risk, find the term best applied situationally, stating that "all children and adolescents are at risk at some time [in their lives]."[44]

The website of Americans for the Arts (www.artusa.org) estimates that our country is home to a staggering four million at-risk youth "growing up in severely distressed neighborhoods surrounded by brutality, violence, and despair."

Economics plays its part in this grim picture. We live in a sharply divided society where the richest 20 percent of the population takes home 50 percent of the total wealth of the country, while the bottom 20 percent survive on just 4 percent.[45] Aaron Kipnis, who spent time on the streets himself, told me that he finds these figures not descriptive but causative: "our economic system is predicated on the assumption that someone must be disenfranchised. We built this country on slavery. Now we have a prison system and a lower class working for the minimum wage."[46] To Kipnis's mind teenagers constitute a disenfranchised class with no right to vote and little likelihood of economic advancement, whose continued disenfranchisement serves the economic interests of adult society. For Kipnis, solving the problem of youth violence entails a major restructuring of our society.

No one doubts that delinquency correlates with poverty: "delinquency rates are highest where infant mortality rates are also high, life expectancies are short, jobs are hard to find, education poor, and hope scarce," writes Richard Lundman.[47] Father Gregory Boyle, a Roman Catholic priest who helps teenage gang members learn a trade and find employment through the Los Angeles–based Homeboy Industries, stresses the connection between violence and economic disadvantage, but suggests hopefully that "nothing stops a bullet like a job."[48]

Kipnis made the point to me that economic class divisions not only cause delinquency but also define what constitutes social deviance: "Deviant behavior is the same in all classes but the consequences are widely diverse based on social status. When middle and upper class kids commit crimes they are diverted into psychotherapy, private schools, drug treatment centers and hospitals. When poor, minority youth commit crimes they go into the juvenile justice system where they are abused."[49]

However, the single greatest predictor of delinquency is not socioeconomic status but gender: male juvenile delinquents outnumber females five to one. Any prevention program, Kipnis argues, must address the reality that teenage boys are at greatest risk. He told me that there is "direct correlation between fatherlessness and delinquency" and that young men lack positive role models and parental intervention to keep them out of trouble.[50]

While Kipnis prescribes an aroused citizenry and a "need to create an infrastructure to support children,"[51] the reality is, in the words of Lois Salisbury, president of Children Now, that "when attention is paid to teenagers it is often negative."[52] In fact, society's response to teen violence has been not nurturing but consistently punitive and coercive and just as consistently a failure. While pointing out that the epidemic in teen violence peaked in 1993, the 2001 surgeon general's report on youth violence admits that "the problem has not been resolved."[53] The surgeon general found no change since 1993 in the proportion of young people who have committed physically injurious and potentially lethal acts and designated youth violence a public health issue that affects our entire society.

Patricia Sternberg, writing about her work as a teacher in our schools, describes the alienated adolescents she encountered on a daily basis. One need only substitute the word "iPod" for "Walkman" to make the following scene familiar to anyone who works with teens today:

> [teenagers] see the world as a place with no future, possibilities, or hope and it makes them angry—at the world, at adults, and at those they consider responsible. They feel alone and fear tomorrow. They slap on their Walkman and escape into a world of rage and isolation. They close their eyes to anything new and anyone unfamiliar or different regardless of their ethnic origin or racial heritage. They disconnect from the world.[54]

Society's consistent response to the problem has been reliance on the criminal justice system, and the solution of choice has been incarceration. We now have more Americans in jail and in prison (two million) than ever before. In fact, with less than 5 percent of the world's population, America is home to 25 percent of the world's prison population. The number of teenagers in adult prisons more than doubled from 3,400 in 1985, to 7,400 in 1997.[55] Rather than signaling social failure, incarceration has become a huge business vital to the national economy, constituting a 40-billion-dollar-a-year industry that employs 400,000 people.[56]

Punishment remains popular with the general public. In California the passage of Proposition 21 in March 2000, supported by 62 percent of voters at the polls, ensured that yet more teenage offenders would be incarcerated. Proposition 21 allows prosecutors to charge children as young as 14 with felonies and to send them to adult prisons. In Los Angeles County 25 percent more youths have been charged as adults since the passage of Proposition 21. Nationally, 200,000 children are tried as adults each year.[57]

The prevailing ideology behind the current system was bluntly summarized recently by nationally syndicated conservative columnist Michelle Malkin:

> If you want to fight youth crime hire more police, take rotten juveniles out of the classroom and put them in separate reform schools, and punish young crooks with more than a slap on the wrists. As for "investing in kids" shouldn't that be the parents' responsibility?[58]

Malkin's operative words seem to be "police," "rotten," "slap," and "punish," all in line with the coercive system that failed last year and will fail next year.

Incarceration has become hereditary. One and a half million children have one or more parents in prison. Five hundred thousand youthful offenders are presently on probation nationally. Generation after generation of youth marches through the system and follows their parents into prison. Lives will be ruined and potential wasted but society can fool itself into thinking it is fighting youth crime even as it assures itself of an ever renewing phalanx of teen and adult offenders.

Like lemmings fixed upon a fatal path, individual states continue to lower the age at which a child may be arraigned and charged and sent to prison as an adult. That age is presently 14 years old in Massachusetts, 12 in Oregon, 10 in Wisconsin and an astounding seven in New York. In March 2001, in a well-publicized case, a 12-year-old in Florida was sentenced to life imprisonment for a homicide, a sentence later reversed in the face of public revulsion. Children and teens, who are years away from being old enough to vote, drive, or buy cigarettes or alcohol, are now routinely treated as adults and sentenced to adult penitentiaries. The thought seems to be that if we cannot halt child violence at least we can, in a legal sense, end childhood and pretend that these offenders are equivalent to adult offenders.

State prison, as you might imagine, is a dangerous place, especially for children who may be subjected to beatings, rape, and worse. In 1994, 45 children were murdered in state prisons across this country.

But teenagers receive little sympathy from adult society. As Robert Fellmeth, director of the San Diego–based Children's Advocacy Institute says: "They're not cuddly. They're not cute. They're awkward and pimply faced and full of glandular emotion and temper tantrums. It's hard to get people to invest in them but they're our future. And we all went through it."[59] Malkin certainly didn't use the word "cuddly" and so we lock teenagers up at least as often as we treat them. A report of the Coalition for Juvenile Justice, created by the U.S. Congress, states that 50 to 75 percent of jailed juveniles suffer from a mental illness. In the words of coalition chair Robert Pierce: "The real crime is that many traumatized and troubled children have to get arrested to get mental health services."[60]

What public money is directed toward the problem is more often spent for punishment than for prevention. California, for example, spends two billion dollars a year for police, courts and jails for juvenile criminals and just $116 million a year for the prevention of youth violence.[61] The California Youth Authority operates 15 prisons and camps to house 7,400 wards of the state. Conditions in such institutions are often primitive and punitive. The Los Angeles Times reported, for example, that teens at the El Paso de Robles Youth Correctional Facility near San Luis Obispo were forced to spend hours on their knees as punishment for minor infractions.[62] A 2001 audit of the Ventura County Youth Correctional Facility "has revealed more than a dozen sets of problems, some so serious that it prompted investigators to propose the possibility of closing the embattled facility."[63] Problems included untreated infections and contagious diseases among inmates. At the juvenile hall in Santa Monica, California, there were 24 suicide attempts by inmates in 2001 alone: "Kids when angry ram their heads against the cinder block walls…. The nurse sees self-mutilation and 'boxer' fractures—hand injuries from punching the walls."[64]

Racial inequalities exist within juvenile jails as well: according to a 2002 report of the Youth Law Center, "Latinos are detained in juvenile justice systems 1.5 times more often and are twice as likely to be incarcerated as their white peers."[65] More and more teens are locked up and the severity of the legal system increases. The Los Angeles Times reported on April 10, 2001, that "since 1992 more than 47 states have made their juvenile justice systems harsher."

The fly in the ointment is that even by the estimates of these state juvenile justice systems, incarceration fails to prevent youth violence in spite of increasing penalties. The California Youth Authority states that 55–60 percent of juvenile convicts return to prison within just two years of release[66] and this figure rises to 96 percent within 15 years. The 4 per-cent who don't return may have died or left the state. In Florida the recidi-vism rate is 55 percent and in Utah it is 79 percent.[67] One jail sentence seems to inexorably lead to the next.

In seeking a more permanent solution, our society also killed children. From 1973 to 2005, more than 200 people were sentenced to death for crimes committed as juveniles and 19 of them were executed. Until 2005, another 74 sat on death row for crimes committed before they turned 18. Such executions were upheld by the U.S. Supreme Court in 1988 and allowed in 23 states.[68] Only in 2005 did the Supreme Court reverse itself and, by the slimmest majority of a 5 to 4 vote, forbid capital punishment for felons convicted of crimes committed at age 18 or younger, removing the United States from a short list of nations, including Iran, China, and Pakistan, that allow such executions. There is no guarantee that a future court case might not return our society to the legal murder of children.

The cost of combating crime is huge: 147 billion dollars in 1997, "the last year for which figures are available [from the Bureau of Justice Statis-tics], up from 36 billion in 1982."[69] Thirty-five billion dollars are spent on building and maintaining prisons alone[70] and incarceration is a growth industry now employing 413,000 Americans (noninmates) who work behind bars.[71] Hallinan's book, *Going Up the River*, paints a depressing picture of the burgeoning inmate population as well:

> In 1939, at the end of the reign of gangsters like Al Capone, we had 137 Americans in prison for every 100,000 citizens—a high water mark that stood for decades. But in 1980 we broke that record and we've been breaking it ever since. By 1999 the U.S. incarceration rate stood at a phenomenal 476 per 100,000—more than triple the rate of the Capone era. So common is the prison experience in America today that the federal government predicts that one in every eleven men will be imprisoned in his lifetime. For black men the figure is even higher—more than one in every four.[72]

Incarceration for one year costs between 30 and 36 thousand dollars per adolescent. By contrast, tuition at Harvard is around 32 thousand dol-lars a year and the cost per child for a year of public school in the South Bronx is about eight thousand dollars; and budgets for prisons grew twice as fast as those for education in the years 1988–1995.[73]

Although Aaron Kipnis told me, "we know how to prevent delin-quency. But as a culture we lack the resolve,"[74] the truth would seem to be a bit more complicated. The data enumerated above demonstrates that incarceration and the many alternatives employed to date have been insufficient to stem the tide of youth violence. Lundman writes categorically that "prevention programs don't work and they waste money."[75] In his book *Prevention and Control of Juvenile Delinquency*, Lundman compared three options: the juvenile justice program; diversion from the system, usually identified as short-term treatment modalities; and no action, that is the release of criminal suspects without incarceration or treatment. His counterintuitive results were that rearrest figures were substantially the same for all three.[76] Does this mean that we ought to do nothing? Doing nothing, "no action," may be the least expensive choice, but it remains just as ineffective as the first two choices.

Surgeon General David Satcher's recent report on youth violence warned: "We cannot afford to waste resources on ineffective or harmful interventions."[77] Dr. Satcher identified as one of these failed strategies the much publicized national program D.A.R.E., which he stated, "has had little or no effect in deterring children from substance abuse." Yet the 21-year-old D.A.R.E. (Drug Abuse Resistance Education) program with its ubiquitous bumper stickers and T-shirts, costing approximately $235 million a year, is now taught in 75 percent of the school districts in the country and in 54 foreign countries. Meanwhile a six-year study at the University of Illinois indicates the D.A.R.E. program "has encouraged drug use particularly among suburban youth by making it seem more prevalent than it is."[78] A parallel 10-year study at the University of Kentucky "found that the D.A.R.E. program had no effect on students by the time they were 20 years old."[79] As a result, Salt Lake City mayor Rocky Anderson labeled D.A.R.E. "completely ineffective," deleted the program from the city budget and removed it from the city schools, labeling it "a complete waste of money, a fraud on the American people."[80] In the face of such criticism, the D.A.R.E. national advisory board nearly shut the program down but finally opted to spend $13 million in 2001, redesigning the curriculum after losing Department of Education funding. D.A.R.E. continues but as a feel-good program that convinces the public that the government and schools are doing something about drugs but with no more positive impact than previously.

This is not the first time a search for remedies has led to the misuse of scarce resources. Twenty years ago, in a highly publicized initiative, tens of thousands of teens were exposed to a program called "Scared Straight." The idea was to take "at-risk" teens to state penitentiaries where they would be exposed to and, presumably frightened by, the wretched conditions and dangerous inmates there. Scared Straight even aired as a prime-time television special, filmed at Rahway State Penitentiary, in 1979. The program seemed so attractive initially that the California legislature passed a bill to bus some 15,000 nondelinquent children to state prisons for confrontations with inmates. Oddly, Scared Straight, in a controlled study in New Jersey, actually increased juvenile delinquency, as measured by arrests, four times over a control group not involved in the prison visits.[81] Other much bally-hooed approaches, such as "community treatment" have proved no more effective than "the necessarily haphazard supervision of probation officers" and no more effective than institutionalization.[82] No wonder, Lundman concludes, that the prevention of delinquency is "a stubbornly elusive goal."[83]

Equally, the drug-free school zone laws, passed by many states and intended to curtail drug use and sale by making drug dealing within 1,000 feet of a school punishable by especially severe sentences, have also proved ineffective. The most recent data shows that 80 percent of drug cases occurred inside drug free school zones.[84] Zero tolerance policies, requiring stiff penalties for even minor drug offenses, have backfired by making students less likely to turn in drug abusing peers who would face harsher penalties, according to a report of the National Center on Addiction and Substance Abuse.[85]

The 1999 welfare reform law passed by Congress included $500 million for sexual abstinence education programs but barred discussion of condoms and birth control. A study of these programs in 2002 found "no reliable evidence that these programs are effective in reducing teen sex, pregnancy or the transmission of disease."[86]

Other tools for dealing with delinquency, like the recent vogue in prison "boot camps" and restitution programs, are similarly unproved. Following the beating death of one teenage inmate by correction officers, Florida closed its boot camps in 2006. Kipnis believes that the very coercive nature of such programs ensures not only their failure but also the failure of our very society: "The current system is a recipe for disaster; no police state has ever been successful in ensuring the well-being of their society."[87]

In his 2001 report on youth violence, the surgeon general tallied a long list of "ineffective strategies." In addition to D.A.R.E., Scared Straight, and boot camps, he listed: "peer counseling, peer mediation, peer leaders, non-promotion to succeeding grades, gun buyback programs, firearm training, mandatory gun ownership, redirecting youth behavior, shifting peer group norms, residential programs, milieu treatment, behavioral token programs, waivers to adult court, social casework, individual counseling."[88] While many of these programs are not coercive in themselves, young people are initially forced into the program and face punishment if they discontinue treatment.

However, past failures do not seem to deter a reliance on old methods. Faced with the problem of school-yard bullies in Minnesota, for example, authorities are sending convicted teen bullies to jail. Minnesota's Dakota County judge, Richard Spicer, when questioned about the new penalties, which he supports, responded: "Is it working? I don't know. Will it work? I don't know."[89] Authorities obviously feel the need to "do something" but have no assurance that anything works. Thus, coercive programs persist, in spite of the fact that a "review of 231 studies of correctional treatment published since 1945 indicates that the present array of correctional treatments have no appreciable effect, positive or negative, on the rate of recidivism."[90] But lack of efficacy has rarely endangered an ever harsher response to adolescent misbehavior.

In his report on youth violence, Surgeon General Satcher stated: "Rigorous evaluation of programs is critical. While hundreds of prevention programs are being used in schools and communities throughout the country, little is known about the effects of most of them ... nearly half of the most thoroughly evaluated strategies for preventing violence have been shown to be ineffective—and a few were shown to harm participants."[91]

In spite of rising youth crime and a punitive social response wedded to failed programs, Aaron Kipnis, who has seen the juvenile justice system from both sides as felon and psychotherapist, is not alone when he sees signs of hope. As he explained to me in an interview, "the majority of difficult, troubled, criminal, and even violent young men can lead whole and productive lives when given the right opportunities and leadership."[92]

The surgeon general agrees: "Youth violence is not an intractable problem. Thus the most urgent need is a national resolve to confront the problem of youth violence systematically, using research-based approaches and to correct damaging myths and stereotypes that interfere with the task at hand."[93]

The line between staying out of trouble and getting into trouble can be no more than a matter of free time. As Pasadena, California, police chief Bernard Melekian has said, "I think everyone knows that the crime rate spikes between 3 and 6 P.M. Auto thefts, burglaries, vandalism ... crimes of opportunity committed by kids left to their own devices. Not bad kids, just bored kids.... We can lock them up or we can find a way to harness that energy." Chief Melekian is a member of a national organization called "Fight Crime: Invest in Kids" made up of 100 police chiefs, prosecutors and crime victims lobbying for more resources for teen child care and after-school programs.[94] After-school programs, their timing and their content, point to an answer.

The problem is that one half of eighth graders are in so-called self-care after school, which translates into "no care." The Website Coming Up Taller reports that "many young people spend 40% of their time without responsible adult companionship or supervision."[95] Children left home alone are twice as likely to start drinking, smoking, or abusing drugs as children with adults in the home.

No consideration of teenage risks would be complete without an analysis of the prevalence of gangs. In his report on youth violence Surgeon General Satcher estimates that there were 26,000 active youth gangs in schools and communities across America as of 1999, with a total membership of 840,000 young people. The surgeon general states that "gang members, a relatively small proportion of the adolescent population, commit the majority of serious youth violence" and offers studies from Denver, Colorado, and Rochester, New York, that show 14–30 percent of youth are gang members but account for 68–79 percent of serious violence reported.[96] However, a gang membership of 30 percent of the population is hardly a "small proportion" and stamping out gangs, a fact of urban life for over 100 years, would appear to be an unattainable goal in any case.

In fact, experts agree that gangs exist for a reason and serve rational functions for young people. Curtis Branch, who studies gang growth, writes that gangs "are the byproduct of young people who have psychological needs that they perceive as only being met through gang affiliation."[97] Martin Sanchez Jankowski, who studied and lived with street gangs for ten years, sees a gang as "organized defiant individualism"[98] writing:

> Much too often we have thought of gang members as the lowest of the lower class.... This view is simply not accurate. A great range of individuals are in gangs, but the vast majority are quite intelligent and are capable of developing and executing creative enterprises.[99]

Indeed, Vance Packard quotes one teacher he interviewed: "By lashing out, kids are trying to tell us something and we aren't listening."[100] Nearly 100 years ago reformer Jane Addams described her settlement house in Chicago as surrounded by youth gangs armed with guns and abusing cocaine and traced the daily petty juvenile crime she witnessed to young people's "quest for adventure."[101]

A fixation on gangs and youth crime has historically meant a punitive police response. Not surprisingly, young people in every theatre program I have studied shared with me anger and personal stories of police intimidation and harassment. As Madame de Sevigne points out: "The humbling of inferiors is necessary to the maintenance of social order."[102] Police stops, frisks, and questioning of teens in their cars and on the street, fall within the category of what James Scott calls "rituals of subordination" and those so dominated "ordinarily dare not contest the terms of their subordination openly. Behind the scenes, though, they are likely to create and defend a social space in which offstage dissent to the official transcript of power relations may be voiced."[103] Scott calls this social space the "zone of constant struggle"[104] and it is a fitting name for the daily interactions of adults and teens.

The schools, like the streets, constitute such a zone of struggle and our educational system seems designed to enforce inequalities of power. In the frontispiece to his book *How Children Fail*, John Holt quotes a fellow educator, William Hull: "If we taught children to speak, they'd never learn." Holt sees this attitude as the basis for adult "oppression" of children:

> We adults destroy most of the intellectual and creative capacity of children by the things we do to them or make them do. We destroy this capacity above all by making them afraid, afraid of not doing what other people want, of not pleasing, of making mistakes, of failing, of being *wrong*. Thus we make them afraid to gamble, afraid to experiment, afraid to try the difficult and the unknown.[105]

Alan Creighton and Paul Kivel call this "the hidden curriculum"[106] of education, where young people are taught to obey, compete, make money, have a career, take tests, follow leaders, conform, and belong, where learning equals memorizing, and individualism is a dirty word.

If, as Ruth Perlstein and Gloria Thrall assert, "conflict is based on unmet needs,"[107] it is easy to see how youth's quest for basic needs like identity, security, control, recognition, fairness, and power will lead to conflict with an adult agenda and what Vance Packard has called "our anti-child culture."[108]

Twenty years ago Letty Cottin Pogrebin, a founding editor of Ms. magazine, wrote an article for the December 1983 issue of the magazine with the arresting title: "Do Americans Hate Children?" It's a question I'm sure most Americans would immediately answer in the negative. However, Pogrebin wrote: "As a society we love children when they are under control. We hate and fear children who defy us, children who are independent, quirky, free thinking, nonconformist, idiosyncratic, precocious, or critical of adults."

Kipnis, for one, sees things getting worse. He told me:

> The prison population keeps increasing. More and more boys are left behind in school. Young men are a dwindling minority of new college students, down I think to first year college classes in 2005 that are only 43% male. There's been no improvement in education, incarceration, or employment. Rather than a wholehearted large scale commitment of resources to multiply alternatives to incarceration, we make juvenile justice more severe, trying more teens as adults, and sending 10,000 boys, some as young as 14, to adult prisons. The future is grim. We have the largest prison population on earth. We've become a two-tiered society where some have advantages and the rest are left behind with an increasingly larger underclass not unlike India's "untouchables" caste of the past. But we know that societies that have disenfranchised young men in the past have eventually collapsed and societies that spend more each year on prisons than they do higher education, as ours now does, are doomed.[109]

Given that youth violence takes a tremendous toll on contemporary American society and that coercive and punitive programs have so far failed to solve the problem, the time is ripe to examine not only new programs but new paradigms and new ways of looking at these problems and a new search for solutions. In searching for new initiatives to stem youth violence, we need to identify programs that counteract the multitude of risk factors that teens face, such as criminal activity, violence, drug and alcohol use, suicide, unprotected sexual activity, dropping out of school, and gang membership. We need to look for new programs that empower and educate youth while offering them "free zones" to work out their own identities and values and remove the "adultism" that has historically left them repressed and resentful. I will argue and, I hope, demonstrate, that arts programs, and specifically after-school theatre programs, offer that unique combination of possibilities.

CHAPTER 3

History and Theory of Community-Based Theatre

A T LEAST SINCE THE TIME OF PLATO AND ARISTOTLE, social philosophers have recognized the potential of the stage to powerfully affect its audience. In each era of human history, social, educational, religious, and political movements adapted or developed theatrical modes to advance their particular goals. In doing so they laid the groundwork for today's community-based theatre. Called community theatre, educational theatre, political theatre, therapeutic theatre, grassroots theatre, popular theatre, "vanguard theatre,"[1] "democratized theatre,"[2] or people's theatre, such projects reject the values of the professional and commercial stage. Aspiring to what they see as higher purposes than box office success, entertainment, popularity, or even artistic endeavor, they seek to instruct, educate, ennoble, liberate, or heal their audiences and, often, their performers as well. As Susan Haedicke writes, "community-based theatre aims to influence and change the real world, not just reflect it."[3]

Today's theatre for social purposes is hardly a new invention. Though too often uninformed about the work of their historical predecessors, today's "community-based" theatre practitioners owe much to the pioneers who came before them. A review of American history finds many early examples of theatre impacting and motivating audiences, from clergy dramatizing sermons and Biblical lessons for performance in churches across the country to the many and varied stage adaptations of Harriet Beecher Stowe's novel, *Uncle Tom's Cabin*, which served as powerful propaganda tools for abolitionists during the Civil War era. The next three chapters are divided more or less chronologically rather than thematically, although three strands of theatre run concurrently through the last 115 years of history; these are described as theatre of reform, theatre of education, and theatre of revolution. To unbraid these strands would do a disservice to the clear interdependencies they continued to exhibit as they evolve, borrowing techniques one from the other, as one practitioner's ideas spread and educate colleagues who may not have shared political ideology but who remain dedicated to the social and moral power of theatre to advance human society. This story can be read as a sort of intricate tapestry of human development.

The first fully self-conscious plan to use theatre to transform American society grew out of the settlement house movement of the late 19th century. Influenced by Leo Tolstoy in Russia and Romain Rolland in France, these social reformers chose theatre as a key component of their community work. Unlike previous reformers, settlement house workers "settled" into impoverished inner-city neighborhoods and established a myriad of social services for the people they had come to live and work with. Where charity workers had once focused on individual cases of need, settlement workers "stressed the social and economic conditions that made people poor"[4] and aimed to change society.

The settlement house movement was America's first concerted attack on poverty, taking on issues like education, housing, employment, sanitation, and the special conditions confronting women and children.

Kindergartens, day care centers, health services, gymnasiums, reading rooms, libraries, and theatres all shared space where these community workers, often recent college graduates from the middle and upper classes, lived in spartan apartments and ate together in communal kitchens. Campaigns for economic justice accompanied the social services offered by these young reformers, typically inspired by Protestant clergy, though including Catholic and Jews. With their consciences awakened by the social gospel movement and Christian socialism, settlement houses served as training grounds for young ministers and seminarians.

The settlement house movement began with the founding of Toynbee Hall in 1884 in East London by two Oxford University students and the idea quickly spread to the United States. The first American settlement house was founded in New York City in 1886. Two years later Jane Addams opened Hull House in Chicago. By 1891 there were 6 settlement houses in the United States. By 1897 there were 74 and by 1900 there were 100. By

1910 the movement had mushroomed to 400 houses across the country, mostly in the east and midwest.

In 1888 Chicago offered deplorable living and working conditions to a growing influx of immigrants from abroad and to African Americans from the South, featuring racial and ethnic strife, organized crime, and gang wars in the streets. Reformers like Addams, Upton Sinclair and William T. Stead stressed the simultaneous need to change social conditions and to educate and train individuals. Hull House offered classes in pottery, metalworking, enameling, wood carving, weaving, dressmaking, sewing and cooking.[5] But like almost every other settlement house, it also had its lecture series, educational conferences, and university extension courses. In an effort to introduce beauty and art into otherwise drab lives, Hull House also offered galleries and exhibitions. The introduction of pageants and festivals, meant to dramatize the heritage of the various immigrant groups, led quickly to the founding of thriving theatres within the settlement houses. Drawing from the classics, mysteries, melodramas and fairy tales, performances of various kinds were created for adults, teenagers, and children. Plays by Shakespeare, Ibsen, Gillette, Shaw, Lady Gregory, Goldoni, and Wilde were offered. Economic necessity gave rise to the "new stagecraft," a reliance on shadow and light rather than elaborately painted scenery. Produced at small cost and in intimate halls, these plays in turn helped to launch the subsequent national movement of Little Theatres.

Dramatic presentations proved immediately attractive for settlement houses. Plays helped to teach English to foreign-speaking and sometimes illiterate amateur actors and audiences. The producers felt comfortable with the moral values of the drama while plays offered a bridge across religious and racial divides, bringing different nationalities together as cast, crew, and audience. Plays were chosen that celebrated the cultures people had left behind in their countries of origin and challenged their participants who most commonly had no previous experience on the stage.

Hull House presented plays in its drawing room and gym as early as 1899 and in 1901 built the Hull House Theatre, the first settlement house theatre in the country. Seating just 230 and presenting plays with "social ideas"[6] at 20 to 50 cents a ticket, the Hull House Theatre drew both local community members and a well-heeled uptown crowd hungry for culture and a taste of the demimonde. The resident Hull House Players, under the longtime direction of Laura Dainty Pelham, recruited and trained two generations of young actors from the neighborhood and even toured Ireland in collaboration with the Abbey Players.[7]

Visiting Italian and Russian troupes offered plays in their native languages. Greeks from the neighborhood presented the plays of Sophocles in Greek. The Young People's Socialist League presented social dramas in both Yiddish and English. One local Italian resident penned a play about the alienation emerging between Americanized sons and their old-country parents. Union plays were presented by trade unionists. There was a puppet theatre for children, a Shakespeare club, and a Young People's Theatre with child actors and a five-cent admission.[8] The theatres reached a large audience; Jane Addams estimated that nine thousand people visited Hull House every week.[9]

Addams saw the Hull House theatre as a response, and good theatre as an antidote, to the 446 commercial theatres operating in Chicago in 1909 which she attacked for popularizing negative human values. She explained that their main theme was revenge, their style melodramatic, offering "a debased form of dramatic art."[10] Addams blamed the theatres for corrupting youth, who filched change and sneaked in to see the tawdry shows. Noting that 15,000 young people under the age of 20 had been arrested in Chicago in 1909 alone, she observed: "May we not assume that this love of excitement, this desire for adventure, is basic, and will be evinced by each generation of city boys as a challenge to their elders."[11] She also wrote:

> Theatre is the only place where they can satisfy that craving for a conception of life higher than that which the actual world offers them.... The theatre becomes a veritable "house of dreams" infinitely more real than the noisy streets and the crowded factories. [At Hull House] we availed ourselves of the use of the play ... not only as an agent of recreation and education but as a vehicle of self-expression.[12]

Once Hull House began its theatre, Addams was amazed at the commitment the young actors were willing to make:

> The Hull House Theatre is constantly besieged by children clamoring to "take part" in the plays of Schiller, Shakespeare, and Moliere, although they know it means weeks of rehearsal and the complete memorizing of stiff lines.[13]

The Hull House experiment was replicated throughout the nation, and in every case, theatre became a part of a settlement house's education and reform programs. In Boston Elizabeth Peabody (1804–1894), a national crusader for kindergartens for the poor, founded a settlement house in the city's West End ghetto, home to successive waves of Italian, Jewish, and Irish immigrants. In 1913 a theatre was built and by 1915 the Intersettlement Players drew together actors from the various Boston settlement houses. On July 4, 1923, the players featured several hundred child actors performing a patriotic pageant before an audience of 10,000 on Boston Common.

The Henry Street Settlement House in New York City founded the Neighborhood Playhouse on Grand Street and, as early as 1911, ten settlement houses in Brooklyn had come together to present a historical "Pageant of Patriots" in Prospect Park. This use of untrained actors in mass theatrical presentations with didactic political messages performed in public spaces foreshadows the street and political theatre of the 1960s and the community-based theatre with teens today.

The settlement house movement crossed paths with an even older tradition of children's theatre in America and gave it new life. Educational theatre, like children's theatre, had been a weak, though recurrent theme in American history. As early as 1749, Benjamin Franklin had urged the inclusion of art as a subject in colonial schools with the entirely pragmatic goal "to improve skills of the professional and the quality of the crafts."[14] By 1798 the Rev. Charles Stearns had published 30 plays, each about 10 pages long and written originally for his pupils in Lincoln, Massachusetts, in his book *Dramatic Dialogues for the Use of Schools*. The short plays examined, and resolved, various moral dilemmas facing young people. Hundreds of copies were ordered for school use by nearby towns.[15]

Tracing the history of the arts in the public school curriculum, George Geahigan notes that music was introduced into the schools in the 1830s, literature in the 1860s, and industrial drawing in the 1870s not only as a path to learning other subjects (drawing, for example, was promoted by Horace Mann as a way to improve penmanship) but also as a "means for fostering ideals and promoting morality."[16]

At the same time, new educational ideals welcomed the arts into the schools. In the late 19th century, G. Stanley Hall, father of the child study movement and working under the influence of Charles Darwin's discoveries in evolution, posited that the development of each child repeated the evolution of the entire race and that children, rather than simply being miniature adults, were qualitatively different from grown-ups. From this view he drew the lesson that the teachers' goal was not to mold the minds of the children in their care but rather, after intense study, to develop a curriculum to meet each individual child's needs.

John Dewey, the most influential philosopher of American education, suggested that it was a teacher's role to challenge his/her students and so induce disequilibrium and develop problem-solving skills. Dewey stressed that children feel as well as think, learn values as well as facts, and benefit most from integrating studies, like art, that allow them to understand their world. He wrote:

> In other words, art is not nature, but it is nature transformed by entering into new relationships where it evokes a new emotional response.[17]

Dewey began using dramatics with children in 1896, seeing drama as part of education. He called it "learning by doing"[18] and the activity quickly spread, becoming a part of the teacher education curriculum at Northwestern University in 1929 under the leadership of Winifred Ward.

Nellie McCaslin traces the origins of children's theatre to social and educational centers rather than theatres.[19] She reports finding records of plays for children written as early as 1810 in the United States, but credits the Educational Alliance, a social services program, with establishing the first regular children's theatre program in 1903, with Alice Minnie Herts as director of its Children Educational Theatre. The alliance proclaimed the dual goals of teaching better communication skills to the children of Russian and Polish immigrants on Manhattan's lower East Side and weaning them away from the adult vaudeville shows by presenting a series of Shakespearean and other classic plays. Beginning with *The Tempest*, the Alliance chose plays that would inculcate "resourcefulness, good taste, and discrimination."[20]

In her groundbreaking 1911 book *The Children's Educational Theatre*, describing her innovative work, Herts notes the theatre's educational impact on students who had previously had little interest in such undertakings:

> At this point in the progress of class work and production an inestimably valuable truth came to our notice—namely that children and young people whose minds could be reached in no other way, in their desire to enact characters, responded under instruction in the character to emotion and interest which stimulated the latent resources of their sluggish minds.[21]

Herts also describes how her young actors came to take on the attributes of their characters:

> We counted the months of careful, patient training well spent when it served to bring the soul of a boy of an East Side tenement into points of contact with the soul and spirit of the chivalrous young Prince [in *The Prince and the Pauper*] and from these points of contact to stimulate him into action.[22]

In later chapters we will examine the ways in which children do indeed emotionally interact with the characters they portray on stage, just as Herts suspected, and how the stage becomes a place to role-play solutions to many real-life problems.

We might feel uncomfortable today, however, with the obvious spirit of noblesse oblige lurking behind Herts' patronizing language, and in 2002 Dorothy Chansky took Herts to task for positing Shakespeare "as an Anglophone savior." Chansky wrote:

> Salvation and social construction cohere in the site that is Shakespeare and non–Anglo-Saxons must rebuild everything about their speech and bearing in order to appear adequate in front of their own families and neighbors. That Herts and the founders of the Educational Alliance were wealthy German Jews attests to the belief in the importance of learning to "pass" on the WASP model.[23]

We will see in chapter 5 how even today's theatre programs like City Hearts finds Shakespearean plays and diction conducive to character building. Early 20th-century American educators soon gravitated to the idea of using theatre in the schools to affect exactly the transformations Herts had trumpeted. Mark Twain was not alone when he called children's theatre "one of the very, very, great inventions of the Twentieth Century."[24]

Herts continued as director of the Children Educational Theatre until 1909 when it closed, only to reopen in 1911 as the Education Players bringing adult actors into the public schools.[25]

In New York City Emma Sheridan Fry also began teaching at the Educational Alliance, where in 1904 she aided in productions of *Snow White*, *Little Lord Fauntleroy* and *The Prince and the Pauper* with casts of children performing for audiences of children. In her 1913 book *Educational Dramatics* Fry describes her work as leading to the new "Science of Educational Dramatics" whose goal was "to develop the whole human being towards life and citizenship."[26] Like Herts, Fry described the salubrious effects of drama:

> There was no isolation of audience from players.... Ideals take shape. Vocabulary is purified; speech sweetened, voices modulated, manners influenced, and the children profit by hours of happy activity and association in a common interest.[27]

The Drama League of America, founded in 1910, created a Junior Department which produced plays for children and established the Children's Drama League. The drama league, before its demise in 1931, helped found and develop the Little Theatre movement, modeled in large part upon Andre Antoine's Teatre Libre in Paris, the Frie Buhne in Berlin, the Moscow Art Theatre, and August Strindberg's Intimate Theatre in Stockholm. These little theatres, often seating 100 to 200 audience members and often supporting themselves by subscriptions, introduced the new drama and plays of social criticism of Europeans like Ibsen and Shaw to an American public unused to serious drama.

From 1911 to 1917, 50 such Little Theatres arose, including the Provincetown Players; the Washington Square Players and the Neighborhood Playhouse in New York City; the East-West Players, which presented the work of Yiddish playwrights; the Negro Playwrights, under the direction of Robert Edmond Jones; the White House Saloon in Galesburg, Illinois, that became the Prairie Playhouse; and a series of Little Country Theatres, the first of which was established in Fargo, North Dakota, by Arthur Arvold.[28] Inspired by a U.S. visit of the Irish Players in 1911, Mrs. Lyman W. Gale founded the Toy Theatre in Boston with just 129 seats.

Constance D'Arcy Mackay called the Little Theatre movement: "One of the newest, freest, most democratic forces in the art of the American stage." Mackay defined the Little Theatre as:

> an intimate stage and auditorium where players and audience can be brought into close accord; a theatre where unusual and noncommercial plays are given ... where scenic experimentation is rife.... For experimentation is the Little Theatre's raison d'etre.[29]

Plays were put on "for intrinsic enjoyment rather than monetary gain."[30] Democratizing the stage and utilizing drama for altruistic social and educational purposes was the hallmark of nonprofit organizations from the late 19th century to our own day.

In 1912 the short-lived National Federation of Theatre Clubs, founded by the Federation of Women's Clubs, brought together 1,300 members, many of them dedicated to children's theatre. The following year the Educational Drama League was formed to promote drama in the schools, settlement houses, and on the new public playgrounds that were then being built across the country.[31]

The Association of Junior Leagues of America was founded in 1901 and grew directly out of the settlement house movement, bringing debutantes together to perform social work activities. Many chose to work in children's theatre and this activity was the main project, for example, of the Chicago Junior League by 1924. Junior league members also founded the Children's Theatre of Evanston, Illinois, in 1925 and hoped to create a national children's theater.[32]

Even as theatre practitioners were reaching out to child audiences, educators were turning to drama as an educational tool. John Dewey had advocated the use of dramatizations to teach reading and as a means of making abstract ideas available to pupils. "Allow him [the student] to act out an idea,"

Dewey observed, "and it becomes real to him."[33] The new educational movement in Britain, reacting against rote learning and the 3 Rs, cast the child not as "learner" but as "creator and doer" as early as 1870. Harriet Finlay-Johnson in her 1912 book *The Dramatic Method of Teaching* popularized the idea of class dramatics as a way to make the learning of other subjects more interesting to students. This was a far cry from the then conventional expectation that child drama meant merely subsidizing seats for school children at professional theatres.[34]

Later, Peter Slade worked with children to draw from them the elements of a story from conversation and improvisations. Unlike Finlay-Johnson, Slade stressed that "experience transcends knowledge"[35] and promoted class dramatics as a value in and of itself. Slade encouraged teachers and students to be coworkers in jointly creating their own plays. He stated explicitly that "if a teacher does it [alone] it is not Child Drama."[36] Echoing Aristotle, Slade argued for the beneficial cathartic effect of drama, encouraging children to move beyond morally inoffensive plays and tackle plays with tragic and disturbing themes, noting, "they [the children] spit out much that is undesirable in their lives this way."[37] By the 1930s Slade's work was being studied by teachers in training in Britain and around the world. His work, continued by his student Brian Way in the 1950s and 60s, grew into the internationally influential theatre in education movement, or TIE, as it is known today.

Way argued that dramatics offered "moments of direct experience transcending mere knowledge, enriching the imagination, possibly touching the heart and soul as well as the mind."[38] He described the contrast, for example, between simply teaching children that a blind person is a person who cannot see and asking children to close their eyes and find their way out of their classroom. We shall explore this type of experiential drama and its effects on its young participants in succeeding chapters.

By 1940s this pioneering work with children's drama had become an ongoing institution. By 1949 there were 200–300 permanent children's theatre groups in the United States.[39] Writing in that decade, Isabel Burger described one adult theatre's work with children that prefigures the work I observed in the contemporary after-school theatre program City at Peace. At the Experimental Theatre of Baltimore, she wrote, adults in 1941 worked with teens and preteens whose ideas were incorporated as the dialogue and action of the plays. With no adult input in the script itself, the children moved from improvisations to dialogue and from short scenes to full-length plays, the end result of the performance being that "timid children became

confident children."[40] The 1950s saw a further expansion of children's theatre with a policy of federal funding.[41] However, U.S./USSR Cold War
rivalry and the 1957 launch of the Soviet space satellite *Sputnik* saw the U.S.
government redirect federal education funds to the sciences and math
rather than the arts. During this time, "music and art ... managed to retain
only a marginal foothold in the curriculum."[42]

In 1959, a national conference at Woods Hole, Massachusetts, brought
together progressive educators and the resultant report, *The Process of Education*, written by Jerome Bruner, that helped to redefine the role of the
arts in public schools. Basing his argument in large part on the writing of
Jean Piaget, Bruner broadcast the idea that aesthetics constituted a unique
domain and source of knowledge rather than, as believed earlier, merely
an instrument for learning other subjects.[43] We shall see in succeeding
chapters how scientists today posit the arts as a unique way of understanding and knowing the world that for many people undergirds all other means
of learning and education.

The 1950s also saw a reevaluation of the role of drama in education
in England and development quite different from the American model. In
the 1950s, while teaching at Durham University, Dorothy Heathcote wrote
a series of works that had a profound impact on drama in education internationally. Heathcote, who had made the transition from actress to teacher,
reacted against the improvisation and spontaneity emphasized by Slade and
Way. She stressed instead the literary content of drama and its unique emotional value for children:

> [Drama] brings classes into those areas that in the main are avoided in school:
> emotional control, understanding the place and importance of emotion and
> language with which to express emotion.[44]

Heathcote insisted that "drama is not something special, rather a technique
most ordinary people regularly employ as a way of coping with new and
unsettling experiences."[45]

The 1960s and 70s saw theatre in education develop further in England
in new and radical ways that slowly spread across the Atlantic. Based on
the ideas of Slade, Way, and Heathcote, TIE emerged as a distinct movement in Coventry in 1965 when a team from the Belgrade Repertory Theatre began working in the schools. According to Christine Redington's
history of the movement, TIE joined elements of educational theory (child-
centered, use of play, learning by doing, an interdisciplinary approach to
school subjects, and problem solving) with theatrical elements like narra-

tive plot, empathy, actor-audience interaction, and social and political subject matter.[46] In this respect, TIE represented a whole new dimension in theatrical activity.

The challenges TIE presents to its young audience may seem surprising to Americans unused to an educational system that questions the status quo and demands change. For example, in a class of seventh graders studying the voyages of exploration of Christopher Columbus, one British teacher took a purse from a student's desk by secret prearrangement with that student. When the student publicly asked for her purse back, the teacher refused, stating it was now hers. The entire class protested what the students called "stealing." The teacher opened the purloined purse and removed what appeared to be a private note. The class protested her action again and the teacher explained, "but it's mine now, I discovered it just like Columbus." The class and teacher then engaged in a discussion of the history and ethics of "the discovery of the New World." The class lesson had become dialogic rather than pedantic, experiential rather than passive.[47] Augusto Boal would later call such subversive drama invisible theatre because people are drawn into a play (the drama of the purse's theft, for example) without knowing it has been scripted by a few participants in the know.

In her book, Can Theatre Teach? Christine Redington presents in some detail the TIE drama Pow-Wow, which had been performed for very young children by TIE teams over six years. It's both startling in its daring and powerful in its call to action. I don't think it could be repeated even today in an American public school:

> Mr. Tex, an American showman, walks into the classroom and talks to the children about the white man and the Red Indian and about his "Black Elk" show. He tells the class Black Elk is a savage Red Indian, like his ancestors who killed the white man in America. After the break, the children go to the school field, or to the hall, and find there a teepee in a circular wire cage. Black Elk emerges and does his "show" acting out how Indians lived, with Mr. Tex providing the commentary. When Mr. Tex leaves to make some phone calls the children are left alone with Black Elk. Slowly he gains the children's confidence until, eventually, he gets them to release him from the cage. He then works with the children to create a Red Indian village, and to fish and hunt the buffalo. They have a Pow-Wow, and smoke a peace pipe. Mr. Tex returns and is furious to see Black Elk out of his cage. He demands to be given the peace pipe and the tomahawk which Black Elk has been showing the children. Mr. Tex then asks the children to vote on who should have the tomahawk and the peace pipe. For the voting the children must decide whether to stand by Mr. Tex, that he should have the two items, or by

Black Elk. There are then, two possible endings depending upon the way the children vote.[48]

Note that the conclusion in theory is open-ended and that the children are empowered to make decisions. Because the children do not know they have been cast in a scripted drama and accept the events for real life, this teaching method might be considered highly manipulative. We will see much the same methodology used with unsuspecting adults by Augusto Boal in his invisible theatre.

Emanuel Shipow notes that the TIE movement was "well established by 1968."[49] There were 21 TIE groups operating in Britain in 1979, but replicating the model in other countries proved problematic. Though Shipow found that "every student in Moscow is involved in the [state subsidized] drama-in-education program, of the three educational laboratory theatres in the U.S. [in Providence, New Orleans, and Los Angeles] funded by the National Endowment Fund for the Arts 1966–70 none were refunded."[50] He cited "financial crises, lack of support by teachers, low quality of productions [for] goals haphazardly met."[51] Compared to London and Moscow, he wrote, "in Los Angeles the most widespread attitude toward theatre [in education] is that of apathy."[52]

In the United States funding for arts education roller coastered. The creation of the National Endowment for the Arts (NEA) in 1965 led to an infusion of money that saw local arts agencies grow from 500 to 3,800 nationwide, and in 1971 the NEA established the Expansion Arts Program to encourage the development of community cultural organizations. However, the school desegregation struggle of the 1960s, the Vietnam War escalation, resultant expenses of the 1970s, and the political cry to move "back to basics" successfully undercut new growth. In 1992 George Geahigan found that not much had really improved writing in his report on the status of the arts in education:

> Ever inclined to the practical, American educators have tended to regard the arts as more enjoyable than necessary, as something to be attended to after the serious business of schooling has been finished.[53]

This long-held attitude undermines funding for drama in education and community-based theatre groups to this day and inhibits our ability to see how drama can engage social problems such as youth violence.

Evolving alongside the settlement house and children's drama/drama in education movements was the political theatre movement. At times all three shared not only dramatic techniques but also social goals that resonate today in the work of after-school theatre programs with at-risk teenagers. Oppressed groups often turned to theatre as a means of protesting their lower status in society. For example, the African Company was founded in New York City in 1821 by a group of African Americans who opened their own facility, the African Grove Theatre, for the production of Shakespearean and original plays. But this theatre was closed just two years later after the attacks of white hecklers and police arrests led the city government to declare it a public nuisance. Ira Aldridge, a young actor with the African Company, had to emigrate to Europe to build a reputation, little honored in his own country, as one of the great actors of his time.

Bruce McConachie and Daniel Friedman, in their valuable book *Theatre for Working-class Audiences in the United States, 1830–1980*, find that:

> ante-bellum [1830–1860] working class theatre ... [largely constituted escapism, featuring] apocalyptic melodrama, special effects, and extravagant scenic spectacle [for exploiting workers who sought relief from] ... frustration through a spectacle of destruction.[54]

The tidal wave of immigration from 1870 to 1920, brought to America a working class with a socialist orientation that seized upon theatre as both an organizing and propaganda tool. Carol Poore points to the German-American immigrant socialist workers' theatre of 1877–1900, especially the Arbeiter-Buhne, which presented Max Kegel's *The Press on Trial* and August Ho-Walster's *Saviors of the State*. Socialist political organizations spawned socialist theatres using amateur, rather than professional, actors to present a mix of German (i.e., Hauptmann's *The Weavers*) and American plays. Some 50 socialist plays were written in the United States prior to 1900 and were included in mass meetings and festivals in cities like Cincinnati, Louisville, Chicago, St. Louis and Milwaukee with the goal of connecting socialist ideology to contemporary events and moving their audiences to political action.[55]

Robert Gard and Gertrude Burley, in their book *Community Theatre*, note the establishment of the "first rebel theatre," the Theatre of Arts and Letters in New York City in 1892. This early attempt to institutionalize political drama died "shortly thereafter."[56] In 1905 Julius Hopp founded the Progressive Stage Society in the same city to marry his twin interests in theatre and social reform. When that effort failed, he also founded the Wage Earners Theatre which proved equally short-lived.

The tradition of using amateur actors to present plays of social significance reached its zenith in June 1913 in a production that foreshadowed community-based theatre of the next 100 years. *The Paterson Strike Pageant* brought a crowd of 15,000 to Madison Square Garden to see a cast of 1,500 striking silk workers, Italian, Jewish, and Polish immigrants, under the direction of John Reed and organized under the auspices of the Industrial Workers of the World, reenact incidents of the strike taking place at that very moment in Paterson, New Jersey. Reed, formerly a member of the Dramatic Club associated with George Baker's English 47 class at Harvard, hoped the play would both win the support of the audience and reinforce the commitment of the actors/strikers.[57]

Everything about the strike was theatrical: the setting, protagonists and antagonists, conflict, and theme. Paterson, know as the Lyons of America, housed 276 silk mills where workers toiled 10 hours a day, six days a week for an average wage of 18 cents an hour.[58] The strikers, demanding a reduction in the workweek and a wage of 30 cents an hour, faced a united opposition of mill owners, media, local government and police forces. When they invited the aid of the Industrial Workers of the World (IWW), they created, in the words of the *New York Times*, "the most serious menace the present system of society has ever been called upon to face."[59]

The nonaction of not working had to be made visible and theatrical to scare off replacement workers, gain public support, and demonstrate the strikers' unity and determination. For five months workers walked daily picket lines in front of the mills while an elected strike committee met in daily public sessions. When the local assembly halls were closed to the workers by police orders, hundreds walked several miles each Sunday for legal public meetings in nearby Haledon where they were welcomed by the Socialist mayor.

A sense of decorum, as severe as at any theatre, ruled. When a girl was seen kissing a boy at one meeting, a striker called out: "Mr. Chairman, there is love going on here." The majority voted to expel the young couple from the hall.[60]

To raise funds for the strike, workers held bake sales, dances, and sold tickets to boxing exhibitions, a benefit football game, touring musicians, movies, jugglers, an opera singer, and "an armless wonder."[61] Locals put up signs along Main Street publicizing their solidarity and offering free haircuts, shoe repair and dental services to strikers. Wobbly (IWW) speakers harangued the crowds and Elizabeth Gurley Flynn, only 22, became a local favorite, so in demand that producer David Belasco, the famous "Bishop of Broadway," offered her a role in a labor play. However, she declined the legitimate stage for the illegitimate stage of revolutionary and street-side agitation.

As the strike dragged on, workers found it more and more difficult to make ends meet. To publicize their financial need in a scene orchestrated to tug at the heartstrings, strikers gathered at the local train station to bid goodbye to 600 of their young children who were being sent to be cared for by sympathetic families in New York City.[62]

The mill owners tried their hand at theatre as well, declaring March 17, 1913, "Flag Day" and draping American flags over each mill gate beside calls for strikers to return to work. The striking workers responded by stretching a huge American flag across Main Street with the slogan: "We wove the flag. We dyed the flag. We live under the flag, but we won't scab under the flag."[63]

Paterson became a single unified theatre set designed coequally by the mill owners and the strikers. In the background stood Lambert castle, home of Catholina Lambert, who led the mill owners in opposing the strike. In the castle, complete with stone turrets, Lambert hosted parties for 400 guests at a time and showcased his magnificent collection of European paintings. Belasco, himself, would have loved the spectacle of the castle as backdrop looming above the strikers as they shuffled along on their picket lines down-stage in the valley below.

In April at the bohemian Manhattan salon of Mabel Dodge, Wobbly "Big Bill" Haywood announced the strike would soon be lost if it could not gain wider support. "Then," said Dodge, "why don't you bring the strike to New York?"[64] Leaping to his feet, Dodge's lover John Reed declared "I'll do it" and in an instant plans were laid to put on a show a la Mickey Rooney and Judy Garland. Reed roped Robert Edmund Jones, who later became one of Broadway's greatest set designers, into doing the program, posters, and set, and artist John Sloan to paint the backdrop.

Haywood introduced Reed to the workers at a rally on May 18 and Reed spent part of every successive day in Paterson scripting and rehears-ing the play. Upton Sinclair described Reed "with his shirt sleeves rolled up, shouting through a megaphone, drilling those who were to serve as cap-tains of the mass."[65]

Reed began by asking the workers to show him what they did and then incorporated their actions (already theatricalized in the street) into staged theatre. The babble of languages was a barrier at first but Reed encouraged the strikers on stage to speak in their own language to their own people. Mass singing and bands were added. "One of the gayest touches," wrote Mabel Dodge, "was teaching them to sing one of their lawless songs to 'Harvard, Old Harvard.'"[66]

Only 300 strikers turned out for the first day's rehearsal but soon 1,000 came daily. Scripting the play was easy, said Reed, because the strike "was drama."[67] Workers, reluctant to take the parts of police and scabs at first, eventually filled every role. There were no actors, only strikers.

On June 7, 1913, just three weeks of publicity brought out thousands in a line snaking for blocks around Madison Square Garden. As night fell, hundreds of red lights, surreptitiously installed earlier in the day on the four sides of the Garden tower, the second tallest structure in Manhattan, spelled out the fearsome letters "IWW" ten feet high, to be seen, wrote Mabel Dodge "from one end of town to the other."[68]

Eleven hundred strikers took a special ferry and train from Paterson; others walked the 23 miles, and so began what John Dos Passos called: "The most exciting meeting either of us had ever been to in our lives ... that was one show where the audience really did take part."[69]

The Garden house lights dimmed at 9:01 P.M. and came up on the stage illuminating Sloan's 200-foot painted backdrop of the Paterson mills. Once again it was 6 A.M. on the previous January morning. "First we saw the mill," wrote the *Paterson Evening News*, "stretching its black stoves menacingly to the sky. Its windows were lit, its whistles blowing. We watched [the workers] ... swallowed one by one through the mill's hungry door. Then the ... whirr of iron-hearted machinery began.... And then—something happened, the machinery stopped grinding ... the workers rush from the mill. They wave their hands, they shout.... They sing the Marseilles. The strike is on!"[70]

The audience rose to sing along and, as Mabel Dodge wrote, "For a few electric moments there was a terrible unity between all these people. They were one.... I have never felt such a high pulsing vibration in any gathering before or since."[71]

Reed employed every technique to foster that unity of actors and spectators: the workers marched down the center aisle as if emerging from the audience; when the strikers recreated the funeral of Valentino Modestino, a bystander shot two months earlier by mill detectives, Modestino's own widow wept again from her seat and the audience joined her in "moans and groans and sobs."[72] Then "they took the lid off the coffin and the strikers filed by each dropping a red carnation," wrote Dos Passos, "they showed such grief on their faces that the enormous audience was silent as the dead."[73] Wobbly leader Carlos Tesca rose to deliver the funeral oration, the same speech for which he had been arrested earlier in Paterson: a crime and the staging of the crime.

The merging of reality and stage show, actors and audience became palpable and the New York Press reported: "The Garden has held many shows and many audiences from Taft to Buffalo Bill, but it is doubtful if there was ever such an assemblage either as audience or show.... In fact it was such a mixed grouping that at times they converged and actor became auditor and auditor turned suddenly into actor."[74]

Critics deemed the pageant an artistic success; most organizers called it a political success, but everyone agreed that it was a financial failure, raising but $300 for the strikers' relief. Seven weeks later, hungry and beaten, workers trickled back to the mills. The strike had failed. But the pageant and strike made their mark on American literature inspiring the future theatre work of pageant attendee Susan Glaspell, who cofounded the Provincetown Players, as well as novelists John Dos Passos, Max Eastman, Ernest Poole, and Harry Kemp, and the poet William Carlos Williams. Most importantly, the pageant presented a model of theatre-for-social-change that made possible the alternative theatrical experiments of Moreno, Boal, and others.

Reed was not the only community-theatre practitioner associated with George Baker at Harvard. Baker is most renowned for nurturing playwright Eugene O'Neill, a student who dropped out of the course. O'Neill redefined American commercial theatre with plays of harsh realism, which soon elbowed aside the popular melodramas of the day. However, Baker's groundbreaking work at Harvard impacted many writers who toiled far from Broadway. George Pierce Baker began teaching at Harvard in 1890 in the English Department and soon added drama to his courses at Radcliffe in 1897 and at Harvard in 1900. A proponent of the Little Theatre movement, Baker tried his hand at community-based theatre, directing "farm hands and textile workers" in outdoor pageants at Peterborough and Plymouth in 1910.[75]

Baker's Workshop 47 at Harvard, growing out of his English 47 class, invited audiences as large as 400 to not only attend the staged work of student playwrights but also to remain after the show to supply written evaluations of the work.[76] Before he retired in 1933, having moved to Yale in 1924 to head their newly endowed department of drama, Baker groomed a generation of new American writers including Samuel N. Behrman, Philip Barry, George Sklar, Albert Maltz, Alistair Cooke, Josephine Putnam Peabody, and Rachel Lyman Field. Most important for our purposes are the somewhat lesser-known theatre practitioners who studied under Baker and went on to make important contributions in educational theatre, children's theatre, and political theater. For example, Radcliffe student Elizabeth

McFadden is credited with writing the very first play on child labor, *The Product of the Mill*, produced in Boston in 1912.[77] Charlotte B. Chorpenning, a playwriting student in Baker's English 47 class, began with children's dramatics at Hull House in 1912, went on to work with Winifred Ward at the Children's Theatre of Evanston, wrote plays for children, and joined the Goodman Theatre in Chicago where she worked for two decades, from 1932 to 1952.

However, it was two other men influenced by Baker's work, Robert Gard and Frederick Koch, who added yet another theatrical strand to a growing web of community-based theatre across the nation. Koch, born in 1877 in Kentucky, secured an appointment as an instructor of English at the University of North Dakota in 1905 upon graduation from Harvard. Like most other universities across the country at that time, North Dakota had no theatre building on campus, not even a stage. Theatre, identified with vaudeville, was considered beneath academic interest. However, Koch founded the North Dakota Playmakers and, when he moved to the University of North Carolina (UNC) in 1918, he continued his experimental work in communal drama, mining country folk stories and rural tales for plays. Koch also nourished native playwrights: Thomas Wolfe was in his first playwriting course at UNC. Koch went on to found the Carolina Playmakers in 1919, an organization he would lead until his death in 1944.

Coining the term "folk play" in his playbill of 1919, Koch explained: "The term 'folk' as we use it ... is concerned with folk subject matter: with the legends, superstitions, customs, environmental differences and vernacular of the common people."[78] In his bid to empower the oppressed and give voice to the voiceless, Koch founded the Bureau of Community Drama, which included subdivisions of Negro drama and tenant-farmer drama, reaching out to poor people and helping even small, rural towns to stage their own plays. Part of this effort included community pageants similar to those previously mentioned. Of these, the most famous was Koch's production of Paul Green's *The Lost Colony*, dramatizing the history of Roanoke Island, a pageant still performed in the area today. The Carolina Playmakers toured throughout the South well into the 1940s.

Alfred Arvold built on Koch's work in North Dakota when he joined the faculty of the Agricultural College in Fargo. When the college opened a new administration building in 1914, Arvold made sure it included a 200-seat theatre and then filled the stage with plays by rural residents of the state, who wrote about the issues they faced, like the financial plight of farmers and the prejudice directed against country folk by their city cousins.

Arvold wrote, echoing Shakespeare's words, that the stage holds a mirror up to life:

> It is through the drama that people learn to interpret human nature, its weaknesses and strength. The sad and the happy, the rich and the poor, the strong and the weak, the young and the old, those with many different ideas see their actions reflected in this mirror.[79]

Born in 1910 on the plains of Kansas, Robert Gard pursued a full theatrical career that never came within a hundred miles of Broadway. In Kansas, upstate New York, the Canadian prairie province of Alberta, and, finally, Wisconsin, Gard collected stories, wrote plays, and encouraged other playwrights in the most unlikely places. His was a lifelong quest for a people's theatre and an unbroken commitment to involve as many people as possible in the process of theatrical creation. He wrote in his 1954 book *Grassroots Theater: A Search for Regional Arts in America*: "The true 'people's theater,' as I see it, will be the creation for the community of a drama in which the whole community may participate."[80]

Gard was a second generation legacy of George Pierce Baker, studying while at Cornell with Alexander Drummond, founder of the Cornell Dramatic Club, who had, himself, been enrolled in Workshop 47 with Frederick Koch. At Cornell, Gard began "to wonder whether the people of America might be drawn together in tolerance and joy ... in a theatre whose stages were everywhere and whose actors were the folks in the cities and on the farms."[81]

Gard grounded his work away from the cities, out in the small towns and farms that constituted rural life because for him "a feeling for place ... seems basic to the creative process."[82] For the first two months he tramped the back roads of upstate New York. Sometimes when he went out searching for authors and stories, he found himself on a farm at evening milking the cows with the farmer. Working with Drummond, Gard dispatched letters soliciting playwrights. One enthusiastic response appended this PS: "What shall I write about?"[83] But others had ideas, and plays poured into his Ithaca office with tales of the Cardiff Giant, rural ghosts, and other New York folktales.

The transition from page to stage was even harder, and Gard, traveling from one small, stageless town hall to another, had to adapt to the circumstances, demonstrating theatre in the round to those who had never imagined stages without a proscenium arch.

Invited to teach in Madison, Gard adopted the "Wisconsin idea" of political reformers like "Fighting" Bob LaFollette, to the theatrical arena.

Meant to democratize society, the Wisconsin idea embraced adult education and university extension programs. Gard founded the Wisconsin Idea Theatre. Combining the first theatre lab on the campus of the University of Wisconsin with annual three-day state-wide theatre conferences, he also reached out to found both the Wisconsin Rural Writers Association and the Rural Arts Project which brought traveling exhibitions into the most isolated rural hamlet.

Prefiguring Augusto Boal and his forum theatre, Gard improvised plays to tackle contemporary controversies, pressing audience members into becoming actors on the spot. The result was hundreds of grassroots plays written and produced on stage and radio. One playwright, Zona Gale, a member of the Wisconsin Dramatic Society founded by Thomas Dickinson, another professor at the University of Wisconsin, Madison, waived royalties to her play *The Neighbors* for

> any country theatre which will use part of the funds so raised ... to plant at least one long-lived shade tree in the community ... furthermore it is understood that the producers, cast, and the audience at such performance shall all be neighbors to everyone, as long as they live.[84]

Gale later won the Pulitzer Prize for her play *Miss Lulu Betts* in 1921.

Gard, who neglected the role of settlement houses in his account of the development of community-based theatre, traced his ideas back to the American tours of W.B. Yeats and the Irish Players in 1903 and 1911 and looked back to the classical Greek theatre and its multiple religious, civic, and aesthetic roles in that society. Gard's emphasis was on social development rather than commercial or artistic success. Never stridently political like John Reed, for example, Gard understood community theatre as playing an educational and unifying role in a democratic society.

The phrase "community theatre" seems to have been coined by Louise Burleigh in her 1917 book *The Community Theatre in Theory and Practice*. Burleigh saw such theatre as a way to "amalgamate" Americans of different faiths, races, and ethnicities.[85] "The community theatre is a house of play," she wrote, "in which events offer to every member active participation in a common interest."[86] Claiming the world's first example of community theatre to be the famous festival performances at Oberammergau, Burleigh recalled how that community overcame the threat of the plague by promising to reenact the passion of Christ every ten years. Burleigh theorized that the involvement of some 700 nonprofessional actors, themselves drawn from generations of townspeople, performing for tens of thousands of fellow residents and visitors achieved "the perfect unity between players and audience."[87]

Beyond theatre circles, political leaders continued to see the efficacy of utilizing theatre for specific political ends as well. W.E.B. Du Bois (1868–1963), a founder of the NAACP and editor of its organ the *Crisis*, looked at the burgeoning movement of community theatres and "became interested in using theatre to advance the cause of black Americans."[88] Du Bois "urged formation of a nationwide movement of little theatres presenting plays 'about us, by us, for us, and near us.' Du Bois' the *Crisis* and the Urban League's *Opportunity* magazine, sponsored playwriting competitions and published prize-winning entries."[89] Du Bois helped found the Krigwa Players in New York City and, in 1950, the Committee for the Negro and the Arts.[90]

CHAPTER 4

Evolution of Community-Based Theatre in the U.S.

THE GREAT DEPRESSION PLUNGED the United States into an unprecedented period of economic collapse and presented the possibility of radical political change. Though Nellie McCaslin describes the previous decade as a time of expansion for children's theatre in recreation centers, Little Theatres, and on the playgrounds of America, sponsored in part by the national publication the *Playground*, economic woes soon brought that expansion to a halt. But this same set of events created the Federal Theatre Project, aimed at employing out-of-work theatre practitioners and bringing entertainment to people suffering through the economic crisis.

Created in 1935 under the direction of Hallie Flanagan, the project produced both classics and original plays but struggled with charges of Communist infiltration and accusations of subversive intent until Congress terminated their funding in 1939. The Living Newspaper, a troupe within the Federal Theatre Project, is best-known for its social and political commentary. Its style, with actors improvising contemporaneous comments on the news of the day in short, episodic scenes, would be copied by many later theatre practitioners including Boal. One of the Living Newspaper's best-known works was *Power*, which advocated the public ownership of utilities, a political goal realized in the Tennessee Valley Authority as well as in Soviet Russia.

The Federal Theatre Project employed 12,700 people at its peak and put on 42,000 performances for audiences of 20 million in its first two years of existence. It is estimated that 65 percent of those audiences were seeing a play for the first time in their lives "for half the cost of a battleship as Hallie Flanagan ... liked to boast."[1]

The Federal Theatre Project moved into children's entertainment with the creation of the Federal Children's Theatre, though this usually involved adult actors performing for audiences of children. This group performed in 15 cities across the country. In their repertory were plays by Charlotte Chorpenning and the Workshop 47 and Hull House alumnus discussed in the previous chapter.

Even this work did not go unscrutinized for political content. The 1937 play, The Revolt of the Beavers, for example, was described by conservatives as Communist propaganda, because it recounted the story of beavers who banded together and rose up against an oppressive Boss Beaver. Brooks Atkinson, critic for the New York Times, called it: "Mother Goose Marx ... a primary school lesson in the class struggle."[2] Though the Federal Theatre Project denied the charges and liberals mocked it as anti–Communist paranoia, the play was closed as too controversial.

Flanagan's career helps demonstrate the interconnections within the evolving community-theatre movement: the production of plays, for both adults and children, with professional and amateur actors, tackling contemporary political and social issues, in traveling shows and unorthodox performance spaces, from town halls to public libraries.

Other theatre groups of the 1930s married theatrical experimentation and original material to explicit political goals. The Group Theatre was the best known and longest-lived of these and its production of Clifford Odet's Waiting for Lefty epitomizes both the success and failure of political theatre and could be compared in effect and intent with John Reed's Paterson silk strike pageant. Odet's tale of the taxi drivers' strike then underway in the New York streets outside the theatre had entire audiences rising from their seats to join the actors on stage in shouting "Strike! Strike!" the final lines of the play, only to then leave the theatre where the wealthier attendees hailed scab cabs for their ride home. The Hungarian Dramatic Circle, the Jewish Artef Group, the theatrical wing of the League of Struggle for Negro Rights, and the New York City–based German Prolet-Buhne each briefly flourished and then expired for lack of finances.[3]

Mike Gold and John Howard Lawson formed the short-lived Workers' Drama League in 1926 and the Workers' Laboratory Theatre in 1930, whose aims were described by a spokesman:

traveling groups must be evolved, ready one day to go to a strike meeting to cheer up the strikers, just as ready another day to accompany a demonstration to inspire the workers; it must be a theatre where the worker may be inspired to fight for his liberation; a theatre of the workers, by the workers, for the workers.[4]

The League of Workers Theatres (LOWT) formed in April 1932, published the magazine *Workers' Theatre* with a circulation of 18,000, and became the Theatre of Action in 1934 before expiring a year later. The LOWT had 400 theatre affiliates and aimed "to propagate the acceptance of radical political solutions." The Shock Troupe faction of the Workers' Laboratory Theatre in New York City publicly embraced the goal of a workers' revolution in America, producing both a play on the Scottsboro Boys in 1934 and the anti–Nazi drama *Who's Who in the Berlin Zoo* in 1935, the year of their demise as well. Professor Sonja Kuftinec, author of *(Re)constructing the American Cabin*, assessed the strength of the movement noting that in the 1930s "400 workers' theatres staged a piece by Langston Hughes entitled *Scottsboro Limited* recounting the story of the 9 young black men in Alabama accused of raping two white women." The Scottsboro boys' convictions on weak evidence personified Southern racism for liberals and radicals across the country.

Looking back on this period, Daniel Friedman writes:

> An indigenous workers' theatre movement developed in the early 1930s. It was the only grassroots amateur movement in U.S. history in which workers created theatre for their fellow workers. At its height the movement involved hundreds of troupes and tens of thousands of workers who wrote, directed, performed, and attended their own theatrical pieces ... they adapted and developed a particular performance style and aesthetic attitude.[5]

This phenomenon of workers creating theatre for their fellow workers was practiced at Hull House 50 years earlier and was to be embraced 40 years later in the community-based theatre of Augusto Boal.

The overtly political theatre of Erwin Piscator and Bertolt Brecht impacted American community-based theatre as well, in its political focus, its redefinition of audience, and its emphasis on social effect. Erwin Piscator's (1893–1966) groundbreaking work occurred with *The Red Revue* at the Proletarishes Theatre and at the Volksbuhne, whose motto was "art to the people," and in his own Piscator Buhne in Germany in the 1920s and 30s. His style, often called agitprop, relied on short scenes, and a mix of drama, dance, song, slide projections, and film, and the cross-referencing of events on stage with real political events. Piscator's work influenced many other groups, including the Living Newspaper, and made a lasting contribution to a stagecraft more interested in ideas than entertainment. As Piscator said in 1928, "our art was created from a knowledge of reality and inspired by the will to replace this reality."[6] His theatre functioned as a collective of practitioners united for a common cause. As he wrote in 1930:

> Never was it more essential than now to take sides—the side of the proletariat. More than ever the theatre must nail its flag fanatically to the mast of politics: the politics of the proletariat. More and more insistent grows the demand: theatre is action, the action of the proletariat. The stage and the masses [together] in the militant theatre of the proletariat.[7]

In exile in America from 1939 to 1951, Piscator influenced actors like Marlon Brando, Tony Curtis, and Rod Steiger, the playwright Tennessee Williams, and people's theatre practitioner Judith Malina, cofounder of the Living Theatre.

Piscator's contemporary and occasional coworker, Bertolt Brecht (1898–1956), also greatly influenced the development of community-based theatre, first in his native Germany and later in exile in the United States. For all of Brecht's theatrical innovations, special attention in this context should be given to his *Lehrstucke*, or teaching plays, which combined elements of political, educational, and community-based theatre that would be seen again in our own time. Brecht reacted against the long-held notion that the theatre was reflective, a mirror held up to nature, arguing that "art is not a mirror held up to society, but a hammer with which to shape it."[8] Brecht aimed to do this by involving his audience in the stage action in new ways and in transforming the audience in the process in a manner that will be further explored in the chapters that follow. Brecht writes:

> In this new theatre I shall feel free to transform my audience into kings. Not only into the semblance of kings but into the real thing. Into statesmen, thinkers, and engineers. What an audience I'll have! What goes on in the world I shall bring before their judgment seat ... it is to become a laboratory for this great mass of working people. I too shall act accordingly: Alter the world; it needs it.[9]

The *Lehrstucke*, consisting of six plays written during years of upheaval in Germany from 1929 to 1934, include *The Measures Taken*, *The Exception and the Rule*, and *He Who Says Yes*. They were "primarily intended as schoolroom exercises ... for the actor-pupil's instruction, not for presentation to passive audiences."[10] These short, didactic works were performed by students, often nonactors themselves, as part of their education in Marxist ideals. No audience was necessary because the participants constituted (foreshadowing Boal's idea of "spect/actors") both audience and performers, changing roles according to the development of ideas in the plays.

Brecht believed that moral lessons were best learned by participation in their action; what John Dewey had called "learning by doing." Brecht wrote, "the *Lehrstucke* ... is designed to clarify the ideas of the authors and all those taking part, not to provide anyone with an emotional experience." Their goal was debate, discussion, and judgment. Not a new form, but one used "by the Jesuits during the Counter-Reformation."[11] Such teaching plays raised problems and questions but often failed to give answers. This is exactly what makes *The Measures Taken*, for example, such a disturbing play. The drama, in which four Russian Communists kill a Chinese comrade after his heartfelt interventions to alleviate other people's suffering undermine their secret mission, asks the question of whether or not the ends justify the means. Such a huge, abstract, moral, and ambiguous question places the play on a much deeper level than mere Communist propaganda.

Of the *Lehrstucke* Brecht wrote:

> Briefly the aristotelian play is essentially static; its task is to show the world as it is. The learning play is essentially dynamic; its task is to show the world as it changes [and also how it may be changed.... These experiments were theatrical performances meant not so much for the spectator as for those who were engaged in the performance. It was, so to speak, art for the producer, not art for the consumer.[12]

Five decades later, Augusto Boal continued this critique of Aristotelian drama and also shifted "control of the means of [artistic] production" (in Marxist terms) from the owners (producers, theatre owners and capitalist investors in theatre) to the workers (the spectators/actors) who actually make the plays.

Inspired by Brecht and others, anarchist-pacifists Judith Malina and Julian Beck picked up the thread of radical political theatre to create the Living Theatre in 1947. Beck and Malina first met in 1943, he an 18-year-old dropout from Yale who had chosen Thoreau and Gandhi as his mentors, and she a 17-year-old who had trained with Piscator at the Dramatics Workshop at the New School. They offered their first plays in their own Manhattan apartment on August 15, 1951, and featured the work of Brecht, Gertrude Stein, García Lorca, and Pirandello. When Beck inherited $6,000, the troupe briefly relocated to the Cherry Lane Theatre but was chased out by the fire department after just eight months. It was an early indicator of the gypsy existence to come. They operated from 1954 to 1956 at Broadway and 100th Street until evicted by the Building Department. They had no permanent home until 1959 when they created a new theatre in a former department store at Sixth Avenue and 14th Street only to be evicted once again, this time by the Internal Revenue Service for nonpayment of federal excise and payroll taxes. This was followed by sojourns, demonstrations, and arrests in Europe, 1964–68; the United States, 1970; and Brazil, 1970–71. They returned to the United States and settled again in New York City in 1984, where Beck died the next year. The Living Theater continues under the direction of Judith Malina and Hanon Reznikov.

Important characteristics of the Living Theatre, a significant influence on contemporary theatre makers, were its emphasis on experimentation on stage, political engagement, and its commitment to erasing the space between performers and audiences. Julian Beck made very clear his rejection of commercial theatre, writing in *The Life of the Theatre*:

> I am a man not interested in the theatre, the entertainments that demean our being, the dissemination of lies. Fun is destructive while joy creates ... I do not choose to work in the theatre but in the world.[13]

In 1968 Beck said, "life, revolution, and theatre are 3 words for the same thing: an uncompromising 'NO' to the present society."[14] To a clear political commitment, the Living Theatre added a commitment to not merely affecting its audience, but also to liberating them. As Pierre Biner wrote in his history of the Living Theatre: "Overall the work of the Living Theatre is one of unification. It strives for unification in reuniting actor and spectator, in abolishing the distance between them both spatially and temporally."[15] In fact, the Living Theatre, attempting to create a community of spectators and actors, often invited the audience to join its actors on stage in plays like *Mysteries and Smaller Pieces*, or the "group grope" of *Paradise Now* where actors invited audience members to remove their clothes and join the naked cast on stage, and ended with the actors leading the audience into the streets where members of both cast and audience were arrested for indecent exposure and breach of the peace. At other times Living Theatre actors would invite audience members to join them in the "subversive" act of smoking marijuana, the goal being again to jolt audiences into a new social and political awareness. The Living Theater's ambition was, in Beck's words:

> to create the spectacle that would so shake people up, so move them, so cause feeling to be felt ... that the steel world of law and order which civilization had forged to protect itself from barbarism would melt.[16]

The Living Theatre's production of Jack Gelber's *The Connection* induced exactly that kind of emotional reaction in its audience: 50 men are reported to have fainted at the sight of drug addicts and actors shooting heroin into their veins or, depending upon the source of the story, realistically simulating the same on stage.

In Brazil in 1970 the company performed *The Favela Project* with and for poor workers and their families in the city slums, known as *favelas*. In one slum outside Sao Paulo they interviewed people and then put their personal stories of misery on stage. The play ends with a scene in which Death binds and gags all of the actors who depend upon the audience members to enter the stage to untie them. Since the company failed to obtain various permits, the performance was illegal, and untying the actors would be an act of rebellion. According to Malina, one of the residents whispered as she released her: "Tomorrow the *favellados* will free the people of the whole world."[17] The authorities responded by arresting 18 members of the company for possession of marijuana and deported them after two months of imprisonment.

In summarizing the work of the Living Theatre, Beck asked and answered his own question: "What can theatre do? It can provoke ... it can unchain."[18] Stage drama that can "cause feeling to be felt," "unchain" spectators and so change lives has often been the goal of political theatre.

The idea that life-changing drama was accessible to nonprofessionals, and nonadults, was continually developing in the parallel worlds of educational and political drama. In 1951 it found expression in the street drama *Dope!*, conceived by a young playwright, and student of anthropology and religion, Mary Attaway Lee, and performed on the streets of Harlem by its own teenage black residents. Though not ideologically political, this community-based theatre clearly aimed at personal and social transformation.

Lee, born in Covington, Kentucky, in 1923, earned her BA from Wellesley College and moved to New York City in 1950 to work as an assistant at the Society for Applied Anthropology Oral History Project, under the direction of Margaret Mead at Columbia University. In the 1950s she studied with Jacob Moreno, the father of psychodrama, and earned her master's degree at Union Theological Seminary where she wrote her thesis, "Practical Inquiry into the Matter of Drama and Religion," and took the professional name of Maryat Lee.

Lee explained her awakening commitment to the healing power of theatre in these words:

> As a young woman, I had the naive idea that one purpose of theatre was to expose specific and universal truths hidden by appearance. Appearances, like

fashions, are specifically designed to divide us. As a southerner I grew up feeling that we were all hiding behind appearances and the roles assigned to us early in life. Theatre offered the chance to step out of that under the protection of whatever character we played, to reveal vital, if hidden, aspects of ourselves. This sharing act of truth would help bridge divisions and create a cleansed and loving community.[19]

Lee began her playwriting career studying and writing adaptations of medieval mystery plays which she felt "spoke to and about ordinary people." She set out to discover the artist in each person:

What if "artists" have separated themselves from ordinary life to such an extent that they have no way to address anyone but themselves? What if there are artists all around us in the community but they've never been recognized? They only feel the presence of some power imprisoned inside them as a vague, restless dissatisfaction with life that they can never still. They must numb themselves in order to forget the ache of idleness brought on by neglecting that power, and that power becomes only a dream that leaks out at inappropriate moments. What if this power were truly aroused and recognized? We are all artists and it is time to unseparate.[20]

Lee drew East Harlem residents into collaborating on a play based on their lives. They were the artists. While *Dope!* featured one professional in the lead role of Louie, the other actors had no training or prior experience. The part of the drunk, for example, was played by a local alcoholic who, unable to memorize his lines, improvised his part differently at each performance. In the play Louie, an addict, tries to get straight but when he sees his 15-year-old sister get hooked, he attacks his dealer "Porse," who shoots Louie. Before dying, Louie claims for himself a final victory in having stood up to the power of heroin, saying "I didn't take it, I won."[21]

At its premier on April 25, 1951, 2,000 people crowded into the street and onto fire escapes to see the play performed in a vacant lot "in the heart of the narcotics traffic for five consecutive nights."[22] *Dope!* included mambo music and featured neighborhood dancers and musicians. Conceived and performed by the community for the community, the play went on to be featured in *The Best Short Plays of 1952-53*, excerpted on television, and reprised in Madison Square Garden.

In 1968 cheerleaders at Ben Franklin High School approached Lee. They explained that they believed members of their basketball team were doing drugs and they sought permission to revive *Dope!* and perform it without paying royalties. In response, Lee went to work with them to develop a new play based on their own experiences and the result was the play *Day to Day* and the birth of SALT, the Soul and Latin Theatre, comprised of black and Puerto Rican teenagers who performed in storefronts and on the streets of their communities. Lee explained:

> The Soul and Latin Theater is an occasion in which an otherwise voiceless community can mobilize and express its strength, talent, character, idiom, and pride in terms that would provide cultural recognition through making something of value and uniqueness for themselves and the community as a whole.[23]

SALT wrote and performed a series of plays developed from community improvisations: *Day to Day*, the story of a teen who steals and sells family possessions to finance a drug habit; *After the Fashion Show*, in which a teen reveals his homosexuality to his hostile father; *The Classroom*, about a middle-class black teacher who bullies a black pupil; and *Lula*, in which a young woman organizes a rent strike. In a moment of audience participation, and possible catharsis (a subject to be pursued in chapter 9), the crowd watching one performance of *After the Fashion Show* carried the lead actor off on their shoulders as a hero for standing up to his father.[24]

Harkening back to Lee's own studies in medieval drama, SALT used an old hay wagon drawn by an automobile as a portable stage in pageant wagon style. The 8-by-14-foot playing area was jury-rigged with loudspeakers for street performances. SALT, with ten actors ages 15 to 18, operated out of LaGuardia House, a settlement house at East 116th street in Manhattan. But then one teen actor died of an overdose and SALT fell prey to internal squabbles.

In 1971 Lee moved to rural West Virginia where she founded EcoTheatre, a rural analog to the work she had done on the mean streets of New York. She cast local, untrained, and unpaid actors to perform outdoors each summer, often returning to pageant-style farm wagons to create performance space. The actors were "mostly teenagers from the surrounding counties, many with troubled home lives and too little money coming in."[25] She used "oral history, taped conversations, gossip, local newspaper items, folklore, diaries, and written reminiscences that townspeople gave her" to create stories of the community.[26]

Lee wrote:

> EcoTheatre has proved to be a good name. It says quite clearly to our audiences that in your own home you can do this too, make a theatre to take its place alongside the professional theatre.... You do not need an interpreter, or an intermediary, or a trained pro. After all, you, and no one else, are the authorities of your lives.
>
> In EcoTheatre we have no actors in the usual sense. EcoTheatre actors per-

form scenes or plays. But instead of studying and playing roles, they experience moments of being themselves.[27]

That last description ties together points that will be made in chapter 9 about the communal nature of community-based theatre and the psychological distancing of drama that allows people to work out their personal issues on stage. Lee died in September 1989 but EcoTheatre performances continue each summer.

What these varied attempts in community-based theatre have in common is their shared aim of making theatre that changes lives. For the settlement houses that meant both educational and socioeconomic changes. For the children's theatre and the theatre in education movements that always meant educational changes and, sometimes, political changes. Commercial and artistic pursuits were tangential or entirely absent from the enterprise. In time each came to believe that their goals could best be met by collapsing the barriers between audience and actors: by enlisting amateurs as actors, by taking the plays into the street to the audience, and/or by soliciting dramatic material from their prospective audiences. Each of these movements helped construct the foundation for today's community-based theatre programs targeting at-risk teens.

Self-consciously political theatre groups that aligned themselves with great social movements also adapted many of these techniques for their work and explored new possibilities for enlisting and energizing audiences and nonactors. In the 1950s and 60s these movements were the struggle for civil rights and the antiwar movement. Most significant of black theatre troupes at mid-century were the American Negro Theatre and the Free Southern Theatre, although many other groups formed, died, reformed, performed, and closed their doors in that time.

Abram Hill and Frederick O'Neal founded the American Negro Theatre (ANT) in June 1940. Hill, born in Atlanta in 1914, studied drama at the New School for Social Research under John Gassner, later a mentor to Augusto Boal, and worked with the Federal Theatre Project as a play reader. It commissioned him to prepare a black history piece for the Living Newspaper. ANT operated out of the 135th Street Library Theatre that had once been home to W.E.B. Du Bois' Krigwa Players. ANT's goal was to "break down the barriers of Black participation in the theatre, to portray Negro history as they honestly saw it, and to fill in the gap of a Black theatre which did not exist."[28] Over nine years the company produced 19 plays, several of which transferred to Broadway; gave 325 performances; trained 200 people; and reached 50,000 more audience members. Harry Belafonte and

Sidney Poitier are products of its drama school. ANT finally closed after several years of decline, its brightest stars seduced away by the commercial theatre. As Hill said years later, "people came into it after trying to get to Broadway. The ANT became a showcase instead of an experimental theatre."[29]

While individual black playwrights like Lorraine Hansberry, LeRoi Jones, Ed Bullins, James Baldwin, and others brought stories of the black experience to black and white audiences in the commercial theatres of the late 1950s and 60s, the Free Southern Theatre (FST) attempted to marry art to politics in an expressed hope to support the civil rights movement and spark social change. FST was founded in 1963 by John O'Neal, Doris Derby, and Gilbert Moses, members of the Southern Nonviolent Coordinating Committee (SNCC), with the aid of Richard Schechner, editor of the *Tulane Drama Review*. Based in New Orleans, FST took as its motto "Theatre for people who have no theatre." To accomplish that goal, FST included people previously excluded from the theatre, telling the *Christian Science Monitor* in 1965:

> FST seeks to present socially relevant drama which reflects life honestly while maintaining high artistic and theatrical standards. The three directors see theatre as a communal experience, an event in which the audience as well as the actors participate.[30]

Just as the civil rights movement put "people power" in the streets in marches, demonstrations, pickets, and sit-ins, FST aimed to put culture, theatre as well as folk songs, in the streets where they would be accessible to all. As Richard Schechner put it: "The Theatre would say in art what the Movement had been saying in politics."[31]

Such goals required courage as well as skill in those dangerous times. FST's August 1964 performance in Meridian, Mississippi, was canceled when the bodies of civil rights workers Andrew Goodman, James Chaney, and Michael Schwerner were discovered buried in an earthen dam nearby. At times, FST took the stage under the protection of armed members of the Deacons for Defense of Equality and Justice.

On tours, FST mixed classics and new plays. The repertoire included: Martin Duberman's *In White America*, Beckett's *Waiting for Godot*, O'Casey's *The Shadow of a Gunman*, and Ossie Davis' *Purlie Victorious*. Performing in theatres, churches, and on campuses, often to people who had never seen a live play before, FST regularly included local nonactors and productions were sometimes unscripted. O'Neal believed that "the strongest art work is that which is most deeply rooted in the folklife and traditions of the people for whom the work is created."[32] But this could be folklife and traditions broadly defined. Fannie Lou Hamer led the Mississippi Freedom Delegation to the 1964 Democratic Convention where they disrupted carefully scripted plans to present President Lyndon Johnson and his chosen running mate Senator Hubert Humphrey as unchallenged champions of civil rights. Hamer had no difficulty in also responding to FST's production of *Waiting for Godot*, a Samuel Beckett play that confounded Broadway critics:

> Every day we see men dressed just like these [tramps] sitting around bars, pool halls, and on street corners waiting for something! They must be waiting for Godot! But you can't sit around waiting. Ain't nobody going to bring you nothing. You got to get up and fight for what you want. Some people are sitting around waiting for somebody to bring in Freedom just like these men are sitting there, waiting for Godot.[33]

Free Southern Theatre's production of *Slave Ship*, on the other hand, drew from the collective memory of a people brought to America in chains in the brutal and dehumanizing Middle Passage. In this performance, the audience was seated in and on the slave ship "becoming participants in the theatrical event" that happened around and to them.[34] After all, wrote O'Neal, "isn't communion the desired relationship between actors and audience?"[35]

Riven by internal political disputes, personality clashes, and ongoing financial challenges, FST was interred with its own New Orleans jazz funeral in 1985.

Dissent against America's war in Vietnam in the 1960s and 70s brought two emerging theatre troupes, the Bread and Puppet Theatre and the San Francisco Mime Troupe, to greater public notice. When Youth International Party leader Jerry Rubin declared "life is theatre ... the street is the stage,"[36] he was describing the mixture of political and theatrical activities that constituted the massive demonstrations against the war that brought millions of Americans into the streets seeking to change government policy.

The Bread and Puppet Theatre was founded by pacifist Peter Schumann who had begun giving puppet shows and dance performances in his native Germany in 1960. Upon arriving in New York City in 1961, Schumann founded the new troupe and with a mix of professionals and amateurs presented 139 separate productions between 1962 and 1981. Operating from the principal that "theatre is like bread, more like a necessity,"[37] Bread and Puppet offered their shows for free and often distributed homemade bread to their audiences, a secular communion. Using larger-than-life puppets, the group addressed contemporary issues, often relying on disturbing visual images rather than text. Utilizing as many as 100 participants or as few as a dozen, performances varied in length from several minutes to three hours. People were recruited to make masks, banners, and puppets and both the preparations and performances were designed to be inclusive of children as well as adults. Spectators were often invited into the roles of actors in the performances, as indicated in one member's description of his experiences in 1972:

> David and I said we would help Bart, Joe, John, and Tom from Coney Island do a Bread and Puppet Theatre pageant at the State University of New York at New Paltz. We drove a truck up from the city packed with puppets. We needed 150 people to present the story of how Mr. Smallman became Mr. Bigman by eating all the people of the world. It was late Sunday morning when we arrived; nobody was around. We had not been announced. We started to unload the truck while a rock band began to play (it was "Spring Weekend"). By the time we were done there were 300 people sitting on the grass listening to the music and looking at the puppets. About 10 people had started to help us unload. The band finished. Bart got a bullhorn and climbed a ladder. "We need twelve people to be inside the dragon." "Who wants to carry the world (a spherical puppet with lots of people growing out of it)?" "We need six capitalist friends of Mr. Smallman's." "Someone has to carry the hot dog Mr. Smallman eats." "Who wants to carry Mr. Bigman's cigar?" We lowered Mr. Bigman's head with its Uncle Sam hat onto his body from the top of the truck. Some of the men pulled the 30-foot devil puppet up on its stand; the afternoon sun was caught behind his scarlet robe, casting horrific shadows. Twenty-five women put on Vietnamese lady masks. Twelve people raised the apostles up, as the whole earth between the dormitories at New Paltz continued to erupt with a fantastical puppet pageant.[38]

For years Bread and Puppet was a fixture of antiwar and antiracism street demonstrations and toured internationally before retiring to Glover, Vermont, in 1974 where they farm communally and maintain a museum. Their best-known productions have been *Cry of the People for Meat*, *The Domestic Resurrection Circus*, and *The Uprising of the Beast* with which they emerged from retirement to tour Russia and Europe in 1990. In 2001-02 they reappeared again in demonstrations against U.S. intervention in the Middle East.

The San Francisco Mime Troupe, still performing today, was founded by R.G. Davis in 1959. Influenced by developments in the 1960s, the group "moved from silent mime, to avant-garde happenings to *commedia dell'arte* styled performance and on to radical politics,"[39] dedicating itself to creating art that supports social change and adopting the motto "Engagement, Commitment, and Fresh Air." By the time Davis left the group in 1970, it had become a quasi–Marxist collective.[40] Known for its outdoor performances that led to arrests for presenting "vulgar" material in public and a court decision that vindicated them in 1965,[41] the Mime Troupe tours nationally and internationally and annually returns for free performances in San Francisco parks where they premier new work.

The troupe scripts new plays on contemporary issues. In 1999, for example, they tackled health maintenance organizations, and in 2001, urban gentrification. Satire, physical comedy, melodrama, rock music, and outlandish costumes and masks mark their productions which aim to educate and energize audiences for radical social change. Frequent Mime Troupe playwright Joan Holden has said:

> When we do the right show at the right time for the right people on the right subject, the energy that surges up from the audience gives a taste of what people really moving could be like.[42]

The 1960s saw numerous community-based and/or political theatre groups flower and then die. The New York Street Caravan, founded in 1968, was a racially integrated troupe that sought out working-class audiences, often performing in union halls or from the back of flatbed trucks. Students for a Democratic Society (SDS) spawned several guerrilla theatre groups as part of their organizing and antiwar work on college campuses, including RATS (Radical Arts Troupe) of the Connecticut SDS, and the People's Street Theatre of the New York SDS.

Perhaps the most important community-based theatre group to emerge in the 1960s was El Teatro Campesino founded by Luis Valdez. In 1964 Valdez traveled to Cuba where he saw for the first time theatre being used in the service of social transformation. In 1965 he joined the San Francisco Mime Troupe after seeing a production:

> A version of "Tartuffe" was the first thing I saw the Mime Troupe do and it really impressed me because of their on-the-spot references to what was happening right there in the street. They had restructured a classical drama and given it new life.[43]

In September 1965 thousands of farmworkers under the leadership of Cesar Chavez and the United Farm Workers Union went on strike against the grape growers in Delano, California. When it became clear that the union needed to find new ways to communicate with, organize, and energize undereducated and sometimes illiterate workers, Valdez founded El

Teatro Campesino with the sons and daughters of farmworkers to present politically pointed 15-minute bilingual *actos*, mixing *commedia dell'arte*, Cantinflas, and Mime Troupe styles in the fields, union halls, and the streets. El Teatro Campesino created the *actos* collectively through improvisation with the single goal of moving the audience to action.

Slowly evolving its themes and styles, El Teatro Campesino moved from the shorter *actos* (agitprop in nature) to longer *mitos*, that drew upon mythic and religious images from Mexican folklore, to *corridos*, full-length plays mixing dialogue, narration, and familiar ballads. Many of its plays, like the *acto Las Dos Caras del Patroncito*, in which two characters wear the masks of Owner and Worker and exchange places, and the *corrido La Carpa de Jesus Pelado Rasquachi*, which follows the alternately hilarious adventures and enraging exploitation of a young man who leaves his family in Mexico to cross the border illegally and find work in the fields of California, tackled subjects close to the personal experiences of their intended audiences and were performed with minimal and portable props and sets. Valdez aimed for "a theatre that is revolutionary in technique as well as intent" which would educate people "toward an appreciation of social change."[44]

El Teatro Campesino spawned a series of similar teatros across the country and then moved to broaden its message from support for a single union to an assertion of Chicano cultural autonomy. It moved into the world of commercial theatre with the play *Zoot Suit* in 1978, a reexamination of the Sleepy Lagoon murder case and the railroading of Chicano teens by an Anglo judicial system in 1940s Los Angeles. *Zoot Suit* proved a great success in Los Angeles but was a bust on Broadway. The company relocated to the little town of San Juan Bautista in northern California in 1971 and became El Centro Campesino Cultural where the "political has now given way to the cultural and the mystical."[45] Today, the company lives and farms communally following a Mayan model.

The Dakota Theatre Caravan, Alternate Roots (Regional Organizations of Theatres South), Teatro de la Esperanza, and Little Flags Theatre Company are but a few more of these community-based politically active theatre companies of the 1960s, 70s and 80s.

CHAPTER 5

Augusto Boal and the
Theatre of the Oppressed

IN THE LATE 1960S YET ANOTHER STRAND was added to the braided history of community-based theatre. The Catholic Church in Latin America embraced liberation theology and spawned not only a new theology but also a new pedagogy and a new theatre of the oppressed.

The meeting of Latin American Catholic Bishops (CELAM) in Medellin, Colombia, in 1968 marked a watershed event for the Church when these leaders declared the Church's "preferential option for the poor" as the cornerstone of what soon became known as "liberation theology." Franciscan theologian Leonardo Boff made the commitment clear: "The Church in Brazil has made an explicit preferential option for the poor—against poverty and in favor of social justice. Who are the poor? ... those $\frac{2}{3}$ of all Brazilians who live in misery."[1] And Boff suggested how this option might be realized:

> To create a theology of liberation based on the practice of liberation it is necessary to participate as an active member in a particular movement, a base community, a center for the defense of human rights, or a trade union.[2]

In response, *comunidades de base* (Christian Base Communities) were organized throughout Latin America. By 1980 there were 80,000 such communities in Brazil alone.[3] The base communities combined theory and practice and depended upon the empowerment of the participants, often the poorest of the poor. Here lay people, often with no priest or other

69

authority figure present, were invited to study scripture communally for the express purpose of interpreting it themselves and applying it directly to their own lives. The formerly passive "flock" now grappled with the challenge of fighting their poverty and oppression for themselves.

Jesuit priest Ernesto Cardenal founded one such *comunidade* in 1966 in Solentiname, a small island in Lake Nicaragua, in the farthest southern reaches of Nicaragua. This occurred during the reign of the last Somoza dictator. When the community met for worship on Sunday mornings, a bible reading and discussion replaced the usual sermon. These poor fishermen and women, functionally illiterate, related the biblical passages to their own lives. For example, Cardenal recounts how when they discussed the story of Jesus' birth in the manger after Mary and Joseph were turned away at the inn, Felix, a fisherman exclaimed:

> God wanted His Son to be born in a pigsty! In a stable. He wanted His Son to belong to the poor class ... right? If God had wanted Him to be born to a rich lady, then that lady certainly would have had a room reserved for her at that hotel, especially arriving in her condition![4]

In 1977 Somoza's National Guard destroyed the community at Solentiname, including the homes of the peasants and the community's library, and Father Cardenal went into exile in Costa Rica. Two years later, after the triumph of the Sandinista Revolution, he returned as minister of culture in the new government. When I interviewed him in 1984, I asked him about his multiple roles of priest, poet, and government leader and he said:

> I am a priest who is a servant of love. I am a poet whose poetry is at the service of love. I am a government minister in this Revolution as a servant of the people and a servant of love.... All this relates to the reign of God on earth ... a kingdom of God which includes justice and an end to class and oppression.[5]

Just as innovative theatre groups sought to break down the barrier between professional actors and nonprofessional audiences, so liberation theology breached the religious barrier between the professional leadership of educated, middle-class, and often conservative clerics, and their audience of undereducated and often poor parishioners. The audience became actors in shaping their own social destiny.

At the same moment, a Brazilian Catholic teacher and philosopher of education named Paulo Freire was attempting to forge new methods for reaching the millions of Latin America's illiterates. His 1986 book, *Pedagogy of the Oppressed*, like the CELAM conclave of the same year, had immediate social effects.

For Freire, traditional educational methods were tools for cultural domination and now "pedagogy ... must be forged with, not for, the oppressed," although he wondered, "how can the oppressed, as divided, inauthentic beings, participate in the development of the pedagogy of their liberation?"[6] His answers were: "thematic investigation," "problem solving education," and what he called "concientization,"[7] a rather unwieldy word signifying the empowerment of people with both information about their world and a new sense of themselves as agents of change rather than passive spectators.

Using the "literacy circles" suggested by Freire, so similar to the *comunidades de base* of liberation theology, *alfabetizacion* campaigns were undertaken in Brazil, Peru, and several other Central and South American countries. In July 1980 I observed firsthand the national literacy campaign undertaken by the new Sandinista government that had overthrown the 40-year Somoza family dictatorship in 1979. As part of a delegation put together by Dr. Benjamin Spock and Jonathan Kozol, I met a handful of young high school students who, with 60,000 of their peers, had left their middle-class, urban homes to go and live with peasants in their shacks in the *campo* for three months, working in the fields during the day and teaching reading and writing at night. The students used Nicaraguan history (recovering, for example, the story of the anti-imperialist Augusto Sandino who the first Somoza had murdered in 1933 and then written into the nation's textbooks as little more than a bandit) and shared contemporary social problems to teach and *concienticize* adults three and four times their age. All this in a country where the annual per capita income was below $600, life expectancy was only 52 years and the illiteracy rate was above 50 percent. As Carlos Tunnermann, the Nicaraguan minister of education, told me:

> Not only did the peasants learn to read and write but the *brigidistas* [the teens doing the teaching] learned for the first time about life in the countryside. They learned about peasant life. They learned peasant songs, art, history, customs. They were also educated. [And] we now have recordings of songs, and art work, and crafts, all done by the peasants, along with recordings of their oral histories, all of which are now displayed and used in any study of Nicaraguan culture.[8]

At the end of five months, 420,000 people had learned the rudiments of reading and writing. In one rural village I watched a 75-year-old man laboriously write his name, which he had just learned to do for the first time in his life. And yet the greatest lessons were learned by the teenage teachers. I will never forget meeting little Felix Vijil. Felix was just 11 years old, which means he was too young to join the 12-to-19-year-old *brigidistas*. But he told me that he had run away from home, a comfortable urban home with multiple servants, and "infiltrated" a literacy brigade. Joining late, he got "the ones that were hard to teach," he said, 12 students between the ages of 17 and 62. He planted corn during the day and taught classes in the evening. He suffered from fleas and worms, and in the middle of the course he came down with ricketsia, a type of typhoid which sent him home for bed rest for two weeks, and yet at the end of the five month campaign, one of his 12 students earned her certificate as literate and the other 11 committed to the follow-up program of adult education. When I asked Felix what he would do if such a campaign were ever necessary again, he replied, "I'll infiltrate again."[9]

On a tropical summer evening in Managua in 1980, I stood in the center of that earthquake-devastated city as trucks rumbled through the streets of the capitol bringing home the young *brigadistas* after their five months in the *campo*. Kids packed the rear open platforms of pickups and dump trucks, singing as they came. Thousands of adults packed the roads and sidewalks welcoming their children home. Banners of welcome hung from the houses and in the gathering twilight the teens jumped from the trucks, formed their brigades, shouted a few revolutionary slogans, bade farewell to their fellow young teachers and embraced their parents. I saw teens who had left just months before as children, some pampered like Felix, others sheltered and protected from the rigors of rural life, return as empowered young men and women who now saw themselves as teachers as well as students. At that moment, over two decades ago, I first saw how teenage energy, fearlessness, and risk taking could be expressed in positive action and how teens could learn selflessness and equality when they were invited to enter the world as actors rather than spectators.

Liberation theology asks "for whom is religion?" Paulo Freire asked "for whom is education?" Augusto Boal was to ask "for whom is theatre?" Each was to answer with a preference for the poor and oppressed and against the exploiters. Equally important, each hit upon a similar methodology for accomplishing their work: the engagement of the oppressed as cocreators of their future through dialogue, empowerment, and active involvement. In a clear acknowledgment of his debt to Freire and CELAM, Boal called his seminal work *The Theatre of the Oppressed*.

Born March 16, 1931, in Rio de Janeiro, Boal studied chemical engineering at the University of Brazil, earning an undergraduate degree in 1952.

He traveled to the United States and enrolled in graduate studies in chemistry at Columbia University. But at the same time he pursued undergraduate studies in playwriting, studying under John Gassner, meeting Langston Hughes, joining the Brooklyn Writers Group, and winning first prize from the Columbia University Literary Exchange in 1955 for his play *Martin Pescador* (Martin the Fisherman). Returning to Brazil in 1956, Boal supported himself by translating mystery novels for six months until being appointed artistic director of the Arena Theatre in São Paulo, a post he filled for the next 15 years.

Traveling the country in the 1960s with his theatre, Boal found:

> Extreme poverty is still an abiding feature in Brazil. Suffice it to say that the average monthly wage is less than $50 U.S. dollars and most of the population doesn't earn that much.... Extreme opulence exists alongside the most abject misery. And as idealistic artists we could not be accomplices to such cruelty. We rebelled against it.[10]

Both Boal and Arena went through several stages of theatre work as Boal slowly developed his ideas of the theatre of the oppressed, whose goal ultimately became:

> rescuing the theatre and giving it back to the people so that they can use it as a means of communication to discuss their problems. We think theatre can be a means of discussing and "rehearsing" revolutionary acts themselves.[11]

In place of the colonial classics, staple fare at the other theatres, Arena offered contemporary realism from 1956 to 1958, with Portuguese translations of works like Steinbeck's *Of Mice and Men*, O'Casey's *Juno and the Paycock*, and Howard's *They Knew What They Wanted*. In 1958, with the founding of the Seminar in Dramaturgy to train native playwrights, Arena embarked upon a four-year effort to produce only Brazilian authors and then switched gears again in 1962 for a two-year period it called "nationalization of the classics" performing Molière, Lope de Vega, Gogol, and Shakespeare but liberally changing the texts to fit the contemporary scene and including "a social interpretation of the times in which the authors worked."[12]

In 1964 Arena ushered in a fourth period it called "the musicals" concentrating on plays of social criticism but including Brazilian music and dance into productions that proved both popular and innovative and attracted international attention. Like the Christians in the base communities who applied bible stories to their own lives and the literacy workers who recovered their nation's sometimes hidden stories of resistance, Boal turned to Brazilian history for stories of rebellion in new plays like *Arena Conta Zumbi* (Arena Tells the Story of Zumbi), 1964; *Arena Conta "Tiradentes,"* 1967; and *Arena Conta Bolivar*, 1968.

Through the use of masks, incantation, primitive myth, and hypnotic music, Arena sought the kind of poetic state Artaud had described in his manifesto for the Theatre of Cruelty, even as they pursued a political as well as artistic agenda. *Arena Conta Zumbi*, the theatre's greatest popular success, retells the true story of black slaves who fled their Portuguese masters. Numbering nearly ten thousand by 1630, they chose a king, Zumbi, and called their free territory "The Confederacy of Palmares." By the time the population of Palmares had grown to approximately 25 thousand, the government organized an army to exterminate them. Destroyed in 1695, the confederacy lasted fully 65 years as a free black state within the Portuguese colony.

Performed throughout Brazil in 1965–66, *Arena Conta Zumbi* was also seen as a comment upon the military coup that had deposed President Joao Goulart the previous year. Political in content, the play was designed to be revolutionary in form as well. As with previous productions, *Arena Conta Zumbi* mixed samba music, songs, and masks but added a wholly new element, the "Joker." This narrator-type figure not only commented on the events of the play but also stopped the action, dialogued with the audience, took the place of the protagonist, and experimented with different plot scenarios within the play. "The Joker System," as it became known, was an adaptation of Brecht's "alienation effect" and his learning plays, the *Lehrstucke*, designed to both educate the audience and to motivate them to act.

Boal's influential book, *The Theatre of the Oppressed*, published in Spanish in 1974 and in English in 1979, had its origins in these plays as the author developed new methods to put theatre at the service of political revolution by empowering his audiences, whom he called "spect/actors" rather than "spectators," as agents of social change.

Saying "our Latin American revolution is against economic exploitation and all forms of domination,"[13] Boal declared:

> the poetics of Aristotle is the poetics of oppression: the world is known, perfect, or about to be perfected, and all its values are imposed on the spectators, who passively delegate power to the actors to act and think in their place. In so doing, the spectators purge themselves of their tragic flaw—that is, of something capable of changing society. A catharsis of the revolutionary impetus is produced! Dramatic action substitutes for real action.[14]

He added: "In Aristotelian catharsis what is being eliminated is always the hero's tendency to violate the law, whether human or divine."[15] He made the point that:

> Aristotle's coercive system of tragedy survives to this day thanks to its great efficacy. It is, in effect, a powerful system of intimidation ... its basic task: the purgation of all anti-social elements.[16]

Believing that theatre, once the equally shared activity of the whole community, had been pirated by the elite for their own political ends and used to divide the community between people who act (i.e., the few who make theatre) from people who watch (i.e., the many who receive theatre), Boal wrote:

> I want the spectator to act, not watch. It is obscene for a human being who is fully capable of doing to merely watch. The first principle in my Theatre of the Oppressed is the liberation of the spectator.[17]

Boal agreed with Brecht, whom he credited as his greatest influence, that "catharsis is not the main object of this dramaturgy."[18] Boal pushed beyond the "alienation effect," which forces the audience out of emotional identification with the action of the play and reminds them that they are an audience that can have its own thoughts about what is happening on stage, to actually collapse the division of the actors on stage and the audience in their seats by making the audience equal participants in the action. As Boal said, this is "something beyond Brecht, who only asked the spectator to think with his head, without giving him the stage space to express that thought."[19]

In searching for theatrical forms toward this end, Boal moved beyond agitprop, feeling that it spoke *at* the audience (in sociologist Raul Leis' terms, "for" the audience but not "by" or "of" the audience, as will be discussed at the end of this chapter and in chapter 9) and so robbed the spectators of their potency. In fact, Boal's troupe found out just how separate they were from the audience for which they performed. As Boal recalls:

> One day ... we were performing one of these splendid musical plays for an audience made up only of peasants in a small village in the North-East—and we sang the heroic text "Let us spill our blood" to our rapt audience.... At the end of the show a huge peasant, a big strapping colossus of a man, came to us on the verge of tears: "Here's a fine thing—people like you, young people, town people, who think exactly like us. We're right with you, we also think we must give our blood to our land."
> We were proud. Mission accomplished. Our message had been received loud and clear. But Virgilio—I will never forget his name, his face, his silent tears—Virgilio went on:

"Since you think exactly like us, this is what we're going to do, we'll have lunch (it was midday), and afterwards we'll all go together, you with your guns, we with ours, and send the colonel's bullyboys packing—they've taken over a comrade's land, set fire to his house and threatened to kill his family— But first, let's eat...."

We lost our appetite. Trying to match our thoughts with our words, we did our best to clear up the misunderstanding. Honesty seemed the best policy: our guns were theatrical props, they were not real weapons.

"Guns which don't fire?" Virgilio asked, in astonishment, "then what are they for?"

"They are for doing plays, they can't actually be fired. We are serious artists, we believe what we preach, we are quite genuine, but the guns are ... fakes."

"O.K., since the guns are fakes, let's chuck them. But you people aren't fakes, you're genuine, I saw you singing about how blood must be spilt, I was there. You are genuine, so come with us, we have guns enough for everyone."

Our fear turned to panic. Because it was difficult to explain—both to Virgilio and to ourselves—how could we be sincere and genuine and true even though our guns didn't fire and we didn't know how to shoot. We explained ourselves as best we could....

"So, when true artists talk of this blood that must be spilt, this blood you sing about spilling—it's our blood you mean, not yours, isn't that so?"

"We are true to the cause, absolutely, but we are true artists not true peasants. Virgilio, come back, let's talk about it.... Come back."

I never saw him again.... Since that first encounter—an encounter with a real peasant, in flesh and blood, rather than an abstract "peasantry"—an encounter which traumatized but enlightened, I have never again written plays that give advice, nor have I ever sent "messages" again. Except on occasions when I was running the same risks as everyone else.[20]

Boal's experience with Virgilio neatly sums up the drawback to agitprop plays as agents of social change: they are, after all, only plays, rather than real actions. The actors who shout "strike" at the end of *Waiting for Lefty*, for example, are not union organizers, but actors. The audience members who join in the shouting and who had the financial wherewithal to buy tickets (*Waiting for Lefty* was performed both in commercial theatres and in union halls) are as likely to be taxi owners as taxi drivers, or simply bourgeois theatregoers planning to take a taxi home after the show. Depending upon the community producing such community-based drama, the play may be an impetus to action or an emotional substitute for action.

Following his encounter with Virgilio, Boal went in search of a new dramatic form that could be "for," "by" and "of" the community. This required inviting the community on to the stage. Describing his ideal theatre, Boal wrote:

There are no spectators only active observers (or spect/actors). The center of gravity is on the audience and not on the stage. The Theatre of the Oppressed has two fundamental, linked principles: it aims to help the spect-actor transform himself into a protagonist of the dramatic action and rehearse alternatives for his situation, so that he may then be able to extrapolate into his real life the actions he has rehearsed in the practice of theatre.[21]

To this end Boal developed what he called "forum theatre" based on his early experiments with *Arena Conta Zumbi*. Usually employing the Joker or a similar device to interrupt the action on stage, forum theatre invites spect/actors (members of the audience) on stage to take the place of the protagonist and solicits from the audience ideas for changing the action of the play, ideas which are then improvised and critiqued by the audience, as several alternatives are suggested in turn. The aim is to empower the spect/actors so that they see themselves as agents of change, first in the theatre and then in life.

In December 1968 a second coup increased repression in Brazil. In response, Arena turned to newspaper theatre, a theatrical revue of the political events of the week reminiscent of the performances by the Federal Theatre Project's Living Newspaper troupe. For example, the report of the minister of economics advocating austerity would be read while an actor gorged himself on a huge meal on stage, thus demonstrating that while austerity is for the poor, the rich will continue as before. Or the newspaper report of the death of a child might be augmented by improvised scenes of his life of poverty.[22]

"Maybe theatre," wrote Boal, "in itself is not revolutionary, but these theatrical forms [forum theatre and newspaper theatre] are without a doubt a rehearsal for revolution."[23] Agreeing with him for once, the Brazilian dictatorship arrested Boal in February 1971. He was subjected to torture, including electric shock and the *pau de arana* (literally the macaw's rod) where the victim is hung upside down from a metal pole behind their knees with their arms tied around their calves and then beaten.[24] Released in May and warned not to remain in Brazil, Boal went into exile in Argentina and then moved again in 1973, this time to Peru to lead a literacy campaign styled on the work of Freire but utilizing theatre and photography rather than written texts.

Boal returned to Argentina, even as that country experienced political instability around the possible return of the former dictator Juan Peron. Amid rising political repression, and the banning of street theatre along with all other political demonstrations, Boal devised, perhaps, his most innovative theatrical form: Invisible Theatre, which had some very strong similarities to the TIE work, like *Pow-Wow*, described earlier. Invisible Theatre combined the performance of theatre in a nontheatrical space, like a restaurant or a train, and the invisibility of the actors as actors, in front of spectators who did not know they had become an audience.

For example, in one Invisible Theatre piece actors boarded a commuter train, getting on in small numbers at several stops. When they were all aboard, one actor began speaking loudly to another complaining about inflation, blaming it on the merchants in the downtown market, while mentioning that he worked for Standard Oil. Another actor, pretended to overhear, and spoke up to blame the truck drivers and the salaries they were paid to deliver vegetables to market for the high cost of living. At this point a woman, a passenger and a spectator, who happened to be married to a trucker, defended her husband and put the blame on the high price of gasoline they need to buy for their trucks.

Soon actors and spectators were adding their opinions in a general discussion of the economic situation that the actors leavened with words about the cost of the country's international debt or the incompetence of the government's economic policies. Having created and fueled a political debate, the actors slowly drifted away while the discussion continued, exiting at various stations along the route without ever revealing their part in the drama. With Invisible Theatre, Boal almost completely collapsed the divisions between actor and spectator and created the stage, real life, upon which the spect/actors were empowered to act themselves.

Elsewhere in the Third World during the 1970s and 80s, governments, nongovernmental organizations and charitable and educational organizations rediscovered the use of theatre groups to educate audiences, especially in rural areas, on issues of health, overpopulation, literacy, sanitation, etc. In 1982 Ross Kidd produced a survey for the Centre for the Study of Education in Developing Countries that found theatre companies touring and presenting educational dramatics in Bangladesh, Guatemala, Jamaica, Columbia, Ecuador, Mexico, Botswana, New Guinea, Sri Lanka, Grenada, Nicaragua, China, Vietnam, Cuba and many other countries.

In her book *Community in Motion*, L. Dale Byam surveyed "theatre for development" programs in Africa. These case studies pointed up some inherent dangers in community-based theatre. Byam documented the work of students and young people doing theatre for undereducated audiences in rural areas around issues the theatre groups had chosen, for the audiences' own good naturally, and often at the behest of and with the funding of oppressive regimes and corrupt state ministries. Lack of financing, lack of follow-up, and the top-down nature of these campaigns (they were "for" but not "of" or "by" the community) brought few long-lasting results to those they were intended to help.

In the United States in the 1970s, a number of graduate students documented the use of similar theatre for development projects at home. Crosby Warren Robertson created a theatre in a black community in Florida with the express goal of increasing the number of black residents registered to vote. Performing pro-voter registration minidramas in malls and on the street, Robertson had cars standing by at each performance to convey audience members to voter registration offices. His record of newly registered voters documented the success of the project.

Elsewhere, Loisetta Williams described theatre performances to promote family planning, while Dorothy Goodwin chronicled the use of theatre, role-playing, and puppetry to teach retarded adults social skills. Beverly Black documented the use of theatre to prevent sexual assault. Success was harder to quantify in these projects and Goodwin, for example, could claim only the "expectancy of, at least, a small change in behavior."[25] More significantly, such programs often remained unpublicized beyond the graduate students' own unpublished master's and doctoral manuscripts.

One program has had longer-lasting effects. Begun in 1986 by theatre artists Bill Rauch and Alison Carey who met as students at Harvard, Cornerstone Theatre Company approached grassroots organizations offering productions and "adapting plays to resonate with the local community."[26] Its mission statement declared:

> Cornerstone Theatre Company was begun with this challenge: go into different American communities, learn what makes good theatre, and try to inspire a love of theatre in new and varied audiences.[27]

In return for original community-specific productions, the community provides performance and living space for the troupe, props, a casting pool, and backstage labor. Cornerstone has offered *The Marmarth Hamlet*, a Wild West reinterpretation of Shakespeare in Marmarth, North Dakota, population 190, where Shakespeare's line "a proud man's contumely" was rewritten as "the shit we take from assholes,"[28] retold the *Oresteia* through Piute oral tradition on a reservation in Schurz, Nevada, the Faust legend in Watts, and *Romeo and Juliet* in Port Gibson, Mississippi, casting the Montagues as black and the Capulets as white, and staging the medieval morality play *Everyman* in an upscale Santa Monica, California, mall.

In 1991 Cornerstone relocated permanently to Los Angeles where they performed *Crossings: Journeys of Catholic Immigrants* at the abandoned St. Vibiana's cathedral on Skid Row. The *Los Angeles Times* described the production:

> its story outlines from the Bible. But many of the incidents and details reflect the experiences of ordinary Southern Californians who emigrated from Cambodia, Africa, Mexico, and Arab nations. It shows each group leaving troubled homelands and finding refuge here, as well as new challenges and discontents.[29]

This description reminds us of how bible stories were retold and reinterpreted by Father Cardenal's parishioners in Solentiname. Cornerstone has encountered numerous challenges and discontents themselves. When they performed *The Good Person of New Haven*, based on the Brecht play *The Good Person of Sezuan*, at the Long Wharf Theatre, for example, they cast 24 local people in the production to act alongside Cornerstone professionals. However, Long Wharf season subscribers, many of them from well-to-do communities beyond the theatre's immediate neighborhood, did not appreciate the work and many walked out in midshow. As Sonja Kuftinec observed:

> A mentality arose among some subscribers that community-based theatre was not for them or about them and represents a kind of social service pageantry that is destroying the experience of "theatre for theatre's sake."[30]

Even more problematic was Cornerstone's collaboration with Touchstone Theatre in producing a version of *Prometheus Bound* at a shuttered steel plant in Bethlehem, Pennsylvania, in 1999. As reported by Sara Brady in her article "Welded to the Ladle," the script was vetted by former workers at the plant and their comments and reactions were incorporated in what became the play *Steelbound*. However, the large Latino membership of the union was never reflected in the cast which had no Latino actors. Cornerstone developed no relationship with the local steel union and depended upon corporate sponsorship from the Bethlehem Steel Company. Brady felt this economic dependence deflected the theatre company from raising questions about why the plant had been closed and the workers thrown out of work. She commented:

> This venture reveals that not all theatre created in a community (however that community is defined) will inspire, change, provide the best social, political, or environmental attitude to a community in need, or even come close to including a whole community.[31]

Brady, who acted in this play herself, felt that the production site doomed the play's potential for social change, even though the staging gave the workers their first opportunity to revisit the plant where they had once worked and from which they had been barred since its closing three years earlier:

> The choice to bring Steelbound into the foundry [where 30,000 once worked] meant that the play would become passive rather than aggressive, an elegy rather than a protest—an ironic gesture in a town with a strong union presence.[32]

And the corporate backing meant that:

> never did the script ask the company to answer for the shutdown, for the failure of the company to keep up with other mills in the U.S. and internationally.[33]

The result, concluded Brady, was that:

> In the case of Steelbound the art of community-based theatre became an opiate for the masses, not an instigator of social change.[34]

Community-based theatre projects continue to grow, however. Prisons and jails have been among the sites of recent work. Rhodessa Jones organized women in the San Francisco jail to begin a theatre program in 1991. This theatre for women in jail is performed by incarcerated women dramatizing their personal stories. In Manchester, England, a group called TIPP, Theatre in Prisons and Probation, has been performing in prisons since 1992. In Los Angeles, University of Southern California theatre professor Brent Blair stages Shakespeare with inmates at Juvenile Hall. At the Luther Luckett Correctional Complex in Kentucky, Curt Tofteland founded Shakespeare Behind Bars: Acting with Conviction, working with inmates, some serving time for murder, to stage Hamlet, Othello and Titus Andronicus. Their production of The Tempest is the subject of the 2005 documentary Shakespeare Behind Bars which was nominated for a Grand Jury Prize at the Sundance Film Festival. At the Framingham Women's Prison in Massachusetts, Jean Trounstine has worked for 10 years with female inmates to stage plays, a project also called "Shakespeare Behind Bars," as described in her 2001 book of the same name.

Community-based theatre projects are turning up on college campuses as well, making explicit the relationship between theatre and education. In New York City, for example, Jan Cohen-Cruz founded the Urban Ensemble in 1994 with funding and students from New York University's Tisch School of the Arts where she teaches. In this project, Tisch students work with Lower East Side community residents in productions designed to reduce violence. Students earn academic credit for this community-theatre work. Further north, Harvard University's Project Zero leads a newly reinvigorated movement using dramatics in middle and high schools believing that producing plays as part of the academic curriculum at public schools can "help students learn to use their knowledge to solve unexpected problems rather than simply parrot back facts."[35]

Community-based theatre, regardless of what it is called, developed over a century and remains vigorous today, intersecting disciplines of theatre, education, social work, history, and religion. In each incarnation the goal, not always realized, has been to improve the lot of the members of the community to which it has been directed. Separated from the commercial theatres' commitment to profit and entertainment and from the avant-garde's dedication to art for art's sake, it stresses social utility. Most often choosing its audience from among the oppressed and downtrodden, community-based theatre has sought to educate, motivate, and empower those seeking to improve their lives.

I had always loved theatre: the storytelling, the vibrant characters, and stagecraft illusions created by lighting, sound, and special effects. But when I began studying Augusto Boal for the first time in graduate school, I was energized to discover that theatre could do more than entertain; it could invite participants to democratically examine personal and social issues, rehearse solutions to problems, and equip them to change their lives and society. Later I trained with Boal himself and then researched the long history of applied theatre that I have briefly outlined here. Each new discovery was a revelation:

1. Theatre tackled political subjects and had historically been employed for social change.

2. Amateur actors took politically charged subjects off the stage and out into union halls and the streets as cultural arms of political movements.

3. Theatre needed no, or minimal, props and sets, or stage to succeed.

4. Plays could be created out of current events and issues by the people who lived them.

5. Most importantly, the audience could participate in theatre actively rather than as passive spectators.

I learned that many groups were using Boal's techniques and, categorized generally as theatre of the oppressed, working with women, seniors, victims of sexual abuse, prison inmates, the differently abled, the mentally ill, racial and ethnic minorities, etc. around the world. These groups can be usefully defined as "the oppressed." Teenagers, especially teenagers labeled "at risk," often define themselves, regardless of race, class, or gender, in much the same way. Certainly incidents noted in the previous chapter detailing violence against American teenagers could lead to the conclusion that they often are oppressed. For this reason community-based theatre groups, theatre of the oppressed among them, have begun to work with teenagers.

But even as I began to get excited about the socially and personally transformative powers of theatre, I discovered one more surprising fact: even though groups had been using theatre for social uplift for over 100 years and even though literally tens of thousands of theatre in education, community development, and theatre of the oppressed groups are at work worldwide at this very moment, not one study had been undertaken to prove that their work was actually effective.

Ironically, as I talked to more and more theatre practitioners and heard more and more success stories for their programs, the less convinced I became that their stories could convince lawmakers, funders, and the general public that these theatre programs could be an effective alternative to the juvenile justice system. The stories of teens whose lives had been turned around by these programs were touching and illuminating but they were entirely anecdotal and unquantified. For every teen who attended such a program, went on to college, and stayed out of trouble, how many failed to complete the program, flunked out of school or went to jail? I didn't know and no one was able to tell me.

Yet sweeping claims were being made for the efficacy of art and theater programs. For example, Academy Award winner and former National Endowment for the Arts president Jane Alexander was quoted making the great claim that "if you put a paintbrush or an oboe in the hands of a 7-year-old that same child, at the age of 13, will not pick up an Uzi."[36]

Similarly, when the Rand Institute interviewed 79 adults who lead arts programs with youth, they answered only one of Rand's 38 questions unanimously in the affirmative: "Do you think that arts education is of value to all students?"[37] What made them so sure, I wondered?

When I asked to see the data to support their claims, people often told me point-blank that the effects of their programs were not measurable. As one practitioner said, "do they learn? It's hard to say."[38] Equally conflicted, Baz Kershaw, a theatre practitioner who has often expressed his commitment to theatre as a way of changing political and social policy, wrote, "a strong case can be made for the potential efficacy of ... theatre,"[39] and added that "surely such efficacy is the fundamental purpose of performance"[40] while admitting that efficacy "will always be open to debate."[41] And he lamented that "socially and politically the movement has left hardly any marks at all; it is just a small footnote in the big text of history."[42]

Some begged to be judged over the long haul: "The effects on individuals of a program may be imperceptible in the short term,"[43] while one researcher admitted that "a foolproof means of evaluating changes in human behavior is a bit of a 'Holy Grail,'" both eagerly sought and impossible to find.[44]

Perhaps as a result, no one was doing any measuring. As Rand reported, "we found too few evaluations to demonstrate convincingly that fine arts interventions improved pro-social behaviors in preteen at-risk youth."[45] Rand didn't say the programs didn't work, only that no one had convincingly demonstrated that they did.

One difficulty was that for every success story, disturbing anecdotes of failure could be found. For example, the *Los Angeles Times* reported that Charles Andrew Williams, age 15, who went to his school near San Diego in 2001 and shot 15 fellow students, two of whom died, had played Linus just the year before in his school's production of *A Charlie Brown Christmas*.[46] No theater practitioner I know who works with teenagers ever repeated that story.

The unanswered fundamental question was whether theatre programs had a positive impact on their teenage participants. Rand found that less than 10 percent of the programs they approached to study did any evaluation at all and only half of those were related to results and effects. No one compared one program's results against another. Rand, which had expended tens of thousands of dollars and hundreds of staff hours, was clearly frustrated:

> Very few studies reported any evidence of collecting evaluation data. Because of this we have been unable to confirm our conjecture that arts interventions with at-risk youth lead to positive prosocial outcomes nor to test the more specific hypothesis that programs with certain features predict successful intervention outcomes.[47]

Two years later Rand reported that "testimonials from practitioners are considered 'anecdotal evidence' and as such do not carry the weight of more rigorous scientific studies."[48] "What is needed now," it said, "is field-experimental research that is designed in advance to test the hypotheses emerging from the body of literature."[49]

The efficacy problem remained unsolved. "In spite of broadly shared beliefs that the arts are more than a luxury, there is precious little scientific evidence to prove this conjecture. The broad goal ... is to provide such evidence."[50] Unfortunately, after publishing three volumes of largely descriptive research, Rand ran out of money before the projected fourth and final volume, designed to evaluate individual programs both against each other and in terms of their own goals, could be undertaken. Once again the question of efficacy went unanswered.

Yet every arts organization engaged in such projects sees the need for evaluation; if for no other reason than to build continued support for its programs. As the *Growing Up Taller* report, which surveyed arts organizations working with teenagers, puts it: "With increased competition for fewer resources, the pressure to demonstrate results is increasing. However, assessment takes time and money: commodities in short supply in these programs."[51]

I was taken aback. It seemed to me that society had only to be convinced that this positive, noncoercive, and nonpunitive alternative worked and then these theatre programs would be endlessly replicated to do good across the country. Since no one else was doing it, I decided to undertake an in-depth study of several theatre groups working with at-risk teens, including an evaluation of their effects upon the teenage participants and an analysis of what makes one program more successful than another. This book is the result.

As I read the available literature, I became more and more impressed with the work of Brazilian writer and director Augusto Boal and his "forum theatre." I decided to investigate the efficacy of forum theatre as one of the kinds of theatre being pursued with teenagers. When I came across an article by the Panamanian sociologist Raul Leis, I decided to apply his differentiation of the three kinds of popular theatre, theatre he identifies as "for, by, and/or of the community"[52] as a lens for my investigations, hypothesizing that theatre that was simultaneously all three, "of, for, and by" teenagers, could have the greatest impact in altering attitudes and behaviors that placed them at risk.

Leis writes that theatre "for" the community is theatre presented by an outside group for the community as the audience. Theatre "for and by" the community involves members of the community performing as actors in theatre for the members of the community who are not acting and who make up the audience. And theatre simultaneously "for, by and of" the community features community members acting before a community audience in scripts that also originate from the community.

I set out to find three theatre groups that fit these three categories. The Rand study, by far the most exhaustive I've found, identified 241 arts groups working with at-risk teens in the Los Angeles area. City at Peace in Santa Barbara was one group I had already worked with and I had begun a spin-off City at Peace in the Isla Vista neighborhood contiguous to the University of California, Santa Barbara. This group seemed to me to best epitomize Boal's ideas of forum theatre and also to fit Leis' category of theatre "by, for, and of" the community since the teens acted in plays they wrote themselves based on real events in their lives.

I began searching for other groups. Some, like STOP-GAP Theatre in Orange County, simply did not want to be observed by an outsider. Others, like BreakThrough Theatre, an outreach program of Santa Barbara Planned Parenthood and Phantom Projects, also based in Orange County, seemed to have such a sharply defined ideological base for their work, the first agitating for "safe sex" and the latter for "no premarital sex," as to be too constraining.

Eventually I settled on the Virginia Avenue Project in Santa Monica and on City Hearts, based in Topanga but with an after-school program in Oxnard. Both worked with at-risk youth and both would allow me to observe their work and administer the questionnaire I was developing. Since the Virginia Avenue Project paired professional writers and actors with teens to produce original work and City Hearts provided actors to work with teens in putting on Shakespearean plays, they seemed to fit Leis' two categories of theatre "for" and theatre "by" the community. On a continuum of teen involvement, City at Peace, involving the teens in applying personal stories to the stage and writing the plays themselves, was at one extreme, while City Hearts, where the teens worked with Shakespearean scripts written 400 years ago, stood at the other. The Virginia Avenue Project, using scripts that might be said to be inspired by the teens, but written by adults, stood somewhere in the middle.

My hope was to develop, or find, an instrument, that would measure a teen's attitudinal and behavior changes as he/she went through one of these programs. I found the literature full of such so-called pretest/posttest surveys. STOP-GAP Theatre, for example, published this kind of self-evaluation data attached to a report on a play they had presented to teens on the subject of date rape. Eleven hundred students in three schools in southern California answered written questions on a survey called the Rape Information Questionnaire seven to ten days before they saw the STOP-GAP play and then took the same survey again one hour after seeing the play. According to the STOP-GAP report, male student scores rose from 35 to 40 on the informational scale and from 73 to 75 on the affective scale. For female students the increases were from 41 to 44 and 72 to 74 respectively.[53] STOP-GAP concluded: "Both males and females in the main study indicated a statistically significant increase in the affective measure of self-esteem.... Both males and females learned new material and responded emotionally to it."[54] "This major study validated the hypothesis that STOP-GAP plays are an occasion of meaningful change."[55]

In addition, "shortly after the performance, several 10th grade girls at one school came forward with information regarding multiple instances of rape between high school boys and girls."[56] This information led to eight arrests. However, the STOP-GAP report makes no convincing cause and effect connection between these two events. One would have to ask whether or not the accusers had seen the play (the report does not claim this) and whether or not they credited the play with motivating their accusations. One would also have to document whether or not the allegations were later proved true, which STOP-GAP also fails to do.

Their short-term survey, as dramatic as some of the results were, was more analogous to an exam after a lecture, measuring little more than the retention of information and does not tell us very much about the long-term changes in attitudes and behaviors that are necessary to impact teens' lives. Such surveys administered immediately before and immediately after a single production are common in measuring reactions to "issues" dramas centered around problems like date rape, alcohol and drug abuse. Even if teens have more information on a problem immediately after a show or even if their attitudes are affected by the show, there is no follow up to see if these short-term emotional changes translate into long-term behavioral changes.

Therefore, I opted for a method described by numerous sociologists and psychologists[57] in which a pretest measuring antecedent, or pre-experience, attitudes and behavior, is then followed by a period of participant/observation, and concludes with a posttest near the end of the program. Such a study includes a description of the program, its methods and goals, the pretest of antecedents, the gathering of data, observation of the transactions over time, the posttest survey and finally, a correlation of outcomes.

Antecedents ⟶ Transactions ⟶ Outcomes[58]

I worked with Dr. Shane Jimerson of the University of California, Santa Barbara to adapt and expand a survey he had previously developed.

According to Dr. Jimerson, I would need to obtain at least ten completed surveys from each theatre program, since ten was the minimum number of questionnaire results upon which one could base general projections. The survey administered at the beginning and end of the program would provide statistical measures of antecedent attitudes and behaviors and outcomes. My ongoing observation of the groups would describe and evaluate the transactions.

I translated these survey questions into Spanish since several of the theatre projects informed me that many of their participants were most comfortable communicating in that language. Though it had been my intention to use the identical survey with all three groups, that became impossible. However, each survey had 26 questions in common, sufficient to make comparisons meaningful.

To undertake this survey I had to work with the Human Subjects Committee at my university, studying the federal guidelines, passing a test, and gaining approval of the committee. The Human Subjects Committee suggested I add a code to the survey so that I could preserve anonymity but still be able to correlate subject's survey answers from the pretest to the posttest and I incorporated this idea.

Because the vast majority of the teens were younger than 18, I needed their parents' permission for their participation. This required drawing up a parental permission paper and also translating that into Spanish. Many more of the parents chose the Spanish language permission form than their sons and daughters chose the Spanish language survey, indicating that the parents were often first generation immigrants and their children were second generation and more acculturated.

The Oxnard superintendent of schools was concerned that his school board would be uncomfortable with the "sex questions" on my questionnaire and although I submitted differing drafts rephrasing those questions, I was forced in the end to simply omit them for the City Hearts participants.

Occasionally, parents decided not to allow their teenagers to participate. One father objected to the questions about suicide. He told me: "I don't think we should put ideas in her head. I'd rather she not do it." I thanked him for his time and cite the incident because, like the Oxnard superintendent's reluctance about "sex questions," I found adults were often out of touch with the thoughts and behaviors of the teenagers they supervised. It seemed to me that they were out of touch precisely because they did not ask the difficult questions.

Occasionally a teenager declined to give permission to be surveyed. I always asked twice and explained the goal but took "no" for an answer in a low-key manner. Sometimes they changed their minds when they saw their peers filling out the survey and sometimes they didn't. Sometimes adults in the school or in the theatre programs suggested that I reward those who did the survey by offering them candy or some other inducement but I had to explain that this was considered unethical under the guidelines for experimenting with human subjects.

It turned out to be much more time consuming to get the permission slips signed than to get the surveys filled out. In the end I obtained 49 signed parental permission slips and 53 completed surveys. The extra four surveys came from students over the age of 18 who did not need parental permission.

The surveys took no more than ten minutes to complete. I usually supplied the teens with pens, placed the teens at separate tables around the room to ensure privacy, announced that I was available to explain any terms they didn't understand ("contraception" was the word they were most unfamiliar with, "conflict resolution" ranked second) and then collected the surveys without looking at them and stuffed them all into an envelope to assure their anonymity.

While the surveys promised the most detailed statistical evidence of efficacy, I pursued the issue on two other tracks simultaneously. I interviewed the directors of each program multiple times to elicit from them the project goals they had set. Success would be measured in terms of reaching these goals. I spent much more time observing the activities of each group, sometimes as a participant.

Although I spent two years studying the three theatre groups and obtained more than ten pretest and posttest surveys from each, basic obstacles to this kind of research must be admitted. Outside of a laboratory we simply cannot account for all of the factors that influence human behavior. If my research should show that a teenager's attitudes and behaviors changed over the period of time they were in a particular after-school theatre program, I really had no certain way of knowing that those changes were solely the result of the program. Other events in their lives, such as divorce, a death in the family, or any one of a hundred other events taking place outside of the theatre program could also be responsible for any positive or negative changes.

The other frustration, of course, was the lack of more data. With more time, more money, and more researchers, even more surveys and observations might have been made in 40 or 50 more programs and with a thousand or more teenagers participating. It became clear to me that this project was going to be a pilot program, an experiment in itself, that could some day be followed up on a much wider scale.

In the next three chapters I look at each of the three after-school theatre programs in detail and in the final chapter I report the results that they achieved and try to explain how and why they succeeded.

CHAPTER 6

The Virginia Avenue Project

I FIRST ENCOUNTERED THE VIRGINIA AVENUE Project in the spring of 2001 when a number of theatre practitioners who knew about my research suggested it to me. Hoping to make contact, I attended a performance on March 18, 2001, at the 24th Street Theatre in downtown Los Angeles that had been publicized in a long and laudatory feature preview in the *Los Angeles Times* the previous week.

The 24th Street Theatre is housed in a converted firehouse in a working-class and Latino immigrant area just north of the University of Southern California campus, not far from notoriously crime-ridden south central Los Angeles. When I arrived, I found the 99-seat theatre filled to capacity. Executive Director Anne Gimbel was handing out programs in the lobby and, at my request, she introduced me to Artistic Director Leigh Curran with whom I spoke briefly before entering the auditorium. Sitting among an enthusiastic audience of project participants' families and friends, I saw six one-act plays, grouped into two acts with an intermission, under the heading *The Small but Mighty Plays*. I learned later that these were the so-called two on twos, plays written and directed by adults each featuring two teenage actors on stage. Each short play also included songs, a minimal set or back projection, and several modest props.

Most memorable for me was the one-act *Horse Sense* set in the Civil War, which featured two young actors as horses, one on the Confederate side and one of the Union side who encounter each other on a battlefield and decide to flee the war for a life together out West. The illusion was surprisingly magical and one of the actors, 16-year-old Carl was particularly

91

good and made a very convincing and sympathetic equine. (In this book I've changed the names of all after-school program participants except those of the adult founders/directors and adult actors who have been publicly identified with the programs.) The afternoon was an upbeat celebration of theatrical achievement by the young actors and their families and, at times, a very impressive production.

I found the mission statement of the project, which works with children ages 6 to 18, in their brochure, also available that afternoon at the theatre: "The purpose of the Project is to bring the children who participate in touch with their full potential through long term collaborations with adult mentors that focus on the development of writing, performing, and business skills."[1]

To get an idea of the history and programs of the Virginia Avenue Project, I interviewed Artistic Director and Founder Leigh Curran two months later. Ms. Curran was a playwright and actor living in New York City in the late 1980s when an actress in one of her plays then in production introduced her to a man who worked with the 52nd Street Project. He in turn introduced Curran to the director of the 52nd Street Project, Willie Reale, who recruited her to work with them. Curran wrote her first play for the project and then worked in collaboration with a teen actor and the adult actor, Paul McCrane, later seen regularly on television's popular *ER*, to stage the play. That positive experience hooked her on working with teens.

The 52nd Street Project began in 1981 when teens hanging out across from the Ensemble Studio Theatre in the Hell's Kitchen neighborhood of New York City began breaking into the theatre. In response, theatre director Reale invited the teens into the theatre to perform once a year, hoping to make them feel a part of a theatre they might value rather than rob. Then Reale, in Curran's words, "invited some friends into the work and it just grew from year to year."[2] Over the ensuing years, theatre and film artists, including Francis Ford Coppola, the late Spalding Gray, Craig Lucas, Frances McDormand, Jose Rivera, and the late Wendy Wasserstein, have worked on over 500 plays with some 600 children through the 52nd Street Project.

52nd Street productions are free to attendees and the plays, in Reale's words, are "for and, occasionally, by the kids."[3] In the film documentary *3 Minutes from Broadway: The Story of the 52nd Street Project*, Reale explains, "it's in the nature of a theatrical event to change people's perceptions; we change the way actors think, not the audience.... We give children the chance to fall in love with something that comes out of themselves.... Power is knowing that something that comes from inside you is valuable to other people."[4]

An unidentified volunteer at the project explains that 52nd Street is "a place where these kids can use their imaginations, where they can be engaged, where they can feel some power."[5] And Reale speaks to the issue of efficacy which has so bedeviled projects like this: "You never really know how you change them [teen participants] because you don't know how they would have turned out without you."[6]

The model that evolved in the 52nd Street Project was to pair up ten teens and ten adults and send them off for a week, at a camp or lodge outside the city. The adult wrote a play for the teen and then both rehearsed a shared performance. This was the origin of what was, and is still called the One on One program.

Curran herself got more and more involved as a volunteer, as a director, actor, and writer. While attending a weekend retreat designed to teach adults how to duplicate the 52nd Street process, Curran had a life changing epiphany. Having had commercial success both in the production of her plays and in acting in television commercials, Curran decided, as she told me, that "I wanted to do something bigger with my life than the pursuit of my career." So she went to the project director and said, "I could get this program started on the West Coast."[7]

Curran, who had attended school in Ojai and grown up in Santa Monica, returned to California in 1991 with great commitment but limited experience. "I didn't even know how to write grants,"[8] she explained to me. But friends led to further contacts and people who could help. One day she flipped open a copy of the Yellow Pages and looked under "Youth Projects" to find the only listing was the Police Athletic League (PAL). So she called the PAL, then housed on Virginia Avenue, and made the connection that has served both organizations for over a decade.

Taking its name from that original location, the Virginia Avenue Project (VAP) now receives free space in the new PAL building at 1401 Olympic Blvd. in Santa Monica, about a mile from the Pacific Ocean. A high school and public park share the block. Students and homeless people can be found nearby in equal numbers.

The PAL welcomed the Virginia Avenue Project as its arts program for children ages 6 to 18, with separate staff and separate fund-raising responsibilities. The PAL rules prohibit entrance to the building to any teen who is a gang member or suspected member or who wears gang colors. "Most kids at PAL," says Curran, "have nowhere to be after school."[9] The VAP program is specifically designed to link at-risk children with theatre professionals. To be accepted into the program, the children must be from homes that are too poor to be able to pay for private acting classes. "Some of our kids," says Curran, "were homeless, all are low income, and many are from single parent homes."[10] In its newsletter the project identifies its constituency as "children growing up under difficult circumstances."

The Virginia Avenue Project today operates on a budget of $225,000 a year and supports two full-time and two part-time staff members. Adult artists who work with the teens receive stipends to cover travel expenses and teachers get paid to teach acting classes. Between 45 and 50 children are active in the program each year and 30 new plays are usually written and produced. Asked to describe the goals of the project, Curran told me: "We strive to turn out well-rounded human beings. We work with the whole child and get them to think about what they can do to take charge of their lives and give them the skills to reach their dreams."[11]

In her October 2001 VAP newsletter column Curran reported that "currently 100% of our young people graduate from high school, 90% go to college, and 85% are the first in their families to go." With these credentials it was not surprising that the Rand Institute chose the Virginia Avenue Project as one of nine Los Angeles programs to study in 1997 and labeled it a "'best-practice' site."[12]

The Virginia Avenue Project is structured by age and experience. All new participants enter either the Creative Dramatics class, or, if they are under 8 years old, the Junior Creative Dramatics class. These hour and a half classes meet once a week for nine weeks. Each participant can repeat each series of classes three times. I attended several of these classes conducted in a brightly lighted and attractive room at the PAL building. The teachers all had some professional acting experience and I watched the younger children and teens, in separate classes, play theatre games and enthusiastically tackle acting improvisations with real creativity.

A wide variety of performance programs are offered as well. When the staff thinks a child is ready, he or she is chosen to participate in the aforementioned One on One program. Usually nine adults and nine kids are chosen to go to a week-long camp in Ojai, a wealthy and historic arts community about 50 miles north of Santa Monica, to write and act in original plays. One child and one adult constitute a production team. At the end of their collaborations, their plays are performed in the Little Theatre at the University of California, Los Angeles. The One on One program takes place in Ojai twice each summer, once in July and once in August, with different participants each session. The performances at UCLA are held in September of each year.

After a child has appeared in at least three such plays or written two, he/she is considered for what is called the Two on Two, a program that occurs every three years or so. It was one of these special events which I had seen at the 24th Street Theatre. This program links two teens as actors with two adults. One adult writes the play and the other adult directs.

A third program of the project is PlayMaking Group. Here a child writes a play for two adult actors and an adult director. When the play is publicly performed, the young writer sits onstage in public view. PlayMaking involves about 8 children each year.

The fourth program is RePlay and is held every second year. Here the children write the plays and receive adult readings and feedback. They then revisit the play several months later to deepen their writing process. After rewriting, the play is publicly staged.

Another program offered is called "PlayBack" and it occurs every third year. It is open to children who have done at least three One on Ones. In PlayBack the child writes the first half of the play and then an adult writes the second half of the play in response. The entire play is then performed by the adult and teen together.

AfterPlay, also called the Teen Entrepreneur Program, is the newest program. Here children learn the business of theatre as a metaphor for the business skills they may need later in life. They learn how to raise and be responsible for the money needed in play production.

The Poetry Workshop completes the array of programs offered. Seventh, eighth, and ninth graders from the Virginia Avenue Project are teamed with deaf students from the John Muir Middle School in Burbank, to learn to write poetry which is then publicly performed. The teens' poetry is often printed in the project's regular newsletter. The poem below, titled "What Hatred Gave to Me," was written by then 14-year-old Franchesca Hladik, who participated in my surveys. It appeared in the October 2001 issue of the newsletter, one of several written in the VAP poetry workshop in response to the terrorist attacks of September 11, 2001, and Franchesca gave me special permission to reprint it here:

My mother always smelled like coconut
She was obsessed with it
She used to tuck me in every night
I never got tired of it
She would brush my hair out of my face

Swoop down, and gently kiss my cheek
I loved those times, I loved her, I love her

She would check if my homework was done every single night
She always gave me nutritious lunches, while everyone else got Fruit Roll-ups
    and Doritos
She would always turn up the radio so she could sing
She tried her hardest to sing
And no matter how loud the music was she could still be heard
I loved those times, I loved her, I love her

Hatred left me: the fragrance called loneliness
Late nights waiting to get tucked in
Even though I'm not going to be
Making my lunch, reassuring myself I have plenty of calcium, minerals and
    vitamins.
Turning up the radio, since no one else will do it.

All I have left is a scrapbook in my mind.
Every day I remember her and see what I can find.

In addition, "Nights on the Town" are regularly scheduled trips to see professional Los Angeles theatre whenever local theatres make free tickets available.

Currently, the Virginia Avenue Project takes in five to eight new kids each year and works with 45–50 children annually. Moving beyond their current PAL quarters, they've replicated their PlayMaking and RePlay programs in four different public and private schools where at-risk children write plays and then see staged readings of the plays at their school assemblies. One person, whom Curran trained at VAP, moved north to begin the Haven Project in Portland, Oregon, modeled on both the Virginia Avenue Project and the 52nd Street Project.

Curran explained that the funding for VAP comes from government agencies and private foundations, as well as private gifts and the City of Santa Monica. The participants never pay for any of their classes or programs and all of their public performances are presented free of charge. She's been fortunate to attract theatre artists like Amy Brennerman (a Cornerstone Theater alumnus), John Glover, and Beth Henley to work with the children in the Project through the years.

For the future she wants to increase programming, add a video component, get the kids on the Internet, and get the teens studying Shakespeare. "This," she told me, "is my life. It's incredibly time-consuming, but it's worth every minute. Really, I'm having a love affair with these kids. They're my family."[13]

In August 2001, I had a chance to observe the One on Ones and talk to participants when I visited the Virginia Avenue Project at one of their two, week-long summer outings at the Happy Valley School in Ojai. This small private school lies to one side of Highway 150, 3 miles north of Ojai on the way to Santa Paula. Set among gorgeous vistas of wooded mountains and valleys filled with cattle, it is a distinct contrast to the urban sprawl that is the usual home for all of these teens. Participation in the summer camp, at no cost to the kids, is presented as a reward to students who have attended and participated faithfully in the VAP classes during the preceding year. "Not everyone," Curran told me, "gets to go."[14]

I joined the group for the last of their seven days at the school and visited for 11 hours, from the 8:15 A.M. warm-up, through line readings, blocking, rehearsals, musical rehearsals, and tech run-throughs that culminated in a performance before an invited audience of adults, mostly family and friends of the teen participants.

The participants included nine youths, ages 9 to 18 and nine adult theatre professionals, paired up one on one. Also present were three "junior counselors," young people who had been through the summer camps before and were on hand to help out, and the VAP staff, which included Artistic Director Leigh Curran, new executive director Merrill Friedman, Production Manager Monica Brunt and long-time musical director Billy Mernit.

Prior to the week-long residency at the school, a theatre professional has met with each young actor individually and crafted a play for the two of them to perform together. In some cases, due to illness, professional work, or child-care commitments, the adult is unable to follow through and appear in their play; in such cases Curran recruits another adult to work with the young person. The adult functions as both playwright and/or director and actor. The young person is the second actor. If the script calls for a third, fourth, or fifth actor, junior counselors fill those roles.

In addition to working on the plays, the group has fun: songs around the campfire, trips to the beach for swimming, lessons in belly dancing from a visiting expert, and visits to the local used bookstore where one adult volunteer buys books all around.

This week had been a particularly tough one as Leigh told me after the fact: "The kids spent the first two days complaining. They complained about the heat, the food, you name it. Wednesday I just got them together and said 'I can't take it anymore. I don't need this and I'm ready to go home rather than listen to anymore of it.' I was impressed that the group responded by problem solving and figuring out ways to stop the complaining. After that everything was fine."[15]

At warm-ups early on Saturday, I watched Merrill Friedman work on cooperative endeavors as she asked all of the actors to place themselves on stage, without talking or gesturing, to form the capital letter A, then an oval, a lowercase letter *b*, a lowercase letter *w* and finally, the lowercase letter *r*. Friedman then asked them to run through scenarios on stage. These included (1) walking randomly, (2) walking the stage in the character of the person they are in their play, and (3) walking the stage in the character of the second person in their play. She then instructed them all to stage a baseball game and then freeze the action. This stage picture was then replaced with one of the beach, freeway traffic, dinner at a fine restaurant, and an audience watching consecutively a horror film, a comedy, and a sad movie. All of the actors, young and old, moved confidently from one scenario to the next without hesitation or embarrassment.

Leigh Curran introduced me to the adult/teen team I would follow for the day. Jerry was 13, just a month shy of his 14th birthday, about to enter ninth grade and a white immigrant from South Africa. His partner was Hubert Hodgin. They had met for the first time the previous Sunday when both arrived at camp.

In our interview Hubert told me that this was his first experience with VAP, his first experience ever directing a play, and his first experience working with a young actor. Hodgin is a professional, who began his career in regional theatre in Cincinnati, spent eight years in New York doing stage work, and moved to Los Angeles five years ago where he has continued to do stage work as well as films (including *Shakedown* and *Whatever It Takes*) and television (*3rd Rock*, *Life on the Streets*, and *ER* among others). Hubert is married and the father of one 9-year-old son. Jerry told me that this was his second summer in Ojai with VAP and that he has appeared in several VAP productions.

Jerry and Hubert, like every other team of one young person and one adult, face the daunting task of rehearsing and performing a 10-minute play (that actually runs closer to 15 minutes) in just one week at camp. These plays are then performed again one week after camp for a much larger audience at UCLA's Little Theatre on two consecutive evenings.

In addition to dormitories and classrooms, the Happy Valley School has a very nice performing space called the Zalk Theatre with seating for 200 which is a perfect venue for these intimate try-outs.

At 9 A.M. Jerry, Hubert, and I moved to an upstairs room to rehearse.

Their play, *Dating Isn't Easy*, chronicles the trials of young Bobby, whom the script identifies only as "an all–American boy," played by Jerry, who calls at the home of young Jenny (played by junior counselor, 16-year-old Beth) to pick her up for their first date. But Bobby must first pass muster with Jenny's Dad, Mr. Smyth (Hubert) who just happens to be an alien and who puts Bobby through several bizarre tests, including a television game show on the distant planet "Cleve Land" and a fight to the death with swords, "ribbon daggers," and "tube spears." When Bobby vanquishes Mr. Smyth, he refuses to kill his opponent and so wins his date with Jenny by this magnanimity. The three cast members close the show singing together an original song called "Dating Isn't Easy." The play lasts 15 minutes and, as you can see, includes a bit of realism, a little fantasy, a *3rd Rock* inspiration, plenty of physical activity, stage fighting, and a musical number.

Dating Isn't Easy was written by Steven Wolfson after a 10-minute interview with Jerry several weeks earlier. Jerry, Hubert, and Beth had not seen the script until their arrival at camp. The original intent had been that the play would be directed by Wolfson's wife, Julie, who regularly teaches acting classes for VAP, but a sick child kept her at home and Hubert got a late call to step in as the director.

I talked to Jerry about the process of creating the script. He told me:

> Mr. Wolfson and I met two weeks ago for about 10 minutes. He asked me a few questions like "What do you like to do in your free time?" and "Who are your friends?" I didn't see the script until I got here and I don't see anything in the script that I talked to the writer about. However, this character Bobby seems like me because he's mellow. I don't know what the description "all–American boy" in the stage directions means, however, since I was born and raised in South Africa.[16]

No one else in the cast had ever met the author and no one made changes in the script during the rehearsal process. The setup and denouement of the script reminded me of various plot devices seen on television's popular *3rd Rock* where the resident aliens have a beautiful daughter who attracts various earthling suitors much to her father's discomfort.

Jerry and Hubert had been rehearsing for four hours each day and this was their seventh day working together. Moreover, Jerry had been up until 1 A.M. that morning visiting with other campers and his energy was flagging. Hubert offered lots of positive encouragement as they ran lines but became increasingly frustrated with Jerry's low energy level. It seemed to me hard to believe that they would be ready for a public performance in just 8 hours.

The script was 10 pages long and both actors seemed to have the lines memorized. Hubert suggested running the lines as quickly as possible and this seemed to revive Jerry's energy. After an hour, they went back downstairs to the theatre and ran through the play for Artistic Director Leigh Curran who offered them detailed notes to improve their performance. Beth joined them for the first time that day to run through her part. She seemed quite comfortable on stage and added a well-trained voice to their song together.

After a 10-minute break Jerry and Hubert got together again to go over Leigh's notes. Hubert asked questions to help Jerry think about his character: "What does Bobby want?" "What does he think about the trip to the planet Cleve Land?" Jerry was yawning and his energy was flagging once again. Hubert pointed this out to him gently and expressed his frustration. At one point Jerry wondered: "Should I fall to the floor at that point?" Hubert asked: "Why would you fall to the floor?" Jerry answered: "I don't know." Hubert responded: "If you don't know why, don't do it." They moved on to a fairly sophisticated discussion of "making choices" and making the most of "moments" in the play.

Hubert tried some "what if...?" questions but failed to get much of a response. He tried: "Let me suggest this...." Jerry accepted his suggestions and they ran through the entire script again. To me it seemed that Jerry has trouble relating to his character. He asked Hubert "What's an all–American boy?" and I wondered how much experience he had in dating at his age and whether he could relate to the set up for the scene. Hubert sat in front of Jerry on a chair he had turned backwards. Hubert is tall and thin and Jerry observed: "You scare me. You're like a spider." It was a striking observation but Hubert did not respond directly or pursue with Jerry why he had made this observation. Clearly Jerry was to play a part but there was little of himself in the role and Hubert and Jerry, while together working on a professional level, were not connecting on a personal basis.

Beth came in and they decided to try the song again. Jerry began the lyrics but said, "I don't want to sing the first lines." Hubert was perplexed: "You want to just speak them?" Jerry replied, "yeah" and Hubert said, "That's fine."

At 11:45 they went back downstairs to the theatre again to work through the blocking with Merrill Friedman, who earns her living as a professional director. After 15 minutes they broke for lunch. There had been no complaining from the young people about what had already been four hours of hard work. Despite all of the input Jerry had from Hubert and

Merrill, it was hard for me to tell what would stick. They still seemed to be flying by the seat of their pants and I feared we would see a ragged performance later that afternoon.

The lunch break extended until 2 P.M. so that everyone could pack up and clean their rooms in preparation for returning home right after the performance. At 2 P.M. everyone reconvened in the theatre to rehearse the mass curtain call at the end of the program as well as the individual plays. Leigh gave notes and advice but the kids didn't seem to be paying much attention. Arturo, one of the junior counselors, complained that his performance was hampered because "my foot hurts." Leigh responded, "well you just have to 'give it up' for the performance. That's what actors and athletes do." Leigh then talked about "commitment" and supporting their fellow actors on the stage. Jerry told me he thought the rehearsals were going well. He seemed unfazed by the public performance now just two hours away. At 3 P.M. Music Director Billy Mernit began working with each of the nine casts separately. I took the opportunity to talk privately with Sara Boucher-Rhodes who wrote the play *The Crayon Is Mightier than the Sword* which she was about to perform with 12-year-old Lawrence. I was interested in hearing about the playwriting experience and I was particularly curious about the amount of creative involvement of the young actor in the process. "Well," she told me:

> I had an idea going in. When we met we talked about Lawrence's interest in video games and I just took off on the anger in that, you know, the video games where you shoot monsters and destroy alien invaders. I wanted to transfer that energy to the imagination, to a more creative way to deal with anger and fear and that's what this script is about.[17]

Having talked to Jerry about his experience with the author of his play and with Sara about hers, I concluded that these plays spoke for their adult authors much more than for their young actors. The initial verbal consultations may have sparked the writers' imaginations but failed to give them a real sense of the teens they were writing for.

A few days later I questioned Leigh Curran about this issue by phone. "What do you suggest the playwrights find out about the young people before they write the plays?" I asked. She told me:

> I give them a little of the kid's background and suggest they talk to them about the theme or their interests. I suggest they write a play that has meaning to them, the adults. For example in the play *The Buddy System* the author, Robert Fieldsteel, uses the activity of rock climbing for his two characters because his teen actor, Henry is into rock climbing. But I don't suggest that

the writer put the kid's life on stage because the young person needs to learn to portray a character on stage rather than feel exposed portraying their own life. On the other hand, if we pick up on the fact that a kid has a problem with jealousy, for example, we might write a character that has that problem but then cast the kid as the "wise one" who helps that character cope with that problem and so learn about it that way. Another time we cast a girl who was homeless in real life and set the play out on the street but had it be about two people who fall into a construction hole in the road and have to figure out how to get out. We didn't use her life as grist for the plot but set it up so she had to deal with the issue of "being rescued." Sometimes we get that close to the young person's real life.[18]

"How do you decide which adults to pair up with which young actors?" I asked. "Sometimes I pair them up as to the same gender and then if they've done that, I pair them up with the opposite gender and I'll do that with race, etc. I go by my intuition and whether or not I think it will be a good mix," Curran said.[19]

When the performances began at 5 P.M. I saw the variety of themes the adults had worked on as part of a two-act bill of nine plays titled *That's the Ticket*. Leigh Curran chooses a title each year and the title then ties the plays together. This year each playwright knew that a physical ticket or a reference to some form of ticket had to appear in each play. Last year's title was *Food for Thought* and a food product had to appear or be referenced in each play. I must admit that if this theme had not been pointed out to me in advance, it might well have escaped my notice entirely in actual production, though it does serve to present a problem or complication for the writers and directors to solve and so keeps them thinking.

The first play was *In the Running* by Leon Martell, acted by 11-year-old Marta and her director, Shawna Casey. It revolved around two women competing in a foot race. The moral, stated more than once, was that the fun of running was more important than winning the race.

Second up was *The Adventures of the Avenging Ranger. Chapter 12, the Gatekeeper*, written, directed, and acted by Demitri Corbin, joined by 10-year-old Nicolai in the title role. This was a mildly amusing piece of whimsy without any particular moral or lesson.

When Horses Fly was performed next, written, choreographed and acted by Jodi Heaston with 9-year-old Sacha. It involved two carousel horses, one of which decides to forsake the boring carousel for life in a western rodeo. The moral is about freedom and following one's dreams. I was amazed by the work of Sacha, a chubby little elf who acted and danced with an assurance well beyond her years.

The Buddy System, written, directed, and acted by Robert Fieldsteel with 13-year-old Jack, was notable for its theatricality (the two actors stood side-by-side on the bare stage but convinced those of us in the audience that they were climbing a mountain together) and also for its intriguing ambiguity. The conflict, whether the two long-time friends might be outgrowing their relationship, was never really settled and it had the unfinished feel of real life rather than a synthetic "message" piece all neatly tied up with a clear moral at the end.

Dating Isn't Easy completed Act One and it was clear that Jerry, Hubert and Beth had indeed gotten it together. Maybe Jerry had been saving his energy for this moment. Whatever the explanation, he came alive, singing and acting up a storm. Not one line was forgotten and the interplay between the two actors appeared flawless. Both actors seemed happy, if surprised, by their success when the play ended.

Act Two opened with The Racing Life, written, directed, and acted by Steven Totland with 11-year-old Alan as father Roger and son Guy. The plot involved Guy (Alan) encouraging his admittedly "simple," or intellectually challenged, father to follow his dreams and audition for a punk rock band rather than remain "a loser" by working in an espresso shop.

Next up was Sara Boucher-Rhodes' The Crayon Is Mightier than the Sword, unfortunately the weakest entry in the show to my mind. In the action, 12-year-old Lawrence is weaned away from his PlayStation 2 video console as he learns to use his imagination to defeat assorted villains. The piece had a "this is the way adults would like to see kids learn to live" feel to it that appeared simultaneously preachy and unconvincing.

The next two plays Someplace You've Never Been and The Totally True Legends of Jessie and Jane both addressed the issue of running away from home but came down on opposite sides of the issue. Someplace, written by Winnie Holzman and Paul Dooley and directed and acted by Judy Heneghan with 11-year-old Meghan, seemed a remake of that old saw about searching the world for a precious flower and then finding it in your own backyard. Surprisingly, however, The Totally True Legends of Jessie and Jane, written by Joy Gregory and directed and acted by Ariel Zevon with 18-year-old Judith, was about empowering a teenager to leave home and start over elsewhere, not an idea you often see endorsed by adults.

The invited audience laughed at all the jokes and applauded the participants lustily at the end. The actors, young and old, hugged each other and seemed pleased with their work. Then it was time for everyone to pile into the vans for the two-hour ride home.

The casts would then take Sunday, Monday, and Tuesday off, and reconvene on Wednesday for a tech rehearsal at UCLA, where they would perform for the last time together on Friday and Saturday evenings.

At lunch on the last day of camp the adults and youth were given separate evaluation forms to fill out. With plenty of blank space for writing, the adult/teacher evaluation form had the following questions:

1. Did the child's interactions with adults and peers change during the time spent in this program? How?

2. Did the child appear to gain confidence in him/herself during the course of the program? If so, when did you observe this change and what did you observe?

3. Were there any changes in the child's life outside the program that the child voiced concern about? Any positive changes shared?

4. During the course of the program, did you see the development of pro-social skills in the child (for example task completion, collaboration, communication, problem solving, etc.)?

This was the only time I saw any of the three programs I studied do any sort of evaluation. Though well-intentioned, it was of a fairly general and superficial nature.

I revisited the Virginia Avenue kids on May 4, 2002. Curran got nine of the same kids I surveyed the previous year to come back to the PAL building on a Saturday morning to do the posttest survey. She told me that one teen moved away and one "is kind of moody and we can't count on him to do the survey." She volunteered to mail copies of the survey to the kids who were not present. I had arranged to have 17 VAP teens fill out pretest surveys a year earlier in May 2001.

I was in awe of how organized Leigh was and how the kids responded to her requests and followed through with what she expected of them. With 9 posttest surveys in hand, I returned home, wondering how many of the six surveys I had left with her would be returned to me by mail. Within two weeks I had received three more completed surveys by mail. When I reported the return rate to Leigh, she contacted the parents and kids who had been mailed the three outstanding surveys that same day and told me they would be in the mail to me shortly. Two more arrived in the mail the following week and in the end, I had 14 posttest surveys filled out from the original group of 17, the best return rate from any of the three theatre groups.

The surveys also highlight the commitment over time that participants made to the project. The 14 teens averaged 6.5 years in the 10-year-old Virginia Avenue Project, with one respondent having been in the project for all 10 years and the three newest participants reporting four years of involvement.

Elizabeth Perez, a graduating high school senior, wrote in the project's April 2000 newsletter:

> For the past eight years the Virginia Avenue Project has taught me much more than just acting and writing. I have learned how to grow as a performer and most important as a person. Everyone in the project has become my family. They've been there for me, cared for me and watched me grow. I remember the first time I ever performed on stage. I was nervous and scared at the same time, but Leigh was backstage, ready with one of her many wonderful pep talks. She told me not to be scared and that I would do a wonderful job. As I was getting ready to go on, I remembered her exact words and that day I got rid of my fear of performing in front of an audience.

The stability and longevity of the project is clearly a testament to the commitment, dedication, and involvement of Project Director Leigh Curran for whom the Virginia Avenue Project truly is, as she told me, "my life."[20] Whether the program would survive without her continued personal investment is an open question but, for now, she is the engine that keeps the project running.

In contrast to the other programs I studied, Curran has convinced parents that the VAP is important and gained their commitment and attendance as well as their children's. As a result, the project is a smooth-running and well-organized program that offers a diversity of classes for the teenagers, who respond by remaining active for many years. Clearly Curran has developed a strong and mutually personal relationship with the teens I met.

Two disappointments to me were:

1. The adult playwrights do not really write plays tailored to their teen actors. Certainly, the teens learn to develop characters and present polished work on stage, but there is very little of who they are invested in the process or product. On the other hand, they are developing their own creativity, allowing them to express themselves in very personal ways, as Franchesca's poetry, reprinted earlier in this chapter, demonstrates.

2. The relationships between adult writers and adult actors on the one hand and the teens on the other did not seem very close or nurturing and often did not extend beyond the very short-lived production process itself. However, teen relationships with the regular adult acting teachers and Curran and her full-time staff seemed much closer.

The good news is that VAP continues to grow. By 2006 they had increased their budget to $325,000 a year and their staff to three full-time and three part-time positions. Curran remains as director and the project now has two permanent sites, having expanded into Virginia Park, also in the Pico corridor of Los Angeles. New programs include Photo Zine, a joint program with Venice Arts, in which the VAP teens contribute the written material to a magazine featuring creative writing and photography and Smart Partners, a tutoring program. New this fall is an improvisation program with Phyllis Katz, formerly of the nationally renowned Groundlings troupe. While the core theatre programs still enroll 45 to 50 teens as in years past, ancillary programs in various L.A. area schools reach another 50 teens each year. And VAP grads still shine after leaving the project with one enrolling at Mills College in northern California and another now doing postgraduate work at the Harvard School of Public Policy. The Haven, an Oregon program started by a former VAP staffer, ran for ten years but disbanded in 2005. As Curran told me most recently when I asked if she ever faces burn out: "Life is great. I love the people and I see the results, especially as I see our teen graduates search out socially relevant jobs and find ways to give back to making this a better world for all of us."[21] VAP keeps a list of the impressive accomplishments of its graduates. Among them now are two whom I quoted earlier in this chapter, poet Franchesca Hladik, who studied with VAP from 1996 to 2005 and now attends Mills College on a scholarship, and writer Elizabeth Perez, who studied with VAP from 1992 to 2001 and is currently earning a master's in education at Mount St. Mary's College.

CHAPTER 7

City Hearts

IN THE SPRING OF 2001 I MADE contact with City Hearts, a Los Angeles-based program offering theatre, dance, and art classes to elementary and secondary school students in a multitude of after-school programs. Husband and wife Bob and Sherry Jason, managing director and executive director respectively, and both former juvenile defense attorneys, founded City Hearts: Kids Say Yes to the Arts in 1984. In a letter to me dated May 15, 2001, Sherry explains the program's origin:

> In 1977 as a new lawyer I toured Central Juvenile Hall where I watched in sadness and fascination as a convicted 13 year old murderer took his first piano lesson. He was a prodigy, the music of Mozart touching his soul. I wondered what would have been his case history if he had met the piano before he met gangs.[1]

As a former ballerina, Sherry turned to the arts for answers. The mission statement of City Hearts reads:

> to intervene in a loving, supportive, and nurturing way to break the cycle of poverty, neglect, abuse, homelessness, delinquency, and violence that destroys the lives of children. Through the discipline and healing of classes, workshops, and performing experiences in the Arts, City Hearts provides positive role models, enrichment, and inspiration for our children to learn to be productive, creative, law abiding members of our society.[2]

To that end, City Hearts offers free classes to approximately 1,000 at-risk youths each year. Most are taught at their downtown studio about a mile from L.A.'s Skid Row, on a budget of $300,000 a year. Actress Jane Seymour serves as their national honorary chair and City Hearts has won both national and local awards and press attention, including an appearance on the *Oprah Winfrey* television show.

City Hearts offers a variety of programs: the Early Years Program, which is classes for 5 to 10 year olds; Circus Arts; For Girls Only, which are classes in theatre, dance, and music for just girls; a photography class; ALITE (Arts Literacy for Tomorrow's Education), which coaches functionally illiterate 10 to 18 year olds; and Sentenced to the Stage, where 13–18 year olds on probation attend classes in playwriting and acting in lieu of more traditional forms of community service.

For purposes of my research I decided to study the City Hearts project in Shakespeare offered as an after-school program to students at the Haydock Intermediate School in Oxnard, California, begun in 2000. A City Hearts press release called the program "highly successful." I was particularly interested in the project because of the long history of using the high culture icon of Shakespeare as a civilizing tool to raise social standards; an idea raised by Alice Minnie Herts, a founder of the American children's theatre movement in 1911, as discussed in chapter 3.

In fall 2001 I attended the second meeting of the academic year of the City Hearts Shakespeare Program offered at Haydock under contract from Expanding Horizons, the after-school enrichment program of the Oxnard School District. Expanding Horizons was founded by Dr. Katherine Larson in 1999 and financed with 3.8 million dollars of federal, state, and local agency funding. Through Expanding Horizons, City Hearts offers after-school theatre programs at five Oxnard schools, the others being elementary schools. As the Oxnard project director Justin Doran told me, "our programs are in the tougher schools. If the school is doing well on standardized tests, we haven't been asked to do a project there."[3]

Haydock Intermediate School is an attractive newer campus set in a working-class subdivision a few blocks off the main arteries of Ventura and Oxnard boulevards, in this city midway between Los Angeles and Santa Barbara. Houses are neat, small, and well cared for. Most have burglar bars on the windows. The first class I attended was led by Justin, a professional actor who often performs at Theatricum Botanicum in Topanga Canyon, an outdoor theatre begun by actor Will Geer and his family when he was blacklisted from acting in the 1950s, and who earned an MFA at UCLA. Justin worked with one assistant, Connor, a high school student being paid part-time to learn how to run these classes for future programs, and the class consisted of six middle school students.

Earlier that day all of the students enrolled in after-school programs had met in the library before going to the program they wished to attend. Choices for students included possibilities as diverse as skateboarding, cake decorating, and art. Justin publicly invited students to come with him for "Shakespeare and sword fighting."

Meeting in the cafeteria, with its raised stage on which their productions would be given, Justin had the students circle up and began by asking them, "What's iambic pentameter?" Referring to a current television ad of a couple attending a Broadway show, one girl responded: "It's 16th-century poetry." "Right," said Justin. "Tell me, what rap song do you know that has a good bass line?" The kids responded with several favorite song titles. "Well Shakespeare had a bass line," offered Justin, "and it's called iambic pentameter. Does anyone know how many beats to a line of Shakespearean poetry?" Guesses started at 26 and worked their way down to the correct answer of 10. "Here's a line from *Romeo and Juliet*," said Justin reciting the words, "Hear the ten beats? Now let's make up our own 10-beat line."

Each student contributed a word until they had a line of poetry with 10 beats. "Okay," said Justin, "get out your pens and everyone write a line of poetry with 10 beats." After each teen had written their lines, Justin asked them to stand and read them aloud. All had written something and all had 10 beats. Some read so softly it was hard to hear them. Justin worked with them until their recitation was audible. One young girl, the class cut-up to date, screamed her line and enjoyed the attention. When they were done reciting, Justin told them, "thank you, Shakespeare's." I noted that the racial composition of the group was one black student, three Latinos and two non–Hispanic whites.

The girl who read loudly was constantly interrupting and seeking attention. When Justin told her to "put a sock in it," she took him literally and removed the sock from her foot and stuffed it into her mouth.

Justin suggested that they play tag. They tried several forms of tag: regular tag, and then "styles" tag where everyone had to copy the outrageous physical walk and vocal gesticulations of the person who was "it."

"Okay," said Justin, "let's do something dangerous." The kids were intrigued by this. "Let's form a circle, standing close together, with our knees bent. Each person will try to cross from one side of the circle to the other by walking on the backs or knees of the other people," explained Justin. The kids took off their shoes for this exercise and began, but the first "people walker" took a misstep and the entire circle collapsed in a pile on the ground. "We really need a mat," said Justin, "maybe we'll try this another time. Let's play a game where everyone has to be standing, sitting or kneeling at all times."

The kids, however, started to suggest their own games. They wanted to play "props" as seen on the television show *Whose Line Is It Anyway?* Justin gave in and divided them into teams, giving them innocuous props, like a shoe, and asking them to improvise a scene. It appeared to me that the kids were into this activity, but Justin seemed disengaged and ended the game quickly.

Addressing the students, Justin told them that the beginning Shakespeare class, this class, would meet every Monday and Wednesday after school, and would be performing *A Midsummer' Night's Dream* at the end of the 12-week semester, while the class with students continuing from the previous year would be tackling *Romeo and Juliet*. He had chosen the plays for the students.

"Okay," he announced, "let's play statues. When I say go, form yourselves into a set of statues portraying what I have asked for. Work together so that you do not repeat actions and make sure no one is moving when I say 'freeze.' You have 15 seconds each time. First, show me Sesame Street." The kids took up positions as Big Bird or Oscar the Grouch but some had chosen the same character and the scene garnered no points. In order Justin chose the following scenes for the young actors: cheerleading, breakdancing, Power Rangers, Rug Rats in Paris, and a family portrait. Most received no points because the kids assumed dynamic poses they could not hold for very long after Justin shouted "freeze."

Then he said, "show me what it's like to attend Haydock School." It was a provocative scenario. He questioned them as to their characters and they named various teachers and students around the school. He asked no follow-up questions, however, and received no feedback as to how the actors felt about their characters or about attending Haydock. A chance to delve into their lives and academic and social struggles was lost and he quickly moved on to a basketball game, and then the Bible, which yielded several actors cooperating for a manger scene while another pretended to be Jesus on the cross and another was Moses with a threatening rod. "Time to quit," announced Justin, at 6 o'clock, the session having lasted the prescribed hour and a quarter. The teens headed out with the same bubbling enthusiasm with which they had entered.

The class featured high energy, fun games, a clear camaraderie between Justin and the teens, and space for the teens to express their creativity through poetry and improvs. Yet each time issues close to the actual lives of the students were raised, Justin moved on as if consciously avoiding such exploration. I saw the same thing happen two weeks later. The class and I were watching a video of the Franco Zefferelli movie *Romeo and Juliet*, the play this class would present. The kids paid rapt attention to the sword-fighting scene that was first up on the tape. Later in the movie, however, as Juliet, her mother, and her nurse discuss marriage, the mother mentions that Juliet is 14 years old, the same age as the kids watching the film, but Justin does not point this out or make any attempt to apply this information to the students' lives.

After the class when we were alone, I asked Justin how the play had been cast. He told me: "We asked the kids to write down what parts they'd like to play and to rank their first five choices. But in the end we'll decide who plays what. It just wouldn't be fair to cast someone in a role that's beyond them and have them struggle, maybe have trouble with the rest of their school work, just to attempt something they're not ready for." While the reasons may have been in the students' best interests, they were decisions made for the teens by the adults, a hallmark of the City Hearts program as I observed it over time.

I returned to Haydock the next day to visit the Monday–Wednesday group which was preparing *A Midsummer Night's Dream* and observed the bureaucratic intrusiveness of the school setting. Seven students were present as we began and four more arrived over the next 20 minutes. Present to teach this day was Stuart Calof, who, like Justin, acted in productions at Theatricum Botanicum. With no games, warm-ups, or further introductions (it soon became apparent that Stuart did not know students' names and had to call them "you"), Stuart asked, "Which parts have you been cast in?" Answers included "wall," "Pyramus," and "Thisbe." Stuart inquired, "Is everyone in the class here?" "No," said the kids, "some are in the library." Stuart asked one student to go get them. Stuart then instructed all the kids to lie on the ground. Before he could proceed he was interrupted by a student sent from the office to take attendance. Between students coming to reclaim paperwork, or just wandering in, and very loud announcements over the school PA system, Stuart was interrupted sufficiently to have to stop his class 10 times by my count in just 75 minutes.

In the midst of this mayhem, Stuart instructed the kids to lie on the floor, close their eyes, and get comfortable. One girl said, "I'm not tired and this isn't comfortable." He replied, "just get as comfortable as you can" and then led them through a relaxation exercise as they became aware of and then relaxed the different parts of their bodies. He had them imagine a white light, "like a ball," above them which gently came to rest on their foreheads and made different parts of their bodies glow. They were told to take the white light, then described as energy, into their bodies. Stuart was interrupted twice during this exercise alone.

The kids were quiet, neither talking nor laughing. Stuart told them, "In a moment we're going to get up but I want you to hang onto this glowing light. Keep it as we do the dance. It's there for you. Now the white light is in your stomach. Breathe. Okay. Open your eyes. Come up to a sitting position. Keep the white light. Get slowly up to a sitting position. You kids are great. Justin said you were great."

I wondered about Stuart's emphasis on the light being white. Of the 11 kids present that day only one could be called white or Caucasian, two were black and the rest Latinos. Would making the light purple, for example, have moved the group beyond the traditional white-black dichotomy in which white is always seen as good and black as bad?

Later Stuart arranged the scene from *Midsummer* in which the actors dance and he said, "At the very end of the play, after the mechanicals have performed, Theseus asks for a dance and the mechanicals and fairies take over. I can't believe Justin is going to take the fairies out of *Midsummer*."

That last comment pointed up the lack of coordination among the drama teachers, another disconnect I saw repeated during my year of observation. At the beginning of class Stuart told me he hadn't known I was coming that day, although I had told Justin the day before, and he didn't know my name or where I was from, but had heard "something about the work" I was doing.

Stuart told the class: "We're going to learn different parts of the dance and then put it all together. Since we have no fairies, we'll skip that part." As Stuart gathered the kids together, I became conscious of my own feelings: as always I felt good in the presence of the energy and lightheartedness these kids were putting out. They were clearly having fun, even when they ignored the teacher and fooled around among themselves but the work of the class seemed too often haphazard and unfocused. Frequently, students asked interesting questions that were ignored and teaching moments were lost.

I returned again two weeks later to observe the Tuesday–Thursday class at the midpoint of their 12-week schedule to find the group now planning elementary school tours of various scenes from several different Shakespeare plays. The actors would be double cast from the same teens doing *Romeo and Juliet*. "We're just rolling along," Justin told me. "But can the kids handle this much material?" I asked. "Remember," he said, "we'll only do about 40 minutes of the script from *Romeo and Juliet*, so they can learn that play and other scenes and this way we get the elementary school kids interested in the project."

I asked about a few students I had met earlier who were not present. "Susan?" said Justin, "I don't know what happened to Susan. Maybe she dropped out. Her phone number seems to change every three months. I don't know her parents and I'm not sure she knows them both. Last I heard she was living with a grandfather and his 19-year-old wife." The second student, A.J., was unknown to Justin and even though I had his name and address from having met him there a month earlier, no one present seemed to remember him.

The new year ushered in more changes. Haydock had decided to reduce the Shakespeare classes from four to two days a week. As the Expanding Horizons onsite director Sophocles Costis explained to me, "we had the kids rank order their interests from all the after-school classes offered and Shakespeare ranked at or near the bottom of most lists. I mean, it was at the top of the lists of the kids who were in the program but there just weren't that many of them."[4] From Costis I learned that Haydock serves 800 students of whom approximately 140 are enrolled in Expanding Horizons. The Shakespeare classes draw fewer than 25 of these students.

Costis also told me that 75 percent of those in Expanding Horizons are "referred," a nice word meaning that parents or teachers tell these students that they must attend because they're in danger of flunking out of school. "These are the most at-risk of our kids," said Costis.[5]

The loss to the program of two days each week meant that there would now be just one Shakespeare class meeting twice a week, rather than two classes each meeting twice in the same week. Two weeks later the meeting of the Shakespeare group was canceled by the school on just five hours notice "to do registrations" Justin told me.

When I returned a week after that, I witnessed the least effective class I had yet seen. Things seemed so haphazard that I began keeping time. Eleven teens and I arrived at the exercise room, new home to the class, on time at 4:30 P.M. but the door was locked. Stuart arrived at 4:35 and went off to find someone to open the door. A janitor arrived to unlock the door at 4:37. We entered and as Stuart set out the mats, the kids ran around the room and swung from the exercise apparatus. Stuart went over the attendance sheets with Connor and then called the group to order at 4:42. Parts had been cast for *A Midsummer Night's Dream* and the teens were supposed to be learning their lines. Without any warm-up, games, or informal conversation with the kids Stuart asked, "do we need to review what you covered last week with Justin or can we forge ahead?" The girl cast as Puck responded, "I need to review my part." This was clearly not what Stuart wanted to hear. In the meantime, Edgar was showing off and resisted repeated calls to sit down with everyone else. At the same time Paul wandered off by himself to the other end of the gym.

Stuart said, "Let's start on page 17 of the script." Several teens responded as a chorus: "We don't have our scripts." "I lost mine," explained Paul. They also informed Stuart that the girl cast as Hermia was out sick. Several of the kids were tipping the stack of mats over. Stuart said nothing, but several of the kids told others to "shut up." Stuart asked, "How many of you are off book?" None of the kids were. "Okay," he said, "I'm going to work a scene with the mechanicals, the rest of you work your lines with Connor or with a partner."

Stuart started to work with the four teens cast as the mechanicals. As those not in the scene made noise, he told them, "Guys, you are being very rude." Only two of the teens cast as the mechanicals had their scripts and the others had to go get theirs. It was now 4:50, 20 minutes into the 90-minute session and absolutely nothing of a theatrical nature had been accomplished.

Shawna screamed suddenly, a high-pitched ear-piercing yelp: "I need a script." One boy threw a shoe at her in response. Connor, Stuart's purported aide, was in the corner chatting with the oldest and cutest girl present. Stuart spied him and said, "Connor, I need you to run lines with some people."

At 4:53 Stuart finally began practicing lines with the teen playing Bottom. While he did so, five of the kids gathered in one corner to talk among themselves. Stuart told them, "Don't make me give you a warning already." After receiving three warnings, I was told, a teen is sent to the library for the remainder of the period. Shawna was running her lines as Bottom. She read from her script and addressed her lines to the floor. She was inaudible.

On the other side of the room Connor had six kids gathered together but was doing nothing with them. Every once in a while he'd say, "you guys should run your lines," but he never followed up and they, in fact, never ran lines. Meanwhile, Stuart continued working with Shawna to help her understand the context of her scene within the play as a whole. He moved on to rehearse some blocking with her. In this chaos, two girls moved over to another corner to run lines between themselves. As she rehearsed, Shawna paused several times in her scene to yell, "shut up" at kids she felt were bugging her. At the end of an hour, only Shawna as Bottom had rehearsed, running all of six lines just twice.

By now some of the kids were messing with the weight machine and hanging from the bars. Stuart began to work with Ursula and Paul as well as Shawna. Connor laid down on one of the mats with a group of kids and they talked while others swung on the equipment. Clearly the move from the cafeteria to the exercise room had provided too many distractions. One girl was swinging from a rope attached to the ceiling while a boy hung from a railing installed in the wall. Three girls left the room at 5:20 without a word of explanation and returned 10 minutes later.

A public address announcement interrupted the proceedings and one teen arrived late at 5:12. Connor roused himself to put the hanging rope away, but as soon as he was done, Edgar got it out and swung from it again. Connor wandered around seemingly without direction. Teens not in the program entered to put equipment away in the closet and walked across the makeshift stage stopping all action. Connor again said, "work on your lines" to the kids lying on the mat, but none paid him any attention.

At 5:20 Stuart started working with a second group of actors for another scene. Connor was hanging out with 10 kids who were doing nothing but making a terrific racket in the enclosed space, and I realized I was developing a headache.

At 5:40 Stuart left the group he had been working with and approached the kids lying on the mats. They quieted down while he was there. He returned to his scene but was back again in a few minutes, telling them, "guys why do you keep pushing me on this?" Without receiving an answer, he returned to the scene work. But he soon returned again in response to the noise and gave Edgar a warning. He told them, "I need you working back here" but when he walked away again nothing changed.

Working with his actors, I heard Stuart allow them the first chance to improvise. He told them, "You decide how you will physically cast the spell and you decide how it will physically affect you. Okay. Let's see it." The kids worked the scene with appropriate gestures. However, it was now five minutes to 6 P.M. and the class was nearly over. Not one teen had spent more than ten minutes rehearsing the play in the previous hour and a half and many had had no rehearsal at all.

Near the end, Stuart called everyone together. It was clear from his interactions that he still did not know their individual names. He asked them, "If you were teaching this class what would you think about what happened today?" One kid offered, "It was terrible." Stuart asked, "What can be done about this?" As he spoke two of the kids were clowning behind his back, Tanya miming puffing on a marijuana joint. It was the best acting I had seen. "What can we do?" asked Stuart, "You tell me. We are trying to get out of this exercise room and back into the cafeteria." Shawna interrupted to yell, "shut up," once again with great gusto and volume, this time at Paul.

Stuart posed the question again: "How can I get something done in here next Monday? Everyone bring your script next time and have a pencil to write down the blocking notes. You know I can give warnings but at the end of class all you'll have are warnings and no on will have learned anything. So come prepared next time." Then Stuart dismissed the class at 6 P.M.

I reflected on what might have made a difference in this chaos: (1) games and warm-ups which might have served to burn off energy; (2) a move out of the exercise room with all its temptations; (3) an aide who actually knew what to do and did it instead of Connor who seemed too unmotivated to be useful; and (4) some discipline and leadership from Stuart. If he knew the teens' names, he could call them on their individual bad behavior and if he removed one goof-off at the first sign of misbehavior, the others might quickly get the message and pay attention.

Four days later I interviewed Stuart by telephone to learn about his background and training. Like the other teachers, Stuart was recruited out of the Theatricum Botanicum troupe by Justin. He earned his degree at the University of California at Berkeley where he studied acting and then continued his training first at the Stella Adler Studio and later with the Howard Fine Studio. He had been teaching at the Topanga Elementary School in their STAR program, an offshoot of Head Start, which offers classes in acting, yoga, and music. Then he taught acting with kids four to five days a week, though he had no formal training in working with children. He'd been working with City Hearts since October and this was his first full 12-week session.

Stuart told me that he had received no formal training from City Hearts and had not attended any orientation with other City Hearts teachers. Rather, Justin had oriented him one on one and served as his mentor.

When I asked Stuart what seemed unique to him about the City Hearts program he told me:

Well, first it's clearly an intervention to give the kids something to stimulate their interest and something to hold on to. It's a new demographic for me and a new learning curve. I've had to evaluate old teaching methods with this new group. They present different challenges and a different attitude towards education. I find myself making more phone calls to the kids and their parents to solidify the idea that there are these programs after school. Attendance is problematic. I work hard to keep them coming back and it's not guaranteed that their parents have an interest in their child's involvement.[6]

When I queried Stuart about any frustrations he might have with the program, he told me:

I've got kids that clearly have an attitude towards authority figures ... a harder-edged resistance than I'm used to. The nature of what I get to present them, the space devoid of desks and projects, lets me break down that conventional resistance. I'm the one who gets to see that attitude recede and the kid come out. Kids have a lot of pressures and I understand why they act out. It's particularly gratifying when I get to turn them on to things. There's a lot of light bulbs going on and they leave with new ideas. I've got a new message for them.[7]

Stuart brought up the discipline problems and chaos of the previous Monday meeting I had attended and said:

I've sat down with the kids and talked about what they like and want. The class you saw was the first after we had a big heart-to-heart. I'm in a unique situation as a new teacher walking into an ongoing class. It's not like that at McKenna and Harrington [local elementary schools] where I'm the undisputed authority. I'm on a learning curve with these guys. They're testing me and I'm trying to be sensitive to that. They're trying to get a reaction from me but it will work out.[8]

Six weeks later, following the spring break, I contacted Justin to schedule another visit to City Hearts. I asked in an e-mail, "Has the Haydock schedule been set for next week yet?" He e-mailed me back: "Still being worked on ... they have restructured ... again." The next day he e-mailed once more: "The schedule at Haydock doesn't resume until the 26th and there are now two classes." Two days later he added: "I anticipate losing some of the kids.... Expanding Horizons keeps changing the rules. The kids are now required to come to the program 4 hours a day 5 days a week to take 2.25 hours of drama. That will not fly with some of them."

A few days later Justin e-mailed: "We may not resume classes until May 6." On Sunday, April 27 I asked him: "Are classes going to resume this week or next?" He e-mailed back: "I should know Monday." In other words, Justin was hoping that by Monday he would be informed by Expanding

Horizons whether classes were to begin that same week or the following week. How he was to schedule his own life and work and that of his two other teachers on such short notice I had no idea. On the evening of April 28 he e-mailed me again: "Off till May 6. The students are equally miffed." We all waited yet another week.

On May 7, 2002, I returned to Haydock School for the first day of Shakespeare classes after a month-long hiatus. Told the program would begin at the new time of 2:30 P.M., I arrived at 2:20 as regular classes were being dismissed for the day. I found no adult staff either in the cafeteria or the activity room. I ran into five of the teens I knew from the program but none of them were sure if there would be classes that day. A janitor who recognized me sent me back to the cafeteria and I ran into Rebekah Brown from City Hearts. We all walked over to the activity room together but found the doors locked. While Rebekah searched for a custodian to open up, the teens briefly disappeared. But by 2:45 Rebekah had gotten everyone together in the now unlocked activity room but then everyone had to move to the room next door when we were told that "dance will be using this room."

I noticed that Rebekah was far more personable than Stuart; she hugged the kids and sat with them. Stuart always maintained a greater physical and emotional distance from the teens.

Rebekah announced that City Hearts classes would take place on Tuesdays and Thursdays that trimester. To my great surprise, Rebekah asked me if I knew how late the classes were to run, just as Stuart had weeks earlier. This time I did not know and neither did she.

It turned out, as I learned in my conversations with the teens, that they had no idea when Shakespeare classes were going to get underway again and had gathered in this room the day before, Monday, in hopes of meeting. However, no adults were present and the kids were admonished for making too much noise that interfered with the dance class meeting next door. In response the kids had put together a petition of their own which they showed me, titled "Upset Drama Kids!!!" which asked for daily drama classes after school and lamented that "all the things you promised us are being ignored." The petition was addressed to the Haydock principal. I was impressed at the initiative the teens had taken and their clear desire for drama classes.

As she initially gathered the kids together Rebekah told them they would be performing for the school board soon. "What scenes do you have ready?" she asked. The kids responded, "none." Her questioning also revealed that with the new meeting time for the group some of the kids from last quarter could no longer attend. At 2:55 Rebekah told them, "Okay. I want to see Pyramus and Thisbe." Shawna whined, "But we've done this play seven times over." Rebekah called "places" and teens fell into several groups around the room.

Many of the youths were just fooling around and talking, although one kid was literally bouncing off the walls. Rebekah told them, "I need the rest of you over here sitting down." She shouted over the din: "Group, group, group, everybody quiet! Anybody who touches this gym equipment will have 5 minutes of time out. What can I do to get you to focus? You're all acting like 5 year olds."

By 3 P.M. Rebekah had arranged everyone for the scene. She had to take a book away from Rosie and then settled those not in the scene into a single area as the audience. She told them, "I really love you guys and I don't mean to be mean but we need to rehearse. You know I love you guys." Rather effectively, she charged the audience members with the job of supplying the forest sounds for the scene, assigning some as frogs and others as owls. Now that they had something to do, they settled down and got into the work.

At 3:05 Justin arrived with his own two young children and with four new students for the group. He interrupted the scene to announce: "Check it out, here's what's going to happen." The kids complained to him that they didn't meet over vacation and hadn't heard from him in what seemed to them like a long time. He pointed out that he did call several of the students by telephone during the hiatus. Having just come from a meeting with school officials to set the schedule for the coming 10 weeks, Justin was shown the "Upset Drama Kids!!!" petition but denigrated it, telling the kids they would now have the program they wanted and that their written complaints "make you look bad." It seemed to me this was a lost opportunity to empower the youths, who had just shown their first initiative of the year. He told them, "You're frustrated. I'm frustrated. But the good news is that we will have two meetings per week and every other Wednesday we will get to go off campus and perform at other schools and nursing homes. We've got a performance coming up. Let's see what you've got."

Justin called on some of the veterans to describe the plot of *Midsummer* to the new students. I counted that the group had grown from five students, when I first arrived, to 17. They ran through the forest rehearsal of Pyramus and Thisbe and then Puck's epilogue to the play.

Justin split the group in two to work with the new students whom he cast as the missing fairies and Rebekah took the other kids into the adjacent room which had remained vacant during this time. At 3:40 they put the two groups back together and played a theatre game. I realized that again there had been no warm-up exercises and that this was the first theatre game I had seen them play in a very long time.

At 4 P.M. the students had to go. In their hour and a half together they had spent perhaps 20 minutes in rehearsal. Rebekah said to me, "See we got some work done today." I did not respond, since I did not share her sense of accomplishment.

The next month I contacted Justin to arrange to survey the kids I hadn't reached earlier but he informed me that the upcoming classes previously scheduled had been canceled. The Oxnard public school teachers were talking about a strike and Expanding Horizons had responded by ending their program a week early. I should no longer have been surprised at how quickly things could change and how the schedules were so quickly altered, but I was.

I attended the year-end production and surveyed two additional students after the performance. Of the 14 students who filled out the questionnaires for me the previous fall, only 7 remained with the program and completed the posttest. The others, Justin told me by phone, had "dropped out of the program or been kicked out of Expanding Horizons."[9] Of the three theatre groups I had been following, this was the lowest ratio (50 percent) of pretest to posttest surveys I completed. Among the missing were Connor, Chris, and Abigail, who had been mentors assigned to the program to be trained as future leaders. They no longer seemed to be with the project.

The public production in June was held in the school cafeteria. About 60 parents and 60 children attended, representing the five Oxnard schools with City Hearts programs. Bob and Sherry Jason and other City Hearts staff served a free dinner beginning at 6:15. Balloons decorated the room and a banner that read "Shakespearience 2002" hung at the front. Rebekah greeted people dressed as Queen Elizabeth as several students played Renaissance music on clarinets. A Renaissance-like fountain made of papier-mâché painted to look like stone dominated the stage and the statue in the center spouted real water from an urn. It was a very impressive bit of stage magic which was easily wheeled off stage when the scenes began.

Students from the four Oxnard elementary schools performed first with short scenes from *Midsummer*, *Romeo and Juliet*, *Julius Caesar*, and *Macbeth*. The scenes were interspersed with madrigals and dances also performed

by the young students, the same dances and songs I'd seen Rebekah teaching the kids at Haydock. The kids were clearly having fun though their lines
were often rushed and inaudible. Several scenes repeated from each school:
the mechanicals from Midsummer, the Marc Antony speech over Caesar's body
(usually featuring a student lying beneath a bloody sheet who then jumped
up and walked off stage after the scene), and the witches' first scene from
Macbeth. The older kids from Haydock tackled Hamlet's "to be or not to
be" speech (with Yorick's skull in hand for some reason) and Juliet's "where-
fore art thou Romeo" speech. The teens also did a lot of sword fighting from
Romeo and Juliet and this was a big crowd pleaser.

While doing the play within the play from Midsummer, Thisbe's pros-
thetic breast fell out and Pyramus helped replace it. As planned, water burst
from Thisbe's chest when she stabbed herself. The crowd roared in response.
The entire stage program took about two hours and also featured short
speeches about the program by school officials and Sherry Jason. The assistant chief of police announced that the Haydock Shakespeare program
received funding from the Oxnard Gang Violence Suppression Grant written by the Police Department and that funding was sufficient for two more
years. Santa Barbara's Channel 3 News, an ABC affiliate, sent a camera and
reporter to cover the event for broadcast later that evening.

In my year studying the City Hearts program, I was struck again and
again by the energy of the students, the willingness of many of them to
work long and hard in rehearsal to earn the opportunity to perform, and
the flashes of creativity they displayed. I was impressed also with the commitment and devotion of some of their acting instructors, balanced by the
lackadaisical attitude of others. All were trained as actors but none had any
background in the emotional and educational development of their young
charges and none had real training in working with teens. In addition, the
program was constantly undermined by the conflicting bureaucratic needs
(roll calls, announcements) and the seemingly capricious scheduling of the
host school. City Hearts' reliance on Shakespearean plays often left teens
with little sense of ownership or understanding of their own productions
and did not seem to touch upon issues they faced in their own lives.
Remember that most of these kids had to be there. They were already in
trouble at school for grades or behavior problems, and participation in
Expanding Horizons, which included the City Hearts Shakespeare program, was required to avoid suspension or expulsion from school.

When I reviewed this project in 2006, I learned that circumstances had
changed greatly, but for the worse. It seems that public school teachers had

demanded higher salaries for those teaching after-hours programs in projects sponsored by the Oxnard School District. Feeling too financially strapped to undertake such raises, Dr. Larson attempted to reorganize and refinance Expanding Horizons as a nonprofit independent of the district but failed. The school superintendent resigned before his contract expired following the firing of the assistant superintendent. Others in the administration also resigned and the district was left with no superintendent for a year. A school superintendent installed in 2004 moved the district in new and different directions. Expanding Horizons went out of business and the City of Oxnard took over after-school programming for short time. As of September 2006, there were no after-school programs in the Oxnard schools, though a new group, Star Incorporated of Los Angeles, was organizing to reintroduce such programs in the future. In just four years a struggling school system with many minority children from economically stressed neighborhoods had gone through two after-school programs and was about to embark on a third. It struck me that this lack of continuity and constant turnover on a district level mirrored, and may even have caused, the dysfunction I observed weekly at Haydock School and the City Hearts program that I have described here.

Recently, City Hearts' Sherry Jason told me she had surveyed parents of the kids enrolled in the Oxnard City Hearts programs last spring and "100% of the parents saw an improvement in how their kids did in school; how they studied better, and got along better at home, and they attributed that improvement to the twice weekly City Hearts classes."[10] Unfortunately, Sherry couldn't find the 78 surveys of 10 questions when we talked and hadn't collated the responses to each question in a quantitative manner.

For their part, Justin, Stuart, and Rebekah had formed their own for-profit company, Much Ado About Shakespeare, and marketed acting classes, "Shakespeare, and swordfighting"[11] targeting homeschooled children. They teach a total of 150 children in 3 programs that meet weekly at three sites in the San Fernando Valley. These kids, whose parents pay nine dollars an hour for the classes, "do not present the behavior problems to be found at Haydock but do include children who were dyslexic and autistic," Rebekah told me.[12] Though Justin moved to Texas with his family two years ago, Stuart and Rebekah also continue to teach with City Hearts which still provides after-school theatre programming in 11 Oxnard area elementary schools as well as in East and South Central Los Angeles.

When I asked Brown about the issue of City Hearts teacher training (the lack of which concerned me) she said, "We meet once a month and this question of training us to deal with problems in class gets raised frequently but there has never been any official training. I don't have a degree. I never studied this and I'm still learning as I go."[13] In a separate interview Stuart agreed: "There have been no formal training sessions. Issues have been raised at City Hearts meetings, about behavior issues and policies, but there have been no retreats, no experts brought in. I didn't feel totally unsupported but it was on the job training."[14] When I asked him about his disappointments of his time at Haydock, he told me, "I'm sorry that we had to divert so much energy to discipline and behavior issues and stop and deal with issues raised about respect and commitment. I wish energies could have been put to more positive use. The class was not about Shakespeare or your part in the play but about self-esteem and working with a group and uniting to do a long-term project. We really needed more support from the after-school program [Expanding Horizons]. They could have built enthusiasm for our acting classes and instead it was presented as a time of obligation. The kids had to be there by and large."[15]

In Houston, Justin continues to teach and act, appearing several times in shows at Houston's renowned Alley Theatre. Reflecting on his time at Haydock, he told me:

> It was an eye opening experience that solidified the concept that there are haves and have-nots in this society. I know I was able to keep some students from making bad decisions. I went into students' homes. I had one visit where I caught the adults mixing methamphetamines in their hotel room so I kept after that student until he moved out and graduated. The teens there weren't getting any sense of team or community anywhere else in their lives. For some of them it was the only place in their day where they were smiling. Having the program in the school was not ideal but it was better than nothing. A lot of the meetings I attended were more about tailoring our program to meet the grant than about meeting the needs of the teens. City Hearts was fantastic. Sherry Jason is an angel. The Jasons stayed in that community all this time, spent their own money on the program because Sherry and her husband are so personally committed.[16]

Sherry and Bob Jason continue City Hearts, now 21 years old, with a paid staff of 12 who serve 2,200 children each year at 14 elementary schools in Oxnard and others in downtown Los Angeles. "We have big plans for the future," Sherry told me, "we plan to buy our own office building downtown and have the greenest space in L.A. where we'll involve kids in environmental and global issues. Finances are always a struggle but we've just gotten one of our biggest grants ever and I'm optimistic for the future."[17]

CHAPTER 8

The Isla Vista City
at Peace Program

I DESCRIBED IN CHAPTER 1 THE unforeseen chain of events that led me to found the Isla Vista City at Peace after-school program and then leave to devote my full time to my academic research at other such programs. I had recruited Jeff Flowers, a 28-year-old 1996 graduate of UCSB's BFA acting program already volunteering at the nearby Santa Barbara City at Peace, to work with me. Jeff had previously run the City at Peace programs in Lompoc and Santa Maria. Both of these programs folded in 2000 due to lack of funding.

City at Peace began as a local organization in Washington, D.C. in 1994. Soon after a teenager was brutally murdered in wealthy, seaside Santa Barbara. Community activist Nancy Davis remembers "a big community meeting was held with everyone asking themselves what could we do to prevent this kind of violence. A few days later a friend told me about this great show she had seen in Washington, the very first City at Peace production. I immediately called Paul Griffin, the director of the program and asked if we could try that type of program in our town and use the same name. He said, 'go for it' and we got started. We've done annual shows for ten years."[1] Five years later, Griffin opened an office in New York City to found a national organization of City at Peace. New groups have since begun in Los Angeles, Baton Rouge, Chicago, Israel and South Africa.

When Jeff Flowers joined me in November 2000, another volunteer, Annie Aziz, hired him to work for Isla Vista Parks and Recreation. From

2001 to 2003, he worked 20 hours a week for Parks and Recs and put in about 12 of those hours with City at Peace. In the summer of 2001 he attended a national training for City at Peace volunteers over several days in New York City under the direction of Griffin. That August, although there was no formal link between the national office and the California local, Flowers began adapting the national program for use with Isla Vista City at Peace. Using their manual, which laid out an eight-month schedule of exercises and organization, he was able to add a level of planning we had previously lacked.

His first goal was to recruit a "production team" of teens while City at Peace was officially closed for the summer but scheduled to get underway again in September. The national program was predicated, Jeff told me, on the idea that at-risk teens may lack many things, such as self-esteem, but that their greatest deficiency is power. City at Peace sees youth violence as a logical reaction to the disempowerment they experience daily at home, in the schools, and in the community at large. As the national guidebook states, "violence stems from power and relationships and it is not a function of the character of people or nations."[2] The goal is explicit: "City at Peace wants to build a city at peace, not just do a show."[3] With their emphasis on power imbalances, City at Peace clearly echoes Boal's discourse in his book *Theatre of the Oppressed*, though their literature never mentions this book. Their list of 11 published resources includes only Boal's *Games for Actors and Non-Actors*, his most practical and least theoretical book.

The *City at Peace Guidebook* offers a series of exercises to expose "who has power and who doesn't,"[4] while making overt forms of both external and internalized oppression. The manual states:

> Why does it work? Because young people lead it, reversing the experiences of disempowerment in their lives. Because you let the young cast decide how to represent and interpret their experiences and current situations, and to envision and define their future. Most young people are denied these opportunities for self-determination throughout their young lives. While this change is an uncomfortable process for some (both young people and adults alike) it is absolutely central to changing the violence and conflict in their lives and our communities by transforming those who do not have power (and are hurt by not having it) into powerful agents for building a city at peace.[5]

On October 25, 2001, I dropped in on the group's evening meeting, then held in a room at the Francisco Torres apartment building, a residence hall for UCSB students. Four teens were present, all of them unknown to me. They were introduced to me as the production team and they laid out a very ambitious planning schedule beginning with their own training in the fall and culminating in a public performance in April and a tour of the show in May. The idea behind City at Peace is that "the cast writes the show,"[6] and that "City at Peace is by youth, for youth,"[7] echoing Leis' categories of community-based theatre "for, by, and of" the community, but, again without mentioning this writer by name.

This was their fifth meeting as a group and they shared with me the mission statement they had devised themselves: "To empower, encourage, change, unify, and bring about acceptance in our community by opening eyes to the problems of violence and prejudice that go on everyday."

That afternoon Jeff broke the group into two pairs of different races and/or genders and led them through a "stereotype exercise." First, one of the two teens, facing the other, had to make a series of statements beginning with: "the problem with you ____" (fill in the blank: i.e., whites, males, Mexicans) "is ____" (fill in the blank with a stereotypical put-down). The statements started out fairly strong (i.e., "The problem with you Mexicans is that you all wear those big hats." "The problem with you boys is that you never put the toilet seat down.") but then dribbled away into statements of "I don't know what to say." Then the power switched to the other teen of the dyad who directed a string of stereotypes back at his/her partner. After the exercise, Jeff led a discussion with the teens asking questions like, "What did it feel like for you?" and receiving answers such as, "I've heard all those stereotypes but I don't remember them" and "It's easier to dis myself than insult someone else."

Jeff then drew from the group, in a sort of free association, a list of stereotypes for each of them as in "male = lazy, love sports, horny" and "female = love to shop, emotional, materialistic." Jeff summed up the discussion and reminded the teens that:

> Some of these stereotypes are true for some individuals but the assumption that everyone in the group is like that causes problems. Stereotypes keep people separate and allows one group to have power over another. When we get stereotypes out on the table a lot of them are funny but when we get beyond them we get to know somebody.

Jeff then asked, Can anybody tell us when they were stereotyped?" Everybody seemed to have an answer: a Latino offered, "Mexicans said I was trying to be white" and another boy said, "Because I live in a certain neighborhood people think I do drugs." Jeff asked if these teens had ever stereotyped others and that brought forth more examples. Then he asked them to get together and choose one of their real experiences to drama-tize. I left as they tackled this next project.

In December Jeff and I sat down together and he told me about his work. He said:

> The best thing about City at Peace for me is working with young people and turning them on to theatre. What hooked me were the relationships I formed with the teens. I saw how valuable it was to them to have somebody really listen to them. My main goal is to empower young people to make changes in their lives. The biggest way I've seen them change is they begin to trust each other and talk about things there's no other place to talk about. City at Peace becomes like a family and a support system for teens where they can be accepted. One girl told me it was the only place she could come and be who she really is. I've seen really immature kids become much more serious about their lives here.
>
> This year I went to Dos Pueblos High School and spoke to the leadership class, the American government class, and other classes and passed around a list for the names and numbers of any students interested. I also went around IV to recruit students. Sadly the only student from last year who has come back this year is Roberto. We've been going about two months so far. The production team meets every Thursday evening, averaging 7 to 8 kids, and the whole group meets each Saturday afternoon, about 12 kids on average. My greatest frustration so far is inconsistent attendance ... and I had hoped for more kids on Saturday. But I'm optimistic because the kids who are coming seem to get a lot out of it.
>
> In recruiting kids I didn't much mention community service hours or acting skills, I asked the kids if they wanted to get involved in something to make a change in their lives and in the world. What we need now is more consistent attendance, money as always, and more kids. In January I hope we'll hire a musical director and a choreographer and we're shooting for a public performance in the spring.[8]

When I attended a Saturday afternoon session in January 2002 it was my first time back at the Isla Vista (IV) Teen Center since the previous June and I saw that a lot had changed. Not only was the center cleaner and more open, with the removal of the old partitions, but the teens were different too: older, whiter, and better behaved than before. Of the 14 teens present, eight were white and six Latino; four were over 18 and none was under 16, and no one was goofing off, talking out of turn, or questioning the directions of Jeff, the sole adult present. Only one teen was present who had been with the program the year before, and he was the only one who resided in IV. The rest came from wealthier areas; several of the teens were children of parents who worked or taught at UCSB. Could the seemingly smoother functioning of the program be due to simply recruiting a "better" class of adolescent, I wondered.

The kids had been divided into four groups of three to four each and were given 20 minutes to share personal stories and come up with a dramatization for one of them. The theme was masculinity and femininity and the limitations these labels place on people. The story chosen for dramatization was, Jeff told them, to have a beginning, a middle, and an end. The teens were talking animatedly, sharing stories, laughing and having fun. They kept on task and at the end of a reasonable amount of time, Jeff took a roll of tape and divided the room in half to create a stage area, explaining to the teens:

> This line of tape divides the room but also divides the real world from the imaginary world of the stage; there are no consequences in the imaginary world for anything you might think or do. It's safe to act out anything you want to try—and make sure that we applaud everyone when they go on stage and when they leave the stage.

The first group that volunteered to perform took their tale from the real-life experience of Roberto, who was now living in IV with his sister. As Roberto enters the apartment, he greets his sister and sits down to talk. Two of the women are frozen in one position, imitating a photograph of two women hanging on the wall. Roberto begins to tell his sister about a new girl he had met at school. He says, "She's really nice and very pretty but she's gay." "How do you feel about that?" the sister asks. "It's okay with me," Roberto says. "Good," replies the sister, "because I'm a lesbian. That's a picture of my girlfriend on the wall."

Just then one of the girls knocks on the imaginary door. "That must be my girlfriend now," says the sister. She lets the other woman into the apartment and introduces her to her brother. Roberto goes up and warmly embraces both women. The scene ends to applause.

The second group chose a wordless mime presentation in which two men and two women appear trapped in boxes. One woman and one man free themselves and begin an exuberant dance to demonstrate their newfound independence. They return to the two people still trapped in the box but these two resist all entreaties to free themselves and the scene ends with two teens free and two still boxed in.

The third group presents a domestic scene in which a mother stops her daughter just as she is about to leave the house with a friend. The mother asks, "Why aren't you dressed better to go out?" The daughter responds, "Because I'm trying to be comfortable." The mother says, "You look like a man." The friend butts in to say, "I'll give her a makeover," and the daughter responds by knocking out both her mother and her friend with wild swings of her purse. This scene, minus the purse swinging, later made it into the script for the final production.

The last group announces that they hadn't been able to come up with a scene at all. This news was received with equanimity. Jeff asks the group, "What did you learn from this exercise?" One girl responds, "We found out we had a lot in common." A second said, "Lower class families have problems with drugs and sex but upper and middle-class families have psychological problems and those can be worse." And Roberto added, "We're in a race to create equality but you can't fight anger with anger. In the one skit she knocked all of them out at the end but in reality you have to rise above that and not sink to their level." And on that note everyone broke to eat the pizza that had been delivered.

I was back again on March 2, 2002, approximately a month since my last visit. Jeff and two teens were present at the 2 P.M. starting time and five more teens arrived later, up to an hour and a half late. I was struck by the fact that all of the teens were female. As I waited for the group to begin, I heard my name called and turned to find two young men from last year's City at Peace, Diego and Pepe, over by the watercooler. We greeted each other and I caught up on events in their lives. They told me that they were now attending Santa Barbara City at Peace. "Why go all that way, when you can just come here?" I asked. "It's better down there," said Pepe. "More Mexicans," said Diego. "Does that make it better?" I asked. "No," said Diego. It turned out that both were now attending La Puente High School, a continuation school for teens in trouble at their local high schools, and that Santa Barbara City at Peace had an ongoing project that met at La Puente. After chatting, Diego and Pepe left.

Jeff began the meeting by announcing: "Today our creative work begins." There were new staff present, hired as hourly employees: Yisell Lopez to teach and choreograph the dances and Anthony Kortick to compose music and lyrics for the upcoming show.

The group began with a brief check-in of how everyone had fared over the previous week. Jeff announced that Roberto, the sole continuing City at Peace member from the previous year and, in my estimation, a talented and sensitive teen, had been arrested for "felony burglary," was in jail, and would be dropping out of the group. Jeff also announced that another teen, Brittany, had been "locked up by her parents" and was no longer allowed to attend City at Peace. I remembered Brittany because when I had sent home the parental permission slip for my survey, her father had taken the unusual step of calling me at home to discuss its contents. Our conversation had been pleasant but I had refused his request to mail a copy of the survey to him, suggesting instead that I could bring it to him and discuss it with him, an idea which he declined. In the end he never signed the permission slip for Brittany. Now Jeff suggested that perhaps he and some of Brittany's friends could intervene with her parents to allow her to attend. I gathered that their refusal to let her participate in City at Peace was a result of something she had done but I received no details. In fact, Brittany never returned.

After the check-in, Jeff asked the group to create a list of "creative agreements" for their work together. Individual teens suggested "keep an open mind," "keep everyone in mind," and "challenge yourself." From the national *City at Peace Guidebook* Jeff also added the following, with a brief explanation of each: "Be seen on stage. Be heard on stage. Concentrate always. Be silent off-stage. Be as prepared as you can be. Give 110% all the time. Tell your story. Be on time and ready to go. Create your role in our show." A teen added, "be flexible" and this list, written on large poster paper, was hung on the wall.

Jeff then raised the problem of a lack of male actors for the upcoming show. The loss of Roberto left them with just three males, only two of whom Jeff felt confident would continue with the group. The teens discussed recruiting more boys to participate but decided that after their bonding retreat two weeks earlier and their session sharing "life stories" the previous week, it was too late to really integrate new people into what had become a close-knit group. The group reached a consensus that they would continue with the people who were already members. Jeff announced that the production committee had scheduled two performances of the yet-to-be-written play for April 26 and 27 at the Multicultural Theatre on the UCSB campus. The group seemed both thrilled to have performance dates and a bit intimidated by their approach.

Next on the agenda was choreography and Yisell spent an hour and a half working with the teens in creating a three-minute dance for the show. For the girls this was clearly an activity they had been looking forward to. I was fascinated by Yisell's ability to draw ideas from the girls and then integrate those ideas into what eventually became a visually stunning dance. First, Yisell asked them to find physical manifestations of emotions that would be part of the play, like freedom and constraint. Then everyone looked at what each person had done and decided by consensus which physical actions looked best and might, therefore, be copied by everyone dancing together. Yisell told the girls, "I'll tell you the structure, you come up with the steps." As I watched the long session, I saw a ragged looking collection of 14 individuals slowly transformed into a coordinated dance troupe performing ideas they themselves had originated. At one point Yisell praised them about one improvisation saying, "That was a great despair."

As the group rehearsed the dance, Jeff and I talked about the work accomplished since my last visit. Two weeks before, he and five of the teens had gone on a retreat for the weekend and, based on the stories of their own lives they had shared over the previous months, had developed an outline of 26 scenes for their play. The themes were familiar to me from what I had seen other teens at Santa Barbara City at Peace come up with the previous year. I attribute this to a common sensibility among teenagers as to the issues affecting their lives. This script equated school with a prison, featured a girl battling bulimia, while another girl fought off a sexual attack. There were lots of dramatic elements all within the context of a group of friends who attend school together and later go to a party together. The main themes were gender relations, parental and school oppression, and the solidarity of the teens themselves. The outline was very rough and lacked dialogue and stage directions. I was curious to see how this sparse outline would evolve into an actual script in the two months remaining to them prior to performance.

I returned on Saturday afternoon, April 6, 2002, to find that a lot of progress had, in fact, been made. Faced with the reality of losing students to spring break, they made the decision to push the performance date back two weeks. The goal was now a single performance on Saturday evening May 11 in the Girvetz Theatre, rather than the Multicultural Theatre on the UCSB campus. In addition, rehearsals had been expanded to three times each week.

When I arrived at the IV Teen Center at 1 P.M., Jeff was just arriving but five of the teenage girls were already there. I caught up on the news with Jeff. Roberto had written him a letter from jail and didn't expect to get out until June. Brittany was still prohibited by her parents from participating in City at Peace. As Jeff set up the room, I spoke with one girl, Stephanie, about the progress of the script. She told me that "people are working individually on their own scenes." The goal, Jeff said, was to have a complete script in one more week, or four weeks prior to the performance.

The meeting began formally with a check-in as people shared events of the past week. Then Jeff showed the group a few excerpts from the movie, *The Dead Poets' Society*. He wanted them to see the climax when students at a private school protest the firing of their favorite teacher. The play being written also included a teacher getting the boot from her principal although this was not the major action of the play. When Jeff asked the group, "what's the message here?" One teen replied, "It's about people taking power to make their own choices." Clearly this was a theme that resonated with the teens.

Next came physical and vocal warm-ups. Stretches were followed by a game of follow-the-leader in which Jeff led them in a conga line through all sorts of contortions and silliness. By 2 P.M. the group had grown to nine, eight of them girls. To my eyes, four were Latinas and four were Anglos. The sole boy was African American. I was struck again by how important the warm-ups were. They invoked a transition from one world, ordinary life for want of a better name, to the world of the theatre. They also signified that the work about to be undertaken required a certain discipline, commitment and preparation.

The warm-ups completed, Jeff turned the group over to Anthony who had been hired part-time as composer for the show. He told them, "I took your ideas and phrases and shaped them into these two songs." He began teaching them the songs. The opening song, titled "The Prison" expressed the teen's unhappiness with their school and lives. One character, Ashley, sang:

Worthless, worthless, tired but can't sleep
Nowhere, nowhere, hungry but can't eat
Worthless, trapped, tired but can't sleep
Nowhere, nowhere, hungry but can't eat.

Various teens got to express similar sentiments and all joined together for several choruses. The teens made suggestions here and there to change lyrics and rhythm. They chose the music from choices offered on Anthony's synthesizer. When they'd learned the rewritten song, Mary opined, "That's cool."

The second song they rehearsed, "Freedom," would close the show and celebrated their newfound liberty. A sample verse:

We know freedom
Throwing away our doubt like stones
Cry, cry freedom
Fly with us, ignore the toll.

And the chorus:

We can dance, we can dress
We can cry, we can curse any way that we want

We can take off the mask
And just scream here I am.
You can like it or not
We can finally say it.

Pauline had brought a drum from school with which she accompanied Anthony on the synthesizer. It sounded very good to me.

After an hour working on the two songs, the group took a 15-minute break and then they were ready to work with the choreographer, Yisell, who ran them through the opening dance number with great energy. At first this looked to me like a cross between the big synchronized dance of *West Side Story* and the flowing scarves of Isadora Duncan. But when Anthony added the hip-hop music they had chosen, it appeared as something entirely new.

When Yisell led them in rehearsing the second dance, she told them, "The opening is like Britney Spears but the second half is a strong woman. Can you think of a strong woman?" Stephanie replied, "Eleanor Roosevelt." Yisell suggested, "How about an athlete so you get to be muscular." Mary offered, "Martina Hingis" and that tennis player seemed acceptable to all. After an hour of rather strenuous dancing the group took another 15-minute break and two of the teens had to leave to go home.

After the break the group met to choose a name for the show. There'd obviously been some previous discussion and they quickly settled on what they called "Jeff's suggestion" of *Within These Walls*. With a title decided, the publicity could begin. Stephanie and Pauline volunteered to make posters and Jeff undertook to contact the media.

Next it was time to rehearse the first scene of a teacher struggling to motivate her students in unconventional ways. She works under the disapproving eyes of her principal, who criticizes her for "not teaching by the book." When the teacher replies, "I believe what I'm teaching is important," the teen actor as principal answers, "That's very touching." As director, Jeff added motivation for the dialogue and actions and encouraged the girl playing the principal when she seemed uncomfortable improvising her part.

I noticed that the teens offstage, some of whom see each other every day at school and some who do not, were quite supportive and generous with each other, encouraging each actor in turn. Their enthusiasm seemed genuine. Just then one of the teens from last year's group, those IV residents who are no longer involved in City at Peace, poked his head in the Teen Center door. Jeff and I greeted him and in a moment Jeff had integrated him into the classroom scene on stage, though he did not return the following week.

Playing the unconventional teacher on stage, Pauline told her class that they must write reports on a social change leader of the 1960s or 70s. Jeff spoke up, "That's an assignment for you as actors as well. Think of who inspires you so you can use that thought in this scene." Marta, a Chicana, chose Dolores Huerta because, she said, "She was the only woman up there in that group," meaning the United Farm Workers. Mary chose "Gloria Gaynor." "You mean Gloria Steinem," said Stephanie. "Oops," said Mary, "I think Gloria Gaynor was a disco queen."

The classroom stage scene exploded in a confrontation when Marta, as a student, spoke in Spanish and the principal intervened, ordering her to accompany her to her office. Many times students had told me they got in trouble with school officials for speaking Spanish at school. Another teen, Audra, used Jeff's video camera to record the scene and Jeff promised to transcribe the tape of the improvised dialogue for the script. The rehearsal ended at 6 P.M. after five full hours of work.

At the end I was struck by two things: the seriousness and dedication of the students and the rather stereotypical material they had come up with. Once again school was seen as a prison, and the plot revolved around parties, resisting parental authority (or as the teens usually see it, authoritarianism), and relations between boys and girls where the girls band together to stop boys from controlling or abusing their girlfriends. But these teens were not copying someone else's script; they were writing about what they knew from their own perspective.

On April 27 I returned to the Teen Center to see a rehearsal featuring a run-through of the now completed script. Eleven teens were present. Before they began, I asked one of the young people, Stephanie, how much time she was committing to the project. Between rehearsal and publicity she figured she was putting in 16 hours each week for four weeks.

Things were ragged at the beginning of the rehearsal. Jeff called for the first scene and kids responded, "Am I in the first scene?" Jeff told them, "Everyone's in it." Quite a few of the girls were missing for the opening dance number and no one was quite sure how to line up to compensate for their absence. With their first performance just two weeks away, Jeff and I shared a few nervous glances. There were two new cast members since my last visit, one male with a very large dyed red Mohawk haircut, and one female. Someone asked about one of the cast members, Paca. "Paca dropped out," Jeff announced. This came as a surprise to everyone else and they seem disappointed.

The rehearsal proceeded and elicited comments from Jeff like: "This obviously needs everybody to learn their lines." Later he told them, "We haven't blocked the next scene. You'll just have to walk through it. We haven't figured out the ending yet." All of the scenes that were not so long ago little more than a single descriptive sentence on a page had now been fleshed out with full dialogue. It was now a real script but not everyone knew their lines and whether all members of the cast would show up on opening night was still open to question. The show logged in at two hours. Jeff told them, "We need to step up the pace. We want to get this down to an hour and a half."

The rehearsal ended and Jeff shared with me his anxieties of getting it all together in time. Then he called everyone together into a circle. "Everyone gets four hugs," he said, "No one leaves without hugs." After the hugs everyone moved furniture to return the Teen Center to a usable state for the next group.

That week Jeff e-mailed me a copy of the publicity for the show that would be sent to the local media:

> Within These Walls is a show created by members of City at Peace to express the isolation and imprisonment that they have felt as a result of the violence and injustice they have experienced in their lives. These experiences have left them with feelings of powerlessness that cause them to feel either unwilling or unable to express themselves and their stories honestly with one another. Their inner feelings and beliefs are carefully guarded behind walls of conformity and social acceptability. These walls, created by individuals and supported by the social norms and institutions, then become prisons which few have had the courage to escape. Within These Walls is a story about some who do.

Two weeks later the group performed in public for the first time. Attractive programs had been printed identifying all of the cast and crew. Original artwork had been produced for the program and flyers but publicity had been slight and I was pleased to see that 60 people were in the audience at UCSB's Girvetz Theatre. The show was delayed for ten minutes when the tech person showed up late, having confused the 8 P.M. curtain time with his arrival call.

The show began with the opening dance featuring 8 of the 15 performers. They'd only been in the space for two rehearsals and the dancing was a bit ragged. As they said their "world views" (spoken statements about their lives), many of the voices were too soft to be heard in the auditorium. However, few people blew their lines and cues were crisply followed. The show featured several simultaneous story lines: the conflict between teacher Ms.

Teek and Vice Principal Mrs. K over Ms. Teek's insistence on teaching about social change leaders of the 1960s and 70s and Mrs. K's demand that the students prepare for their upcoming state-mandated standardized tests; student Amy's conflict with her mother over Amy's desire to be a singer and her mother's demand that she study something more practical; student Ted's physical assault on fellow student Ashley, and student Roxy's conflict with her boyfriend, James, who jealously tried to control her interactions with fellow students.

Ashley got a laugh when she addressed the audience and demonstrated her lack of self-esteem, by saying, "I'm so ugly ... but I'm prettier than she is." But the biggest laugh of the evening came when Ms. Teek told Mrs. K she was concerned with the development of her students as whole people and Mrs. K informed the teacher that "their development as people is not the school's concern."

These stories were told over 26 scenes and several songs. The show's title, *Within These Walls*, refers to the various walls that keep people from the freedom to follow their dreams. The conflicts among students were resolved when Amy's mother allowed her to pursue her singing, Ted apologized for his behavior toward Ashley, and Roxy dumped James. However, Mrs. K removed Ms. Teek from her classroom at the end and the students then defied Mrs. K by following their teacher out of the school in spite of Mrs. K's threats to suspend them. The "Freedom" song and dance brought down the curtain at the end.

With an intermission the show took less than two hours and the audience rewarded the actors with a standing ovation and obvious enthusiastic appreciation. The student performers were beaming after this first performance before family and friends. At least a third of these student actors admitted to having never performed on stage before. Their second and final performance was two weeks later when they shared Center Stage in Santa Barbara with the annual Santa Barbara City at Peace show. The plan was then for these actors to choose a new production team that would continue to meet over the summer, recruit actors in the fall, and begin the whole process over again the following year, culminating in another public show in the spring and so on into the future.

As I ended my visits to City at Peace, I was left with many feelings and observations. We had struggled to get the program started in the first year and faced numerous cultural clashes and misunderstandings between the Latino/a teens and the Anglo/a adults. However, it was clear that the teens enjoyed the theatre games, the attention we adults gave them, and the weekly pizzas we ate. But the teens had never really bought into the adults' central goal of producing a theatrical show. Many of our improvs had addressed and, I think, impacted gender and racial stereotypes for the better and students had certainly been able to express themselves creatively, doing so energetically and imaginatively.

The program functioned much more smoothly in its second year. This was due to its reliance on curriculum materials produced by the national City at Peace organization, the training the national organization made available to Jeff Flowers, and the fact that these teens were recruited with the explicit goals of producing a public show and working for social change. In contrast to the other two programs I studied, City at Peace overtly and consistently put the teens in charge of the theatre they were making and the teens responded in a creative and disciplined manner.

Jeff Flowers continued as director for the next two years and the number of actively involved teens doubled as the Isla Vista and Santa Barbara City at Peace programs joined. Their largest show, in 2004, put 45 teens onstage and, according to Jeff, brought back several of the Isla Vista Latinos with whom we had begun the program. Flowers moved to New York in the summer of 2004 and shortly after became artistic director of New York City's City at Peace with offices at the national headquarters.

In Santa Barbara, City at Peace went through a rocky time with a new board and new director that ended in financial difficulties and, for the first time since their founding in 1995, no show was presented in 2006. However, a new board and director are now in place and Santa Barbara City at Peace, including outreach to Isla Vista teens, will, according to local founder Nancy Davis, be back on track in 2007.[9]

Nationally, City at Peace added projects in Los Angeles and New York in 2002, Baton Rouge in 2003, and Capetown, South Africa, in 2005 to their earlier program in Charlotte, North Carolina, and their founding project in Washington, D.C., which dates from 1994. Over the last 12 years they claim the participation of 2,000 teens and the production of 38 original musicals performed before over 100,000 audience members. City at Peace director Paul Griffin told me that their future goals include building the number and size of their local projects and building a presence on the national level through their new National Youth Council which brings together teens from each of the individual projects to tackle a legislative and political agenda. "Right now," Griffin told me, "you don't hear teen voices on teen issues and they have something important to say and a lot to contribute to the debate."[10] Each City at Peace theatre program now also includes a community action project in conjunction with putting on a show. Such projects have included Eye to Eye, which brings parents and teens together for workshops in communication; Adolescents for Change, which adopts an underperforming elementary school and works collaboratively to improve conditions for students; and Window of Opportunity, a teen-designed website of choices for teens not planning to go to college. As Jeff Flowers told me, "we're always teaching activism as well as theatre."[11]

CHAPTER 9

How Theatre Can Save Johnny
and a Million Other Teens

W E KNOW THEATRE AND OTHER ARTS boost academic skills for students. The series of studies titled *Champions of Change* tracked 25,000 high school students nationally over ten years, and concluded that "involvement with the arts is the most powerful factor for success in and out of school."[1] The survey compares after-school programs in the three categories of sports, community involvement, and the arts and found "to the researchers' surprise ... the youth in the arts programs were doing the best."[2] In addition they found:

> substantial student involvement in theatre arts ... associates with a variety of dividends for youth; gains in reading proficiency, gains in self-concept and motivation and higher levels of empathy and tolerance for others.[3]

Through an involvement in the arts, "rather than see themselves as 'at risk,' students became managers of risk who can make decisions concerning artistic outcomes and even their own lives."[4]

These effects of arts involvement were seen equally strongly among students of lower and higher economic status. Students from both groups with a high involvement in the arts had higher grades in English, reading, history, and geography and scored better in standardized tests than those with lower arts involvement.[5] On a creativity index scale of 0 to 50, students with a high involvement in the arts scored 37 while students with a low involvement in the arts averaged 12. Students with a high arts involvement outscored those with a low arts involvement in expression by 37 to 9, in imagination by 41 to 14, and in originality by 41 to 11.[6] The report concludes unequivocally that "students involved in theatre are doing better in school than those who are not."[7]

Empirical evidence comes from other studies as well. A report of the College Entrance Examination Board shows that students with four years of arts education in high school outperformed peers with no arts education or arts work experience on the SAT (Scholastic Aptitude Test) by "59 points on the verbal and 44 points on the math."[8]

These studies measure increased success in school, academic proficiency, and in learning skills. But my study is the first to measure the impact of after-school theatre programs on teenagers' nonacademic lives, an area where claims have too long outdistanced evidence.

According to the website of Americans for the Arts, "the number of local arts agencies in the 50 largest U.S. cities with arts programs for youth at risk increased from approximately 20% in 1986 to 82% in 1997."[9] Great claims are made for the efficacy of these programs. For example, Marc Morial, then mayor of New Orleans, offered this glowing endorsement in 2000: "In New Orleans we found that the youth participating in our arts programs are less likely to revisit our legal system, are likely to achieve academic success and become contributing members of their community. Art is a way for you to find their hidden talents."[10] Certainly the staffs at the Virginia Avenue Project, City Hearts, City at Peace, and the 100 other programs listed in the appendix, would all assert the effectiveness of their programs.

But no one has previously produced evidence for these claims. And if they are effective, no one has yet explained the reason these programs dramatically affect teens. How does art work as a prosocial force to lessen risk factors? And most importantly: are some programs more effective than others? And if the answer to that question is yes, then what is it that makes one arts program more effective than another? Might one particular proven and effective theatre technique be repeated, like a scientific formula, yielding the same positive result each time?

In my fieldwork I was repeatedly told by theatre program practitioners and administrators that their theatre programs teach teens "empathy," "cooperation," "discipline," nourish their "self-esteem," and provide "emotional release," but none offered quantifiable evidence of such results. The 2001 release of the study *Arts in Focus* reveals this quandary: "There is a universal belief among respondents [teachers and school administrators] in the value of arts education to classroom learning," and yet:

the arts in Los Angeles County schools are not an integrated part of the learning process because they have found it almost impossible to convince government and taxpayers to make the investment in arts education they think is necessary.[11]

What if the public at large, school administrators, and elected and appointed bureaucrats who disperse public funds, could be convinced that money spent on good art programs could lead to a decline in teen violence, school drop-out rates, drug use, gang membership, and teen pregnancy? Could we see fewer juveniles in jail and less blood on the streets? These are the questions I set out to answer.

The three after-school theatre programs I studied were sufficiently similar (in that they worked with the same population of teen participants by age and socioeconomic status) and sufficiently different (in their goals, structure, and approach to theatre) to weigh their relative strengths and weaknesses in terms of efficacy. Ideally, a study such as this would include programs that are widely diverse geographically, in structure, and in philosophy. The greater the number of programs and participants that could be studied, the greater the odds that such a study would be not merely representative but definitive. I can only hope that this, the first such comparative study of efficacy in after-school theatre programs, might inspire further research on a wider scale.

There is national and large-scale data available about teen attitudes and behaviors which the 2001 surgeon general report has used for defining teens at risk: sexual activity, alcohol and drug use, truancy, dropping out of school, criminal activity, gang membership, and violence, including violence turned inward in the form of suicide, and these national statistics can be compared against these three theatre programs.

A survey of 10,000 teenagers by the Centers for Disease Control found that 49 percent of high school boys and 48 percent of high school girls reported having had sexual intercourse.[12] The survey also found that 1.7 percent of girls age 14 and younger and 7.5 percent of all girls ages 15–17 became pregnant.[13]

A survey of 8,238 students in 113 California middle and high schools by the California State Attorney General's Office found that 30 percent of seventh graders, 50 percent of ninth graders, and 63 percent of 11th graders reported drinking alcohol in the previous six months.[14]

According to the same report, 10 percent of California high school students had tried the drug Ecstasy, while 7 percent of seventh grade students, 19 percent of ninth graders, and 34 percent of 11th graders reported smoking marijuana in the previous six months.[15]

A 1998 report of the American Psychological Association found that 36 percent of teen boys reported all-day truancy, and 39 percent had been suspended from school at least once.[16] As noted in chapter 2, dropout rates for students through high school were 30 percent overall; 53 percent for Latinos, and 63 percent for economically disadvantaged youth.

Violence is also a fact of teen life. The Joseph and Edna Josephson Institute on Ethics surveyed 8,600 teens and found that 68 percent said that they had hit someone in anger in the previous year.[17]

In his 2001 report on youth violence, the surgeon general reported that 14–30 percent of youth in Denver, Colorado, and Rochester, New York were gang members.[18]

Most significantly for this study I found that on average, all of these national statistics for risky teen behavior are much higher than what I found among the teenagers in the three theatre programs I studied. Like most of the national studies my results are based upon the self-disclosure of teens filling out written surveys. While such surveys certainly admit the possibility of untrue responses, the anonymity of the survey and the absence of repercussions for answers does encourage truth telling.

The raw responses I received in surveying 37 teenagers in three theatre programs over a period of one year should be analyzed in three different ways:

1. within each program to see if the teens changed over the time they were enrolled in the programs

2. between each theatre program and the national statistics cited above to see if the programs had a positive impact on teens as compared to teens not enrolled in such programs

3. between the programs themselves to see if one of the programs is more effective than the others in changing the attitudes and behaviors of teens at risk

The results of the pretest and posttest for each program, the changes in the responses for each set of participants over the academic year, and the difference in responses between groups begin to answer those questions. Listed below are the survey questions and the pretest and posttest results for each program. CH is City Hearts, CA is City at Peace, and VA is the Virginia Avenue Project.

QUESTION	Pre CH	Post CH	Pre CA	Post CA	Pre VA	Post VA
1. How often do you engage in meetings, field trips, or club activities?						
Every Day	1	0	3	2	0	1
Several Days per Week	4	3	7	7	8	3
Once a Week	3	1	0	0	7	5
Once per Month	2	1	0	0	1	4
Never	3	2	1	2	1	1
2. How often do you use conflict resolution skills?						
Every Day	3	0	3	2	2	0
Several Days per Week	4	3	3	4	5	4
Once a Week	6	3	2	2	5	5
Once per Month	0	0	3	1	4	3
Never	1	1	0	1	1	0
3. How often do you engage in verbal fighting at home?						
Every Day	3	3	0	1	1	2
Several Days per Week	4	3	3	1	3	3
Once a Week	2	0	2	4	7	3
Once per Month	1	0	2	3	5	5
Never	3	1	4	1	1	1
4. How often do you engage in physical fighting at home?						
Every Day	0	0	0	0	0	0
Several Days per Week	1	1	0	0	0	0
Once a Week	1	2	2	0	0	0
Once per Month	4	0	1	3	1	1
Never	8	4	8	8	16	13
5. How often do you engage in verbal fighting at school?						
Every Day	1	0	0	0	1	0
Several Days per Week	1	3	1	2	4	1
Once a Week	4	1	1	2	3	2
Once per Month	2	2	2	2	5	7
Never	6	0	7	5	4	4

QUESTION	Pre CH	Post CH	Pre CA	Post CA	Pre VA	Post VA
6. How often do you engage in physical fighting at school?						
Every Day	1	0	0	0	0	0
Several Days per Week	1	0	0	0	0	0
Once a Week	0	0	0	0	0	0
Once per Month	1	3	0	0	3	3
Never	9	4	11	11	14	11
7. How often do you engage in verbal fighting in the community?						
Every Day	3	0	0	0	0	0
Several Days per Week	1	0	1	1	1	1
Once a Week	1	1	0	0	1	3
Once per Month	3	1	0	1	4	0
Never	6	5	10	9	11	10
8. How often do you engage in physical fighting in the community?						
Every Day	1	0	0	0	0	0
Several Days per Week	0	0	0	0	0	0
Once a Week	2	0	0	0	0	0
Once per Month	1	0	0	0	2	0
Never	10	7	11	11	15	14
9. How often do you violate probation without getting caught?						
Every Day	2	1	0	0	0	0
Several Days per Week	1	1	0	0	0	0
Once a Week	0	0	0	0	1	0
Once per Month	2	1	1	0	0	2
Never	9	4	10	11	16	12
10. How many times have you been arrested?						
Never	14	7	8	9	17	14
Once	0	0	1	1	0	0
Twice	0	0	0	1	0	0

QUESTION	Pre CH	Post CH	Pre CA	Post CA	Pre VA	Post VA
11. How often have you thought of suicide?						
Every Day	0	0	1	0	0	0
Several Days per Week	0	1	1	0	0	0
Once a Week	0	0	4	0	0	0
Once per Month	4	1	3	8	4	3
Never	10	5	2	3	13	11

QUESTIONS 12–17 COULD NOT BE ADDRESSED TO CH TEENS

QUESTION	Pre CH	Post CH	Pre CA	Post CA	Pre VA	Post VA
12. How often are you having regular, consensual sex?						
Every Day			0	1	0	0
Several Days per Week			0	0	0	1
Once a Week			1	3	0	0
Once per Month			1	2	0	0
Never			9	5	17	13
13. How often are you having unprotected sex?						
Every Day			0	0	0	0
Several Days per Week			0	0	0	0
Once a Week			1	0	0	0
Once per Month			0	2	0	0
Never			10	9	17	14
14. How often do you use contraception?						
Every Day			0	1	0	0
Several Days per Week			0	0	0	1
Once a Week			0	3	0	0
Once per Month			1	1	0	1
Never			7	6	17	12
15. How many partners are you having sex with on a daily basis? Write a number or zero.						
Zero			8	6	16	12
One			0	3	0	2
Two			0	1	0	0

QUESTION	Pre CH	Post CH	Pre CA	Post CA	Pre VA	Post VA
16. How many partners are you having sex with on a monthly basis? Write a number or zero.						
Zero			8	3	0	12
One			3	5	0	2
Two			0	1	0	0
17. With how many partners did you have sex with during the past year? Write a number or zero.						
Zero			8	3	16	12
One			2	5	1	2
Two			1	1	0	0
Three			0	1	0	0
Ten			0	1	0	0
18. How often do you read a book?						
Every Day	7	3	3	2	5	3
Several Days per Week	4	1	4	6	5	3
Once a Week	2	1	0	0	2	2
Once per Month	1	2	1	1	4	6
Never	0	0	1	2	1	0
19. How often do you go to the movies?						
Every Day	0	0	0	0	0	0
Several Times per Week	0	3	0	0	0	0
Once a Week	4	2	3	2	5	9
Once per Month	3	1	8	9	12	5
Never	2	1	0	0	0	0
20. How often do you go to concerts?						
Every Day	0	0	0	0	0	0
Several Times per Week	0	0	0	0	0	0
Once a Week	0	0	0	0	0	2
Once per Month	5	3	8	7	6	5
Never	9	4	3	4	11	7

QUESTION	Pre CH	Post CH	Pre CA	Post CA	Pre VA	Post VA
21. How often do you go outside of school for personal enjoyment?						
Every Day	4	0	2	3	1	3
Several Times per Week	4	2	2	3	2	1
Once a Week	3	2	6	5	6	1
Once per Month	2	3	1	0	1	5
Never	1	0	0	0	5	4
22. Have you ever been in a gang?						
Yes	1	0	1	2	0	0
No	13	7	10	9	17	14
23. Are you currently in a gang?						
Yes	0	0	0	0	0	0
No	14	7	11	11	17	14
24. Have you ever been jumped by a gang?						
Yes	2	1	4	3	1	1
No	12	6	7	8	16	13
25. Have you ever attempted suicide?						
Yes	0	1	2	3	1	0
No	14	6	9	8	16	14
26. Have you ever been suspended from school?						
Yes	3	1	2	4	3	3
No	11	6	9	6	14	11
27. Have you ever been expelled?						
Yes	0	1	0	0	0	0
No	13	6	11	11	17	14
28. Have you ever dropped out of school?						
Yes	0	0	0	1	0	0
No	14	7	11	10	17	14
29. Are you currently dropped out of school?						
Yes	1	0	0	1	0	0
No	13	7	11	10	17	14

QUESTION	Pre CH	Post CH	Pre CA	Post CA	Pre VA	Post VA
30. Have you ever been in a serious romantic relationship?						
Yes	9	2	8	9	4	7
No	5	5	3	2	13	7
31. Are you currently in a serious romantic relationship?						
Yes	3	2	8	6	1	3
No	10	5	3	5	16	11
32. Have you ever been pregnant or gotten someone pregnant?						
Yes	0	0	1	1	0	0
No	14	7	10	10	16	14
33. Have you ever been employed?						
Yes	7	0	9	11	5	6
No	7	7	2	0	12	8
34. Are you now employed?						
Yes	3	0	3	3	3	4
No	11	7	8	7	14	10

QUESTIONS 35–37 WERE NOT ASKED OF CP TEENS

QUESTION	Pre CH	Post CH	Pre CA	Post CA	Pre VA	Post VA
35. Have you ever taken drugs prescribed by a doctor to improve your behavior in school and home in the past three months?						
Yes	3	2			0	1
No	11	5			16	13
36. Have you taken illegal drugs in the last three months?						
Yes	1	0			2	3
No	12	6			15	11
37. Have you gotten drunk in the last three months?						
Yes	2	1			2	1
No	12	6			15	13

At City Hearts the pretest was administered in October 2001 and the posttest in May 2002. Fourteen teens took the pretest and seven took the posttest. All seven who took the posttest also took the pretest but seven students who took the pretest were no longer with the program when the posttest was given.

Significant changes occurred over the seven months that I studied this program. Half of the original participants dropped out of the program during this time. This was the worst retention rate (50 percent at City Hearts over 7 months, compared to 82.4 percent for the Virginia Avenue Project over 12 months, and 72.7 percent for City at Peace over 7 months) of the three programs and, based on my observations as detailed in chapter 7, I would attribute this to the ever-changing school scheduling at Haydock that meant students were rarely sure when, where, or, even if, the program would be meeting in any given week. I would also attribute it to the disorganized, unprepared, and untrained leadership of City Hearts which failed to provide an attractive and challenging program. Though individual staff members, like Justin and Rebekah, were often warm and welcoming with the teens, a lack of discipline, tardiness, and disorganization were hallmarks of the meetings. In addition, this was the one group that rarely played theatre games before acting classes and rehearsals. As a consequence, I rarely saw the teens having fun at these meetings which were all about work and about the adults trying to rein in the high energy of the students. In addition, on the one occasion teens showed real initiative, in generating a petition to school authorities for more drama classes, that effort was squelched by City Hearts staff.

If we define significant changes in attitudes and behavior as those that showed up as changes of two or three from the pretest to the posttest, I would note City Hearts' answers to Question 8 as a significant improvement. Although four teens reported physical fighting in the community on the pretest, no one on the posttest engaged in physical fighting in the community, though there is always the possibility that these might be four of the seven students who dropped out of the program between surveys.

Also significant changes occurred on Question 3 where four fewer people engaged in verbal fighting at home but on the posttest two fewer never engaged in verbal fighting at home. Also, on Question 25, one person said they had attempted suicide on the posttest although no one had said so on the pretest. On Question 27, we learned that one of the continuing students had been expelled from school. On the other hand, onefewer student was taking prescription drugs to improve their behavior at school on the posttest (Question 35) and one fewer student had gotten drunk according to the posttest as opposed to the pretest (Question 37). Responses to the other questions showed little change from the pretest to the post-test.

In sum, City Hearts posttest scores improved significantly in two areas, less significantly in two areas, declined slightly in two areas, and remained more or less constant in the great majority of categories. Certainly the fact that not one of the seven continuing participants was arrested, joined a gang, got pregnant, dropped out of school, or took illegal drugs over that seven month period must be seen as extremely positive, especially as compared with the national statistics.

At the Virginia Avenue Project the pretest was administered in May 2001 and the posttest in May 2002. Seventeen teens took the pretest and 14 took the posttest. The Virginia Avenue Project had the highest continuity of any of the three programs with 82.4 percent of students still in the program when the posttest was administered a full year after the pretest. I attribute this to the determination and organization of the project's founder and director, Leigh Curran, who made extraordinary efforts to keep students involved. As Ms. Curran told me, "the Virginia Avenue Project is my life."[19] She clearly brought a commitment to the work unrivaled in any other program studied. As I observed the program, the teens related to her as both a surrogate parent and a professional and tried to match their commitment to her example. Parents were also much more involved here than in the other programs studied by design and by dint of Curran's hard work.

Contrasting the pretest and posttest responses of the participants shows less significant variations than elsewhere, perhaps because the teens were already veterans of the program when they took the pretest. The greatest number (6) had been in the program for 3 to 5 years by May 2001 and the average length of participation for all 17 was nearly 5 years. The average length of involvement for the 14 teens on the pretest was over six years. This is an impressive record of longevity which I attribute to both the continuing presence of founder Curran over 10 years and the graduated and varied programs the Project offers to keep teens coming back. In addition to weekly acting classes and the One on One Program described in chapter 6, the Virginia Avenue Project offers two weekly summer sessions in Ojai as a reward to teens in the weekly classes and increasing artistic challenges in the Two on Two and Playback programs which give continuing students a chance to act in larger casts and to write plays, respectively. I would contrast this variety, for example, to City Hearts which seemed stuck in repeating scenes from a small number plays such as *Romeo and Juliet, Julius Caesar,* and *Midsummer Night's Dream.*

For the Virginia Avenue Project surveys the distribution of answers to the questions about verbal and physical fighting in the home, school, and community did not vary much from the pretest to the posttest. No one joined a gang, attempted suicide, dropped out of school, or got pregnant over the year. One more teen had taken illegal drugs in the preceding three months but one less teen had gotten drunk in that time.

The only significant change, defined as a change on the order of two or three teens, occurred in regard to sex. The number of teens who said they were currently in a serious romantic relationship (Question 31) increased from 1 on the pretest to 3 on the posttest. The number answering how many partners they had sex with during the previous year (Question 17) increased from 1 to 2, a less significant change of one, and perhaps attributable to the increasing age of the group one year after the pretest.

At Isla Vista City at Peace, the pretest was administered between December 2001 and February 2002. The posttest was administered in May 2002. Eleven teens took the pretest and 11 took the posttest, though only 8 took both. Significant changes in attitudes and behaviors between the pretest and posttest responses, defined as a change of 2 or 3 can be found in Question 3, showing an increase in verbal fighting at home once a week but a decrease in several times a week; Question 11, showing a decrease in the number of teens thinking about suicide frequently; Question 12, showing an increase in the number having sex each week; Question 14, showing an increase in the number using contraceptives; and Question 26, showing an increase in school suspensions. No teen joined a gang, was expelled from school, became pregnant, or got someone pregnant over the course of the study.

The dropout rate of participants was 27 percent, or three out of 11. Of these three, one teen was in jail, one was grounded by her parents, and one said she was too busy to continue with the group. This was the newest of the three groups studied and their dropout rate fell between that of the two other programs. As a beginning group, then unaffiliated with a larger organization, and with a small budget and a single full-time staff member, it may be too early to judge its long-term efficacy.

A second important comparison to make is between the national statistics that are available for at-risk behavior among teens with the statistics (posttest) I gathered for these three theatre programs individually and (last) averaged from the groups. Remember that I was not allowed to ask City Hearts teens "the sex questions" and added the drug and alcohol questions too late for the City at Peace surveys.

Having Sex: 48% nationally

         9% VA   73% CA   Theatre avg. 41%

Pregnancy Rate: 1.7% age 14 and younger; 7.5% ages 15–17

  0% CH   0% VA   10% CA   Theatre avg. 3%

Drinking Alcohol: 30% 7th grade, 50% 9th grade, 63% 11th grade

  14% CH   7% VA   Theatre avg. 11%

Use of Illegal Drugs: 7% 7th grade, 19% 9th grade, 34% 11th grade

  0% CH   21% VA   Theatre avg. 18%

School Suspension Rate: 39%

  14% CH   21% VA   40% CA   Theatre avg. 25%

School Dropout Rate: 30%

  0% CH   0% VA   9% CA   Theatre avg. 3%

Violence: Teens reporting they had been in a fight in the previous 12 months (on the posttest survey: physical fighting at home, school, or in the community): 68% nationally

  28% CH   9% VA   13% CA   Theatre avg. 17%

Gang Membership: 15% nationally

  0% CH   0% VA   0% CA   Theatre avg. 0%

As can be seen, the percentages of teenagers in these theatre programs engaging in behaviors that place them at risk are significantly lower than the national averages with the exception of the teens in the City at Peace program, who exceeded the national averages significantly in sexual activity and slightly in the pregnancy rate. Although only one of the 11 teens in that group answered that they had ever been pregnant or gotten someone pregnant, one in 11 made for a high percentage. Only with a much larger number of participants could we know if this is an accurate statistic or an anomaly. The fact that nearly half the members of the City at Peace group were over the age of 18 and enrolled in college could explain the higher figures for sexual activity.

The average percentages of all theatre programs answering these seven questions were lower in every case than the national averages. The combined numbers for all three of the theatre programs yield a more significant statistical average than any one of the programs alone.

The third comparison I make is between the three groups in comparing their pretest and posttest responses. The change in the responses over the course of the program should indicate the efficacy of that program in influencing the attitudes and behaviors of the participants.

The difficulties in making comparative judgments are numerous. Because teens left and entered both City Hearts (7 of 14 left) and City at Peace (3 left and 3 entered so that the total number remained constant at 11), I did not have constant populations to survey and it is not possible to directly correlate numbers from the posttest to the pretest to show absolute changes. Percentages, however, may give us a better idea of what happened. It makes sense to compare the results for survey questions which measured continuing behavior or behavior that occurred in the three months prior to the survey. Questions that measured single events in the past (i.e., Question 22, "Have you ever been in a gang?" and Question 25 "Have you ever attempted suicide?") covered time before the teens entered the theatre program.

Seven high-risk behaviors were compared and yielded slight or no differences between programs, though they are significantly lower than the national averages:

1. The percentages of program members who said they never got into physical fights at school (Question 6 on the posttest) were 60 percent for City Hearts, 79 percent for the Virginia Avenue Project, and 100 percent for City at Peace.

2. The percentages of program members who said they never got into physical fights in the community (Question 8 on the posttest) were 100 percent for City Hearts, 100 percent for the Virginia Avenue Project, and 100 percent for City at Peace.

3. The percentages of program members who said they never had unprotected sex (Question 13 on the posttest) were 100 percent for the Virginia Avenue Project, and 82 percent for City at Peace.

4. The percentages of those who said they were not currently in a gang after their time in the program (Question 23 on the posttest) were 100 percent for City Hearts, 100 percent for the Virginia Avenue Project, and 100 percent for City at Peace.

5. The percentages of those who said they were not dropped out of school after being in the program (Question 29 on the posttest) were 100 percent for City Hearts, 100 percent for the Virginia Avenue Project, and 91 percent for City at Peace.

6. The percentages of those who said they had used illegal drugs in

the previous three months (Question 36 on the posttest) was zero in City Hearts and 21 percent in the Virginia Avenue Project.

7. The percentages of those in the program who said they had gotten drunk in the previous three months (Question 37 on the posttest) was 14 percent for City Hearts and 7 percent for the Virginia Avenue Project.

However three questions yielded what I feel are significant differences among the participants in these three programs:

1. The percentages of those who said they never got into physical fights in their homes at the end of the program (Question 4 on the posttest) were 57 percent for City Hearts, 93 percent for the Virginia Avenue Project, and 73 percent for City at Peace.

2. The percentages of those who said they never got into verbal fights at school at the end of each program (Question 5 on the posttest) were 0 percent for City Hearts, 29 percent for the Virginia Avenue Project, and 46 percent for City at Peace.

3. The percentages of those who said they never got into verbal fights in the community at the end of each program (Question 7 on the posttest) were 71 percent for City Hearts, 71 percent for the Virginia Avenue Project, and 82 percent for City at Peace.

So in these significant areas the City at Peace teens outperformed teens in City Hearts in all three, while the Virginia Avenue teens outperformed City Hearts teens in two categories (#1 and #2 above) and tied in the third. City at Peace teens outperformed teens in the Virginia Avenue Project in two out of the three categories (#2 and #3) but were surpassed by Virginia Avenue Project teens in one area (#1). City Hearts teens ranked last in two of the three categories.

It must be remembered that the great difficulty in making comparisons is that we simply cannot be sure that the programs themselves are responsible for the changes that occurred. This is always the difficulty in working with human subjects. We cannot control all of the factors that impact them over time. I do not know what changes were occurring in their home lives, school lives, etc. during the time I was studying their approximately three-hour-a-week involvement in these theatre programs. Equally, we do not know how they might have been changed, or not changed, if they had not been in these theatre programs. As 52nd Street founder Willie Reale said, "you never really know how you change them because you don't know how they would have turned out without you."[20] However, the surveys do show significant improvement in these areas.

Why are the students in these programs more successful than their peers, who are not enrolled in theatre programs, in resisting factors that place them at risk? What are the programs doing that affect teens so positively?

The answer is threefold:

1. Theatre is transformative.
2. Drama is a powerful system for learning and self-exploration.
3. And, unlike any other activity, it offers emotional and spiritual catharsis.

Aristotle, in *The Poetics*, first described this effect he called "catharsis." What Aristotle actually meant by the term has been debated, interpreted, and reinterpreted through the intervening centuries by theatre scholars and practitioners, including Corneille, Goethe, Lessing, and Brecht. Catharsis may have a medical context, as a purgative; a religious context, as a rebirth or initiation; and a moral context, as in the relief of soul and spirit by purification.

Plato had wanted theatre banned from the ideal state he described in *The Republic* because he believed it incited and aroused powerful emotions in the audience. His student Aristotle accepted this theory but reversed the argument. Agreeing that theatre incites emotions, he argued that they then purge their audiences of these feelings through fear and pity, giving theatre a valuable role in sustaining personal and social harmony. It was this purgation that Brecht rejected centuries later as an insidious method of social control to quiet the disenfranchised of Greek society and accused Aristotle of being in "the emotions racket."[21] The question of whether catharsis is a good or a bad thing, or whether it occurs at all, repeats through history.

In chapter 4 I discussed how numerous theatre groups like the Living Theatre and Soul and Latin Theatre, following the ideas of Bertolt Brecht, tried to induce in their audiences such strong emotional reactions that their lives would be transformed by the experience. I noted instances of strong emotional reactions by audiences to the Living Theatre's *The Connection*, that resulted in mass faintings, and to SALT's *After the Fashion Show*, where the crowd treated the actor like a real-life hero after he stood up to his "father" in the play and carried the actor off the stage on their shoulders. These emotional audience reactions resemble those which the radical political dramatists had aimed for in agitprop plays like *Waiting for Lefty*, where the audience rose at the end shouting "Strike! Strike!" with the actors/

characters on stage. In each instance the separation of stage and audience was broken, as was the separation between make-believe and reality.

Richard Schechner, a founder of the Free Southern Theatre, allows for these emotional effects by differentiating between theatre that is "transportational" and theatre that is "transformational" in his article "Performers and Spectators: Transported and Transformed." Schechner writes:

> I call performances where performers are changed "transformations" and those where performers are returned to their starting places "transportations." Transportation because during the performance the performers are "taken somewhere" but at the end, often assisted by others, they are "cooled down" and reenter ordinary life just about where they went in.... I do want to point out that if a change occurs within the performer or in his status it happens only over a long series of performances, each of which moves the performer slightly ... a series of transportation performances can achieve a transformation.[22]

Schechner differentiates between performances that are designed to be transportational, as in staged theatre, and those that are intended to be transformational, as rituals and initiation rites, where the performer (i.e., a young person going through a tribal or religious initiation) at the end will, by the act of having gone through the ritual, have become an adult. Schechner refers to the goal of 1960s community-based, or alternative, theatre as the introduction of the transformative into transportation theatre. Examples of this might include the rituals of the Open Theatre, the invitation to the audience to come onto the stage by the Living Theatre, and the seating of the audience within the ship in the Free Southern Theatre's *Slave Ship*, all previously described in chapter 4.

In his observation of Schechner's Performance Group production of Ibsen's *A Dollhouse*, Victor Turner noted that one of the actresses cast as Nora was actually in the process of deciding in her own life whether or not to leave her husband and two children, just as the character Nora was in the play. In rehearsal the actress wrung her hands at the climactic moment and instead of slamming the door at the end of the play rushed back to stay with her family. Turner noted that director Schechner decided to keep the hand wringing "as the bit of reality" in the final performance although the script dictated that she leave her family on stage.[23] The actress portraying Nora may or may not have been experiencing a transformation or catharsis, or she may have been rehearsing for action in her real life. The actress might have been able to expunge her desire to leave her family by acting out the abandonment onstage, the kind of catharsis Aristotle suggested as a healthy purgation. On the other hand, the acting out of Nora's departure onstage might have sealed the actress' personal decision to leave her family, in what Boal calls a "rehearsal for revolution." Turner, however, does not tell us what the actress portraying Nora decided to do in her own off-stage, real life.

Psychotherapists Michael Nichols and Melvin Zax describe how individuals, like the actress portraying Nora, bring their personal lives to the dramas occurring around them. Recalling that millions of Americans wept when President John F. Kennedy was assassinated on November 22, 1963, they point out that:

> it seems unlikely that most of those who wept were attached deeply enough to this particular man to account for their sadness. Rather, his death probably restimulated various losses and frustrations in their own lives and provided the occasion for, but not the cause of, their tears.[24]

This might help to explain why we cry when King Lear is betrayed or when Juliet dies. Imagined losses onstage touch real losses in our own lives; stage deaths reminding us of our own future deaths. As sociologist Erving Goffman wrote, "all the World is not, of course, a stage, but the crucial ways in which it isn't are not easy to specify."[25]

Also struggling with the concept of catharsis was one of the first psychiatrists to exploit the use of theatre in his therapeutic practice, Jacob Levy Moreno (1889–1974), who is credited with founding sociometry, psychodrama, and group psychotherapy. Moreno first began working with drama as a young doctor in Vienna in the theatre that was part of the sanitarium. He wrote:

> It was the central task of the Vienna Theatre of Spontaneity (1921–1923) to bring about a revolution in theatre, to entirely change the character of the theatrical event. It tried to achieve this task on four levels: 1) The elimination of the playwright and the written play. 2) Audience participation, that is "theatre without audience." Everyone is a participant, everyone is an actor. 3) Actors and audience as the only creators. Everything is improvised—the play, the action, the motives, the words, the encounters and the solution to the problems. 4) the disappearance of the old stage; instead there is the open stage, ... the open space, the living space, life.[26]

The goal of the psychodrama is to reenact the past to create liberation in the present through a catharsis, which Moreno defined as "spontaneous states of short duration, extremely eventful and sometimes crowded with imagination."[27]

Accepting Aristotle's description of catharsis from Greek drama,

Moreno agreed that the goal was the reestablishment of equilibrium but redirected it from the audience, who Moreno said experienced only a "passive catharsis,"[28] to the actors themselves. "It [the psychodrama] produces," he wrote, "a healing effect not on the spectators but in the producer-actors who produce the drama and at the same time liberate themselves in it."[29] He labeled this the "catharsis of integration." Playing "patient" onstage puts the actor in a new world with a new miniature society where "a lifetime is condensed into an hour or two."[30] Moreno says:

> What the aesthetic drama has done for deities like Dionysius, Brahma, and Jehovah and for representative characters like Hamlet, Macbeth, and Oedipus, the psychodrama can do for every man. In the Therapeutic Theatre an anonymous, average man becomes something approaching a work of art ... not only for others but for himself. A tiny, insignificant existence is here elevated to a level of dignity and respect.... On the psychodramatic stage he is put into a state of imagination ... he is the dramatist of himself.[31]

Using role-playing, or the assignment of emotionally challenging characters, or improvising drama to solve personal problems or address issues, Moreno felt that in psychodrama participants would "find themselves discarding evasions, reticences, and equivocations and revealing their true, naked emotions and feelings."[32] The ventilation of suppressed feelings would lead to spontaneous new behaviors, the goal being "both a mastery of the past and a rehearsal for the future."[33]

Moreno recounts the vivid story of Barbara, a young actress who came into his asylum in Vienna to act in plays for the inmates. Barbara was beloved within this community for her heartfelt portrayal of ingenues and good-hearted heroines on stage. One day her husband shared his problem with Moreno: Barbara was a terror at home, abusive, foulmouthed, and always out of sorts.

Without disclosing the problem or his therapeutic goal, Moreno asked Barbara to stretch her acting skills by undertaking the roles of vulgar and stupid women. The end result was that, after playing abusive women onstage and getting that out of her system, Barbara was able to reduce her fits of temper at home and live more harmoniously with her husband. Calling it a "catharsis," Moreno highlights Barbara's story as a model for his work.[34]

In 1940, after coming to the United States, Moreno continued to explore community-based theatre. His communities varied from asylum inmates to temporary communities of psychotherapists gathered at conventions. Interviews with and observations of the participants became the subject matter of the dramas which, like Boal's later experiments in forum theatre, allowed participants to interject and suggest alternative plot resolutions.

With the exception of Moreno, few theatre people have taken the concept of catharsis very seriously in the modern age. An exception is Dr. Thomas Scheff, UCSB professor of sociology and a licensed marriage and family counselor, who sees catharsis as a means to the end result of regaining mental health. In his book *Catharsis in Healing, Ritual, and Drama*, Scheff begins with the premise that stress, a psychological state with physiological effects, is the result of a buildup of grief, anger, fear, and boredom. He argues that "what is needed is a repeated emotional discharge of fear, grief, anger, and so on."[35] This discharge, which he identifies with catharsis, "is a necessary condition for therapeutic change."[36] "Those who cry, laugh, shiver, and so on, in therapy," he states, "make rapid progress and those who don't, progress slowly or not at all."[37] His analysis of a study of 68 therapy sessions found that success in 59 of them followed an emotional discharge, success in seven followed the interpretation of the situation by the therapist, and two related to a change in perception by the patient. Scheff writes:

> Before the abreaction can take place, the client must perceive the situation in a different way than he is accustomed to perceiving it, that is, as non-threatening ... an abreaction [can take place] which reduces tension, removes threats, and makes ... change in perception possible.[38]

"After catharsis," writes Scheff, "the individual's sensitivities to the outside world and to his own inner stimuli are heightened ... his or her thoughts are clearer, and his or her behavior is more creative than before or during catharsis."[39] On the other hand, the effects of a lack of catharsis are less tolerance for the discharges of others, diminution in clarity of thought and perception, and a decrease in cooperativeness leading to isolation. Scheff writes, "unresolved emotional distress gives rise to rigid or neurotic patterns of behavior and catharsis dissipates these patterns."[40] Such patterns are laid down by negative personal experiences: "Events are traumatic to the extent that, first they result in powerful negative emotions and, second, to the extent that these emotions have been retained and not discharged."[41]

Scheff, himself, relates this theory to both children and theatre:

> It would seem, in fact, that in modern societies, for most people there is considerable interference with discharge. Children, especially males, are not allowed to cry nor are they, especially females, allowed to express all the anger they feel. Interference by parents, teachers ... and peers is more or less continuous

and systematic.... Given the fact that a person can usually expect his emotional expression to be met with punishment, an almost universal strategy, is to learn to interfere with one's discharge: one learns to avoid expressing emotional distress ... most individuals accumulate massive amounts of repressed emotion.[42]

Scheff told me:

The problem is that emotion is a bodily state of readiness. If you allow yourself to feel these feelings then you can purge yourself of the feelings and this tense state but if you don't deal with these emotions you remain in that state of tension. Fear is actually a life enhancing emotion. It's a warning of danger that we need to respond to protect ourselves, but if we identify fear with cowardice and suppress fear then we become emotionally blank, but that state of readiness, those emotions, have to go somewhere. Men especially are taught to suck in grief, shame, and fear and mask them with anger. Depression is one result of shutting off emotions. Acting out is another result. Men learn to mask shame, grief, and fear with anger and that leads to male violence.[43]

Scheff points out, for example, that many violent teens have themselves been victims of violence at home and at school. Having no way to work out their emotions, they will at some point explode. One solution is to seek out opportunities for catharsis:

The theory of catharsis argues that thrill seeking is an attempt to relive and therefore resolve earlier painful experiences which were unfinished. When we cry over the fate of Romeo and Juliet we are reliving our own personal experiences of overwhelming loss but under new and less severe conditions. The experience of vicarious loss, in a properly designed drama, is sufficiently distressful to awaken the old distress. It is also sufficiently vicarious, however, so that the emotion does not feel overwhelming.[44]

In fact, drama, for Scheff, provides the delicate balance of offering distressful situations but keeping them far enough removed from real life to be endurable:

Drama then does not create new emotional distress—it simply "restimulates" old distress. We assume that the audience comes to the theatre with accumulated emotional distress which it has been unable to discharge. When the play restimulates this distress, under appropriate conditions it can be discharged.[45]

Scheff had been writing about conventional plays in the commercial theatre where a spectator attends a stage production and watches the play as a member of the audience. I asked him whether he believed that catharsis could occur in a community-based drama or in Boal's forum theatre where the spectator may actually be involved in the action onstage or where his/her own story, the original story that caused the distress, is being acted out by others. He responded:

I think so. There still needs to be the right amount of distance from the original event that caused distress; neither too close to make them uncomfortable nor too distant as to be uninvolving, that is avoiding both under-distancing and over-distancing. If the person was asked to act out their own distressful story on the stage that would be too close and would induce all the pain and fear of the original traumatic event. But if they had some emotional distance, as in seeing another person act out their event, it would be safe for them to express their pent up emotion in a catharsis that could relieve the distress they'd been building up since the original event.

One thing I didn't write about is the "ricochet effect" which I discovered later in a psychology class. A person telling a very personal story would find the material too close to have a catharsis themselves but their audience does—likewise if they see the traumatic event that happened to them happen to someone else, and this could happen in the drama where their own event is being reenacted by other people.[46]

This seems to be exactly what often happens in community-based theatre.

Augusto Boal began his career by declaring he was creating a theatre that was consciously anticathartic and anti–Aristotelian. At that time he saw catharsis as a method for curbing the desires of the oppressed for change. He identified Aristotle as the spokesperson for an oppressive Greek society that excluded a majority of the population, women and slaves, from the benefits of Greek "democracy." He saw Aristotelian tragedy as having a covert political agenda: to disempower the spectators and render them pliable to governmental control.

Boal finds the Aristotelian system of tragedy repressive specifically because its goal is catharsis. Boal describes the action of Aristotelian theatre in this manner: the audience attends and passively experiences the drama taking place on stage. They see the dramatic hero violate the rules (i.e., laws of the city or of the gods) and then pay a terrible price for this violation. In seeing the suffering of the hero (i.e., Oedipus, Antigone, etc.), the audience members experience a "catharsis" which removes from them the impetus to emulate the hero and violate the laws themselves. This leads to an inner sense of repose. Dramatic action onstage has taken the place of real action in people's lives. Analyzing a modern play, Henrik Ibsen's *The Enemy of the People*, Boal writes of Dr. Stockmann, a hero who stands alone against an entire town, in his book, *Games for Actors and Non-Actors*: "I sympathize with his heroic attitude. He drains me of my desire to behave like a hero myself."[47]

Boal claims that his forum theatre aims at an opposite effect: "Forum theatre does not produce catharsis; it produces a stimulant for our desire to change the world."[48] Boal adds:

when an actor carries out an act of liberation he or she does it in place of the spectator, and thus is, for the latter, a catharsis. But when a spect/actor carries out the same act on stage, he or she does it in the name of all other spectators and is thus for them not a catharsis but a dynamization.[49]

It was during his 1973 work in Peru with a literacy crusade that Boal experienced a perplexing situation that led directly to the creation of forum theatre:

> But one fine day, a shy woman came to see me. She said: "I know you do political theatre, and my problem is not political, but it's a very big problem and it's mine. Perhaps you could help me with your theatre?"[50]

It turned out that the woman's problem was that her husband was cheating on her. She had just discovered this and her husband was due to return the next day from a trip away from home. She didn't know what to do when he returned. So that evening Boal arranged for his troupe to construct a scenario:

> We enacted the play using the "simultaneous dramaturgy" mode [with this technique audience members suggested ideas to the actors on stage but did not enter the theatrical space]. Came the moment of crisis—the husband rings the doorbell—what to do? I myself had no idea. I appealed to the audience for ideas. Solutions came pouring in.[51]

People suggested using tears to evoke guilt, locking the husband out of the house, forgiveness, and having the wife abandon the home, among others. Each suggestion was dramatized. None of the solutions seemed right to the wife or the audience.

Finally, Boal called on a woman spectator seated in the third row who looked dissatisfied. She responded: "This is what we should do, let the husband in, have a clear conversation with him, and only then, forgive him."[52] The actors tried this and the scenario didn't seem to go anywhere. The spectator was still unsatisfied. The actors tried again and then again. Finally Boal said to the woman, "If you are still not satisfied, why don't you come on stage and show us what you mean by a 'very clear conversation'—what is that?"[53]

Boal describes what happened next:

> She came up on stage, grabbed the poor defenseless actor-husband (who was a real actor but not a real husband and, moreover, was skinny and weak) and laid into him with a broom-handle with all her strength, simultaneously delivering a lecture to him on her complete views on the relations between husband and wife.... Finally she stopped of her own accord and, satisfied, planted her victim on a seat at the table and said:

"Now that we have had this clear and very sincere conversation you can go to the kitchen and fetch my dinner, because after all this I am tired out."

As clarity goes, this was pretty clear.... Even more clearly, this truth dawned on me: when the spectator herself comes on stage and carries out the action she has in mind, she does it in a manner which is personal and unique and non-transferable as she alone can do it, and as no artist can do it in her place.... This is how Forum Theatre was born.... A theatre which is not didactic ... but pedagogic, in the sense of collective learning.[54]

This is a perfect example of how imagined events in a play call forth real emotions in the participants/audience, whom Boal calls the spect/actors. At least two things happen: (1) those emotions (which may or may not be socially acceptable) can be safely expressed, shared and released in safe place; and (2) solutions to problems can be attempted, rehearsed, if you will, and the best solution can then be chosen for use in real life.

Boal's attack on Aristotle cleared the stage for the creation of the spect/actor and a new interpretation of catharsis. Boal envisioned new theatrical practitioners, the spect/actors, who move from observers to actors and back again, making theatre based on the oppressions they face in their lives. The old model of catharsis rested upon the idea that actors onstage did something to the emotions of the spectators and that this affect moved in one direction, from stage to audience, only. Boal felt this monologue was oppressive and needed to be replaced with a dialogue of equals. And so actors become spectators, spectators become actors, and all shared equally and democratically in making the drama and solving the problem.

The key to a new understanding of catharsis seems to lie in the linking of *mimesis* with *kinesis* to effect a change among the participants (or spect/actors, in the terminology of Boal). In theatre *mimesis* is the imitation of an action on stage. *Kinesis*, also from the Greek, is related to dynamism and action and is defined as the movement or activity of an organism in response to a stimulus such as light. In Boal's forum theatre, for example, plays are constructed out of the true life experiences of the actors. The stimuli that are applied are the action, reaction, intervention, and reconsideration of these true stories by the other actors and audience, all of whom constitute the spect/actors. The real scripts are then changed, become kinetic, or open ended, as people suggest and try out various new possibilities for solving real-life problems.

Boal grounds his forum theatre in body work, physical games, and group play; activities which inevitably lead to laughter at oneself and others. The very activities themselves open the participants to change. Their goal is to break down inhibitions (internal authority, social conformity), and to center the spect/actor in their body. The human body is in many ways quite ridiculous, as exemplified in the Rabelaisian emphasis on the bodily functions of eating, digestion, defecation, fornication, etc. Boal's physical body work and games prepare participants for moving beyond the normal expectations of decorum and so beyond the bounds of both external authority and internal inhibitions (what Boal calls "the cop in the head").

But the body is also a tool for learning and this suggests yet another implication of the term *kinesis*. In his book, *Introduction to the Dance*, John Martin suggests adding a sixth sense to the usual five human senses of touch, taste, smell, sight, and hearing. He calls this sixth sense "kinesthesis." He writes that people, in his case dancers, remember past physicalizations in their bodies. They learn empathetic reactions, as when someone puckers up just from watching someone else suck a lemon, as their own body remembers the sour taste. And so the physicalization of theatre becomes another mode of learning.[55]

To *kinesis*, Boal adds the term *metaxis*, to indicate the interplay between the actual and the fictitious. For him *metaxis* is a heightened state of consciousness where we may inhabit two worlds completely and simultaneously: the real world and the world of the play. At a performance, for example, we enter the world of the play *and* we watch ourselves entering the world of the play. Likewise, as Aristotle pointed out, a play relies on mimesis, the imitation of an action onstage rather than the action itself: we see someone act out a murder onstage but we do not see a real murder committed onstage. This offers us the necessary balance, as Scheff described, to approach neither too near nor remain too far from our own traumatic past experience; to be able to relive traumatic events in a safe manner and in so doing free ourselves from their emotional power through catharsis. Gavin Bolton encountered this effect in his theatre in education work with children in Britain:

> In a game the pain of life can safely be recaptured, encountered, and switched off as required ... all forms of playing ... are deliberately created second-order experience removed from the rawness of living.[56]

And Dr. James Garbarino, professor of human development at Cornell University, saw it among children in Chicago:

> In play situations children can recall unpleasant events more easily because they can pretend the occurrences happened to other characters.... Play also offers children the opportunity to reverse the roles they play in reality. Instead of being passive they can take on active roles.[57]

What Boal finds predictable, and what serves as the basis for participatory community-based theatre, is that when involved or active audience members (the spect/actors) take the stage, interrupt the action, and rearrange the plot, the theatre piece becomes a "rehearsal of revolution."[58] These people are practicing, trying solutions, for off-stage, real-life issues. If they have an emotional reaction, a catharsis, it is within themselves as spect/actors; it is what they do to themselves rather than what is done to them by others. And this emotional reaction, this new self-knowledge empowers them to change their lives off stage.

The efficacy of community-based theatre to create social change may depend in large part upon how deeply within the community the theatre is based. As I discussed in chapter 5, the Panamanian sociologist Raul Alberto Leis, in studying popular theatre in Latin America (popular theatre being defined as theatre that concerns the masses rather than the economic and political elite) differentiates among three categories of community theatre: (1) "theatre produced by a theatrical group but oriented towards the people" (theatre by professionals that addresses community concerns as in agitprop dramas like *Waiting for Lefty*); (2) "theatre organized by and for the people, with spectators" (amateur actors and writers from popular groups, i.e., trade unions), perform theatre for their constituency and address their issues; and (3) "theatre organized by and for the people without spectators."[59] This last, of course, describes Boal's forum theatre and it is theatre *by*, *for*, and *of* the people, since they are all making it together.

Leis' analysis is fruitful for categorizing different theatre groups working with at-risk teens. Teens, like women, racial minorities, older people, and differently abled people, are a specific community defined in this case not only by age but by a shared oppression. Their perceived oppressors— adults, parents, the school system, the judicial system—are all working hard to make teens "fit in," to socialize them to conform to the mores of the dominant group of adults and to rein in rebellious attitudes and behaviors

Teens have a highly developed sense of themselves as oppressed. Their very psycho-emotional developmental stage defines them as rebels pushing against the limits placed upon them. Adults, who fear that this rebelliousness may lead to anarchy and violence, often respond by imposing ever stricter controls, so that those who have rebelled, as truants avoiding school, face progressively harsher measures ending often in actual incarceration.

Boal, with his emphasis upon freedom rather than repression, dialogue rather than monologue, and a method that is both means and goal, has a program that works where others have failed. As Michael Rohd, a forum theatre practitioner, writes, students in forum theatre "learn by doing, not by being told or even shown" and what they learn is freedom.[60] In other words, they do it of, for, and by themselves.

Leis writes, "A people's theatre should concentrate on awakening the latent capacity of the people to take part and to make their own decisions, to organize themselves for common action."[61] On the free space of the forum stage (which, of course, is not literally a stage as we know it, above and apart from the audience but rather the common ground, a rec hall, school gymnasium, teen center, etc. upon which the entire group gathers), teens create theatre out of their lives, connecting the political, economic and social realities of society in their own daily existence.

The focus on catharsis highlights the role of emotional engagement in social and personal change. But theatre also has an intellectual component (and a liberatory component to be discussed at the end of this chapter) that has been largely overlooked but which provides a second theoretical basis for understanding its efficacy. By and large our society equates education with rationality, intelligence, and the mind, as if there were a single way of learning and knowing. Yet, we are now discovering that, in the words of Howard Gardner, a past codirector of Project Zero, a research group at the Harvard Graduate School of Education, there are "several relatively autonomous human competencies"[62] often overlooked by our educational system. Interestingly Gardner, proponent of the theory of multiple intelligences, speaks of education in words we are familiar with from our discussion of theatre: "mimetic" and "transformative."[63] By mimetic he refers to the rote learning common to schools, where students are expected to soak up knowledge from their teacher within an authoritarian system of monologues delivered by the person who knows, and is therefore powerful, the teacher, to the person who does not know, and therefore does not have power, the student. Education becomes imitation and the highest value becomes conformity.

On the other hand, Gardner describes "transformative" education as education that places children in situations where they are challenged to become active agents in their own education and to develop new skills, and are subsequently changed by the experience. This is reminiscent of Schechner's distinction between transportational and transformative theatre. Transportational education fills up young minds with data and moves them ahead one grade level at a time. Transformational education, on the other hand, creates critical thinkers who become coeducators in the learning process.

Instead of an "educational system that assumes everyone can learn in the same way and that a uniform, universal measure suffices to test student learning," Gardner posits the existence of seven human multiple intelligences:

> We are able to know the world through language, logical-mathematical analysis, spatial representation, musical thinking, the use of the body to solve problems or to make things, an understanding of other individuals, and an understanding of ourselves.[64]

Of these seven equally important "intelligences" or "competencies" through which individuals perceive the world, many have an obvious basis in art. Linguistic intelligence depends on writing and speaking; musical intelligence on music; spatial intelligence on drawing; bodily, or kinesthetic intelligence, on acting and dancing; and an understanding of others and ourselves from role-playing (acting) and empathy (through portraying other characters on stage).

Gardner's theory accounts for individual differences in learning styles and helps bridge the dichotomies our educational system has created. As Elliot Eisner writes in his book, *Educating Artistic Vision*:

> The models of mind that have typified U.S. educational psychology ... have made tidy separations between thinking and feeling, feeling and acting, and acting and thinking. The view of thinking has been that the mind and body are distant, and, of the two, body is base while the mind is lofty.[65]

But now we begin to see the body itself as a medium of learning. Something dancers and actors already knew.

And within the arts, drama has a place as a unique way to learn. As Richard Courtney points out:

> Dramatic activity affects human intelligence by improving cognitive processes.... We come to know what we play. Dramatic activity improves learning. Learning is synonymous with the change in knowing achieved by replay, an element of dramatic transformation that brings about cognition. This is particularly the case with intrinsic learning and the improvement of judgment, problem solving, and motivation to learn ... dramatic activity improves intelligence by activating the fundamental structures and dynamics of mind.[66]

In fact, Courtney argues for adding an eighth intelligence, "dramatic intelligence" to Gardner's seven multiple intelligences:

> [Dramatic intelligence] provides a fictional experience we live through in the here and now with a way of knowing; it combines "as if" thought and action as a fictional double of what is actual ... it provides metaphoric meaning and understanding of the human condition ... it ensures as Marshall McLuhan has said that "replay is re-cognition" ... it teaches genuine skills—those skills required in adult work and leisure, such as human negotiation.[67]

This dramatic intelligence begins at an early age: "For young children dramatic play is a very serious business. It is the way they learn to grow up, and the way they learn to learn."[68] Courtney's concept is similar to Schechner's category of the transformative, though the change he notes is as much intellectual as emotional: "Imagining and dramatic acts work by transformation; they change what we know. This change is learning."[69] Courtney feels that the greatest education is not in adding to what we know but in how we know:

> The ideal model of the act of learning is the "Aha!" moment when we feel we are changed in a highly significant way.... Significant learning is aesthetic, a change in the quality of thought. There is an alteration in how we think more than in what we think.[70]

And, for Courtney, this dramatic intelligence functions throughout our lives:

> Dramatic action returns us to fundamental structures of our early life by encouraging us to see ourselves as similar to others and vice versa. They promote cooperation and de-emphasize stereotypical thinking.... The baby, from an initial consciousness of similarity, develops the first forms of differentiation—similar/different and part/whole.... In all forms of later development these structures remain tacitly constant. These are precisely the same structures as those of dramatic thought and action.[71]

The learning theories of Gardner and Courtney provide a basis for understanding why drama and art students do better in school. Gardner's theory of multiple intelligences demonstrates that individuals have different ways of perceiving and learning about the world. The traditional educational system that insists on a single way of learning and privileges the rational accumulation of facts and logic-based thinking, ignores these additional capabilities and plays to the strengths of only a certain percentage of students. The arts, however, open up a wider range of potentialities and allow students to learn and develop in other ways. Courtney's addition of an eighth intelligence, dramatic intelligence, widens this theory to include the very specific and unique aspects of drama: The playing of multiple roles onstage and off, and the empathy and self-knowledge this requires; the physicalization of learning in the body through gesture, image, costume, and sound; the openness to novelty and change; the need to openly express a myriad of emotions required of all actors; the need to work collectively and to place the social needs of all of the company above one's own; and the internal discipline of participation, whether it involves learning lines, showing up on time, knowing cues, etc.

Theatre educator Joe Norris relates a discussion at his school that supports this judgment:

> A science education colleague and I recently came to the conclusion that drama students may, in fact, practice more science than those in the science classroom. In drama classrooms students continually generate and test hypotheses through the magic of "what if."[72]

Director and acting guru Konstantin Stanislavski called this science the "magic if." He asked, for example, actors preparing to portray Hamlet on stage, to imagine how they would act and feel if their father had recently died and their mother had married their uncle. A corollary activity of this "what if" must also be a growing empathy as actors inhabit and dig within themselves to understand the character they are trying to portray convincingly. The "what if" transports actors across racial, gender, age, and class divisions and contains the power to transform them by that dramatic experience.

As theatre historian Nellie McCaslin notes, "of all the arts, drama is the most inclusive, for it involves the participant mentally, emotionally, physically, verbally, and socially,"[73] an attribute especially important within a society where most teenagers have been rendered passive spectators by the technologies of the cinema, television, video games, and computers, and treated as passive consumers of education by the school system.

In summary, there is substantive evidence for the unique attributes dramatic art offers at-risk teenagers in our society. In addition to the psychological and emotional benefits of catharsis and the diverse intellectual benefits of dramatic and multiple intelligences, theatre also offers a liberatory space, free of coercion and punishment, for youth development. Theatre empowers teens by making them the agents of their own dramas. Ethnographer Dwight Conquergood, who has worked extensively with gangbangers in Chicago, writes:

> Refugees, undocumented migrants, street youth—the subordinate people with whom I have done fieldwork—typically do not speak in public, they are spoken about and for [and, I would add, to]. They and other displaced people enter the public sphere not as active agents but as objectified problems to be surveyed, solved, and administered, through public policy, police, and the law.[74]

As Alan Creighton and Paul Kivel have noted, "the primary goal of violence in the United States is the systematic, institutionalized, and day to day imbalance of power."[75] These enforced imbalances of power are of men over women, adults over children, rich over poor, heterosexual over gay, able-bodied over physically impaired, and white over black, brown, red, and yellow. Specific to the subject of this investigation, teens are ordinarily allowed little or no power over their own lives and so are regularly restricted, disrespected, controlled, and abused by adults.

Boal calls his theatre a "rehearsal for revolution" and that remains its potential, and power, today. The most eloquent description of the liberatory function of theatre within a repressive social order may be found in Fatima Mernissi's memoir *Dreams of Trespass*. Mernissi, who became a professor of sociology and a widely read commentator on Islam, feminism, and the Arab world, grew up in a domestic harem in Morocco in the 1940s and 50s. Denied access to the life of the city around her and to school because she was female, Mernissi lived the life of a caged bird: "Our harem in Fez was surrounded by high walls and, with the exception of the little square chunk of sky that you could see from the courtyard below, nature did not exist."[76] To escape their confinement emotionally since they could not escape physically, the women engaged in dreams, songs, and plays of freedom. One member of the harem, Chama, regularly organized plays on the terrace, out of the sight of the men of the family. Mernissi recalls that Chama

> would stage the lives of all kinds of heroines, but the romantic Princess [Asmahan] was by far the most popular. Her life was as fascinating as any fairy tale, although it had a tragic end, as one would expect—an Arab woman could not seek sensuous enjoyment, frivolous entertainment, and happiness, and get away with it.... When Chama staged the first part of Asmahan's life she threw a green carpet on the terrace floor so that we could visualize the forests of the steep Druze Mountains where Asmahan was born. Chama then pulled a sofa on to the stage to represent the Princess's bed and smudged kohl powder around her eyes to suggest the Princess's dreamy green ones. The hair was more of a problem—the heroine's had been jet black—and so Chama was obliged to pull a charcoal-covered turban over her disturbingly red locks.... A wooden horse would be standing near Asmahan's bed. For you see, Asmahan had started running early in life. What else could a woman do who was born extremely beautiful into a princely family ... where everyone ... watched a woman's every move. Asmahan rode ... liberation meant running. To be free was to be on the move. Riding fast, even when you had no purpose, could give you a taste of happiness—movement for the sheer joy of it. So Chama would get off the bed and ride the immobile horse while the voices behind the drapes continued to sing about how depressing it felt to be trapped in a dead end situation ... sometimes I would push the horse back and forth a few times to give the scene a sense of movement.... As I watched Chama perform I vowed to myself that when I became a grownup woman ... I definitely would be affiliated with a theatre of some sort. I would dazzle Arab crowds ... and tell them about how it felt to be a woman intoxicated with dreams in a land that crushes both the dreams and the dreamer....

Theater, that spelling out of dreams and giving up the body to fantasy, was so essential. I wondered why it was not a sacred institution.[77]

Theatre is politically and socially contested space where a battle of liberation can be waged and, even won. In theatre, teens (or any oppressed people) can role-play their struggle and experience freedom. Offering emotional release, a special way of learning, and a rehearsal of revolution against repression, drama uniquely presents a multitude of methods to help at-risk youth reach their full potential.

On the basis of my research I make the following points:

1. More research is called for in at least two areas. Larger studies are needed to establish the cause-and-effect relationship between after-school theatre programs and the alleviation of attitudes and behaviors that place teens at-risk. Simultaneously, further comparative research needs to be done among such programs to further refine the elements that make each program successful.

2. There are literally thousands of after-school programs currently in operation. They need help to communicate and coordinate their activities so each can learn from the others.

3. I have established a correlation, at the very least, between involvement in after-school theatre programs and lower rates of at-risk behavior. This correlation, sustained by further and broader research, should lead to political/social decisions to invest public funding in what is so far the only proven effective strategy for lessening teen violence. The good news is that these programs are less expensive than other programs like the juvenile justice system and are expressive rather than repressive, creative rather than coercive.

4. I have established that some theatre programs work better than others.

5. Several intersecting theories explain why theatre programs are uniquely equipped to have a prosocial effect and why some theatre programs, as evidenced by my data, are more effective than others.

Finally, based on my research, I want to dissect what makes for an effective teen theatre program. The report of the surgeon general on youth violence states:

Studies of program effectiveness depends on the following principles.... The project addresses a pressing local problem. The Project has clearly articulated goals that reflect the needs and desires of the "customer." The project has a receptive environment in both the parent organization and the larger system.

The organization has a leader who is committed to the objectives, values and implications of the project and who can devise practical strategies to motivate and effect change.[78]

Let's apply this list to effective theatre programs like the Virginia Avenue Project or City at Peace. Both have clearly articulated goals that address local problems (theatre training for the Virginia Avenue Project and "peacemaking through art" for City at Peace). In contrast, the less successful City Hearts program mission is more defuse:

> to intervene in a loving, supportive and nurturing way to break the cycle of poverty.... Through the discipline and healing of classes, workshops, and performing experience in the arts, City Hearts provides positive role models, enrichment, and inspiration.[79]

Secondly, the surgeon general notes the important role of meeting the "desires of the customer." This happens most clearly in the City at Peace program where, in the words of their national guidebook:

> Why does it work? Because young people lead it, reversing the experiences of disempowerment in their lives. Because you let the young cast decide how to represent and interpret their experiences and current situations, and to envision and define their future. Most young people are denied opportunities for self-determination throughout their young lives.[80]

At the other extreme, the least effective of these three programs, City Hearts, was entirely a top-down affair, indistinguishable from the authoritarian and disempowering structure the teens face every day in school.

The surgeon general's emphasis upon a receptive environment is also borne out by my research. The greatest failure of the City Hearts program was that it operated at the constantly changing whim of the Oxnard School Board, superintendent, and Expanding Horizons. The constant shifting of meeting rooms, the last-minute cancellations, and the inappropriate environments offered, especially the exercise room with its mats, weights, and hanging ropes, and the constant interruptions of taking attendance and the office public address system announcements, made it impossible to plan, concentrate, or work seriously.

Fourthly, the surgeon general's emphasis upon the necessity of a leader to effect change is also borne out by my research. The unwavering and long-term commitment of the Virginia Avenue Project's director is a vital component of its success. Likewise, the two-year leadership of Jeff Flowers certainly began to establish such leadership at City at Peace. On the other hand, the continued rotation of three leaders and the recruitment and dismissal of teen aides at City Hearts means that participants did not know who their leader would be from week to week and undermines both consistency and the development of long-term relationships.

Sadly, I have also come to believe that successful programs cannot function in the public schools. I say sadly because public schools have the resources, the buildings, parking lots, and tax dollars which could give such programs lots of needed support. But such support, as I saw at City Hearts in the Haydock school, comes with crippling strings. There are simply too many constituencies to satisfy: The bureaucratic needs of administrators for attendance forms, announcements, and strict scheduling; the political needs of not upsetting parents by raising questions about uncomfortable issues like suicide, drug use, and sex; and the competition among interest groups all work against allowing teens to exercise the personal freedom that they need to develop. When I asked Paul Griffin, director of City at Peace if any of their projects were ever sited in school buildings, he replied:

> I thought ten years ago that we were headed for partnerships with the schools but we learned that while schools are good for teaching academic subjects they are not very good about the developmental needs of teens. Young people are practicing to be adults. If they don't get to make choices until they're adults it's likely that their first choices will be the wrong ones. They need to practice making choices now in an open dialogue with other teens where they can examine those choices and talk to other people and learn to be responsible. Schools can be battlegrounds in many ways and we just didn't think our program would work in that venue where the teens' freedom would be limited.[81]

To the surgeon general's list I would add several more ingredients. Each of the three programs depends upon trained theatre artists and these adults are quite capable actors and acting teachers, but none of them has training in child development or educational theory. Each of these programs need leaders who are trained educators as well as artists.

Also necessary is a dynamic program to keep the interest of the participants. The Virginia Avenue Project has accomplished this through multilevel classes and its summer camp experience. Unlike the unvaried work routine I observed at City Hearts, rehearsals and preparations for performance must include warm-ups, to set the world of the stage apart from the everyday world and to help participants become present in the space and in their bodies. In addition, theatre games that are fun and build cooperation, trust, and confidence are key components in building regular attendance.

Teen participants need to buy into the program and embrace its activities and goals. This is more easily accomplished in voluntary programs (i.e., the Virginia Avenue Project and City at Peace) than in programs where enrollment is enforced from above or where the alternative is suspension or expulsion from school (i.e., the City Hearts program at Haydock).

To succeed, programs must empower their participants to make decisions and to share responsibility for their success. The dismissal of the City Heart teens' petition for more classes by the City Hearts staff ended the only initiative and ownership those teens took for that program. As Judith Weitz, of the President's Committee on the Arts, noted, "programs shaped by the youth themselves have the immediate value of 'not being like school' and the kids ... make the choice to change because they aren't being made to."[82] Theatre, in the words of the 52nd Street Project "gives children the chance to fall in love with something that comes out of themselves."[83]

In much the same way, the material for youth theatre, the very stuff that gets onstage, must come out of the youth themselves. As the 1998 RAND study found:

> Arts programs create environments that "put the youth on the edge"—situations that combine heightened risk, through socially visible performances and peer critiques, with dynamic rules that structure participants' behavior and encourage personal accountability.[84]

Boal's forum theatre, Leis' community-based theatre for, by, and of the community, City at Peace's construction of plays from the real-life experiences of its actors, all create an environment where teens are empowered to share, consider, and solve their own real-life problems and where cathartic changes of attitude and behavior can occur. Such theatre, unlike the standard political theatre of the past, offers no pat answers but poses an unending series of questions. This is important because, as the late educator John Holt wrote, "the true test of intelligence is not how much we know how to do, but how we behave when we don't know what to do."[85] Such theatre is unique within an educational system where but 5 percent of class time is spent in discussion and "fewer than 1% of teachers' questions require students to respond with more than a remembered fact."[86]

Today, we face a crisis of youth violence. We face a simultaneous crisis in arts funding for youth. According to the Los Angeles Times, "the ratio of arts instructors to students in Los Angeles County is a grim 1 to 1,221."[87] The time has come for our society to invest in our empowering teenagers, rather than in controlling them. By making a concerted investment in the arts now, society can act to significantly stem the tide of teen violence and save lives.

Appendix: Selected After-School Theatre Programs

THE 106 AFTER-SCHOOL THEATRE programs described below are but a sampling of programs springing up across the country. Program descriptions have been gleaned from individual Websites and have been severely edited here for space. We need to continue to build a national directory of such programs and get participants talking to each other about best practices and common challenges.

About Face Youth Theatre
1222 W. Wilson, Second Floor, Chicago, IL 60640
Phone: (773) 784-8565
Fax: (773) 784-8557
E-mail: mailbox@aboutfacetheatre.com
Website: www.aboutfacetheatre.com/AFYT

About Face Youth Theatre (AFYT) is dedicated to giving voice to lesbian, gay, bisexual, transgender, and queer (LGBTQ) youth, creating performance opportunities for young artists, and connecting young activists and artists to LGBTQ leaders in the community. Programs include: Activist Theatre workshops (fall, winter, spring), the Playwright's Forum, About Face Open Mic at Las Manos Gallery, and History in Voices: A Documentary Project about HIV and AIDS. About Face received the prestigious Human First Award by Horizon's Community Services and was one of just five organizations in the United States to receive a major capacity building grant from the Diana, Princess of Wales Memorial Fund (U.S.).

ACT IT OUT Peer Performers
555 Amory Street, Jamaica Plain, MA 02130
Phone: (617) 524-1160
Fax: (617) 983-2237
Website: www.cominguptaller.org/profile/pr20theater.htm

ACT IT OUT was founded in 1992 and mainly serves kids ages 15–21. Its goal is to integrate training in violence prevention, conflict resolution, teen health issues and creative decision making with drama. Participants are recruited from the high schools where the group has performed. The intensive program runs year-round. Between October and May, youth meet after school and on weekends to learn acting techniques, develop an original theater piece and perform in Boston-area schools and throughout Massachusetts. During the summer, the group performs almost every day, often creating a new work for the summer tour. The group also has produced material for television and video and is working on a new CD-ROM about violence prevention.

ALPHA TEEN Theater
83 Hanover Street #8, Manchester, NH 03101
Phone: (603) 627-5127
Fax: (603) 627-1650
Website: www.cominguptaller.org/profile/pr03theater.htm

ALPHA TEEN Theater was founded in 1992 to serve kids ages 12–19. During the school year, teens attend the program twice weekly after school for 1 hour of academic tutoring and 1 hour of theater work. The teens do theater exercises under the guidance of an artistic director. The theater work helps them develop decision-making skills, address social issues, improve coping skills and build their self-esteem. Teens write five scripts based on issues or conflicts in their own lives. They perform these and other skits before audiences of peers in community settings.

American Variety Theatre Company
2027 W. Broadway, Minneapolis, MN 55411
Phone: (612) 374-8426
Website: www.cominguptaller.org/profile/pr05multi.html

The American Variety Theatre Company (AVTC) is an outgrowth of a 4-H garden project that developed to meet the changing needs of youth in the program as they grow older. They offer students, ages 4 to 19, classes in jazz, tap, ballet, acting, improvisational theater, piano, voice and recording. Each discipline is split into different classes by age and proficiency level. The classes all culminate in a production at the end of each session. Transportation is provided, and the $10 annual fee is waived for those unable to afford it.

The Arena Stage: The Living Stage
1101 Sixth Street SW, Washington, DC 20024
Phone: (202) 554-9066
Fax: (202) 488-0405
Website: www.cominguptaller.org/profile/pr08theater.htm

The Living Stage Theatre Company, an outreach arm of the Arena Stage, began in 1966 and focuses on kids ages 3 to 18. It is an improvisational theater program that draws from the lives and concerns of audience members to develop the content for its performances. The four ongoing workshops, for physically disabled toddlers, impoverished second graders, teen mothers and incarcerated youth, give traditionally overlooked populations a voice. The first part of each workshop focuses on a scenario in which the main character is always the same age as the participants and faces a dilemma. At a crucial moment, the scene freezes, and the group improvises how the scenario can be resolved. During the second part of the workshop, the participants work on theater exercises to develop skills in communicating emotions and creating characters, on building sets and more. Then, each group works together to create an improvisational performance of its own.

The Artists Collective
1200 Albany Avenue, Hartford, CT 06112
Phone: (860) 527-3205
E-mail: info@artistscollective.org
Website: www.artistscollective.org

Founded in 1970 as an interdisciplinary arts and cultural institution, the Artists Collective emphasizes the cultural and artistic contributions of the African Diaspora. The Artists Collective serves over 1,200 students per year in its several different training programs.

The After-School Program serves 200 students at 12 Hartford Schools two days a week.

The Rite of Passage/Yaboo Ceremony focuses on traditional African family values welcoming adolescents into adulthood.

The Youth Jazz Orchestra performs regionally and its members are racially and economically diverse. Young musicians 13 to 21 years of age are selected to audition for placement.

The Choreographer's Workshop is comprised of selected advance dance students 9 to 17 years of age. The dance ensemble performs traditional African, modern, jazz and tap throughout Connecticut.

The Summer Youth Employment Training Program provides summer employment for Hartford youth and develops work readiness skills and training in the arts.

Camp Culture is a 6-week, full-day cultural summer program, serving over 200 children, many of whom receive scholarships.

Beyond Borders: Literacy Intervention
761 Terminal Street, Los Angeles, CA 90021
Phone: (213) 572-0121
Fax: (213) 572-0125
E-mail: laura.rice@eastlaclassic.org
Website: www.eastlaclassic.org

East L.A. Classic Theatre (ECT), a bilingual (English/Spanish) classic theatre for young people, seeks to provide comprehensive language acquisition, literacy instruction, and engaging theatrical adaptations of literary masterpieces to disadvantaged youth in the Latino community. Programming is designed to serve three complementary goals: to develop literacy skills; to cultivate minority readers, writers and audiences; and to create a new bicultural theatre aesthetic emphasizing great classics of world drama. Professional actors (with degrees and training in classical theatre and education methods) work with classroom teachers and engage students in English-language acquisition and literacy activities. The curriculum incorporates Gardner's theory of multiple intelligences, with students applying "different ways of knowing" to classroom activities and interpersonal relationships.

Biola Youth Theatre
12625 La Mirada Blvd., Suite 100, La Mirada, CA 90638
Phone: (562) 906-4574
Fax: (562) 906-4586
E-mail: byt@biola.edu
Website: www.youth.biola.edu

Biola Youth Theatre's (BYT) mission is to provide La Mirada and surrounding Southern California communities with a quality theater program that incorporates solid theater training with spiritual principles, led by highly skilled and dedicated professionals in a caring and nurturing environment for children and youth.

Courses offered include basic classes, where students learn the basics of acting, stage presence, how to build a character, improvisation, and audition techniques. Intermediate and advanced classes, for students who want to sharpen their skills and build on the basics of BYT theatre can audition to take intermediate or advanced classes during summer camp.

BYT has a partnership with Biola University. It is one of only two Christian programs in Southern California. Since 1996, they have produced 24 shows.

Blue Apple Players
PO Box 4261, Louisville, KY 40204
Phone: (502) 587-7990
Fax: (502) 587-7928

E-mail: info@blueappleplayers.org
Website: www.blueappleplayers.org

Founded in 1976, Blue Apple Players brings original musicals and educational theater programs to youth throughout Kentucky, Indiana, Tennessee, Georgia, Ohio, and West Virginia. These programs reach across social, economic, and geographical boundaries and use drama to ignite children's imagination and change lives. Blue Apple tours over 150 performances of its original musicals each year, reaching nearly 100,000 youth.

The Drama for Learning and Drama for Life programs provide drama-based education focused on academic and social growth for youth at more than 70 different schools and community sites a year in the Metro Louisville area and in Southern Indiana. An inventory of 36 original musicals addresses topics ranging from teen pregnancy to adolescent suicide and includes musicals based on American history and traditional folk tales.

The Boulevard Arts Center

6011 S. Justine Street, Chicago, IL 60636
Phone: (773) 476-4900
E-mail: boulevard_arts@msn.com
Website: www.boulevardarts.ccts.cs.depaul.edu

Boulevard Arts Center is a multidiscipline, multicultural community arts center, grounded in the African American community, and serving all residents of Englewood, Back of the Yards, West Englewood, and adjoining south-southwest Chicago neighborhoods. It consists of three interconnected entities: the School of the Arts, the Cultural Center, and the Arts Business Development Center. Together these programs train about 1,500 community residents each year and influence another 100,000 through performances, exhibitions and public artworks. Youth work 20 hours per week for 8 weeks in July and August in groups of 10 to 12 under the guidance of a master artist to conceive, design, create, critique and present an artistic piece of public art to their community. Projects have included stone and wood sculptures, murals, photographic billboards, silk-screened posters and videos.

Boys and Girls Club of Broward County: The Creative Arts Unit

1401 NE 26th Street, Fort Lauderdale, FL 33305
Phone: (954) 537-1010
Fax: (954) 537-1070
Website: www.cominguptaller.org/profile/pr31theater.htm

The Creative Arts Unit, founded in 1994, serves kids ages 12–18. As an alternative to sports, games and computer programs, the Boys and Girls Club of

Broward County created a musical theater program for youth. Program auditions are held each January at participating Boys and Girls clubs, which are located in high-risk neighborhoods. Selections are made on the basis of interest and commitment as well as talent. For 14 weeks, the participants are transported to the Creative Arts Unit where they brainstorm themes for their production by drawing from issues in their own lives. Previous themes have dealt with inner-city violence, teen pregnancy and domestic abuse. At the end of each session the show is performed at a major theater.

California Youth Theatre
1605 Ivar Avenue, Hollywood, CA 90028
Phone: (323) 461-7300
Fax: (323) 461-7707
Website: www.cytivar.org

California Youth Theatre (CYT) is a nonprofit educational corporation founded in 1962. CYT's productions and workshops provide opportunities for young actors and technicians to develop their talents. In addition, there are community outreach programs which particularly target disaffected young people and those from disadvantaged areas.

The Migrant Education Performing Arts Workshop is a 3-week performing arts workshop for California migrant students in cooperation with the Los Angeles County School Migrants Education Program. Students from 13 Southern California school districts participate in a performing arts interdisciplinary study bringing together drama, music, and dance as well as contemporary folktales and other ethnic literature.

The W.R.I.T.E Program is a workshop devised to enhance the quality of life of underserved and at-risk youth through imaginative use of theatrical writing and puppetry to strengthen communication skills. The workshop is offered in cooperation with the Housing Authority of the County of Los Angeles.

Chautauqua Alcoholism and Substance Abuse Council
2-6 E. Second Street, Jamestown, NY 14701
Phone: (716) 664-3608
Fax: (716) 664-3661
Website: www.cominguptaller.org/profile/pr43visualarts.htm

The Chautauqua Alcoholism and Substance Abuse Council (CASAC) was founded in 1985 and is geared toward children ages 14–18. Two troupes of youth are recruited at the beginning of every school year to perform scenes about alcohol and substance abuse before student audiences throughout the county. Performers receive intensive theater training and then meet once a week for two and a half hours for rehearsal and discussion. Once a month, guest speakers and trainers meet with the youth to work on special issues such as AIDS and alcohol and substance abuse treatment. In the performance, youth and peers talk about substance abuse and alcoholism, thus creating an inter-active program between performers and audience members.

The Children's Theatre
2400 Third Avenue South, Minneapolis, MN 55404
Phone: (612) 874-0500
E-mail: info@childrenstheatre.org
Website: www.childrenstheatre.org

The development of original plays for young people is a priority for the Chil-dren's Theatre (CTC), founded in 1965. Touring brings CTC's best produc-tions, workshops, professional artists and teacher training materials to dozens of Upper Midwest communities. More than 58,000 people in 50 midwest com-munities saw the 2001-2002 tour. CTC's Theatre Arts Training (TAT) Program provides in-depth training that is not necessarily geared to train future actors, but to develop confident people who understand the power of working with others to achieve success. Each year, 800 students, ages 8 to 18 take part in this training. CTC offers programs in storytelling, acting, music, dance, and play-writing.

Children's Theatre of Charlotte
300 E. Seventh Street, Charlotte, NC 28202
Phone: (704) 973-2800
Website: www.ctcharlotte.org

The Children's Theatre of Charlotte offers multiple classes and programs for young people. The School of Theatre Training is for grades 4 through 12. The children meet once a week and the training culminates in a large performance. For the youngest students, preschool and primary classes are available which help the students develop self-confidence and socialization skills in a comfort-able setting, using story dramatization, music, art activities and movement.

Elementary classes, appropriate for both beginning and returning students in grades 2–5, encourage creative thinking by exploring character, voice, move-ment and improvisation. Middle school classes, for grades 6 through 8, build on the principles of character, voice, movement and improvisation, while incor-porating more advanced skills like script analysis and scene study.

For teens, the Children's Theatre of Charlotte offers the Ensemble Com-pany program, a free pre-professional training to high school actors who pos-sess evident theatrical talent, a strong commitment to theatre work, and a good sense of humor. Most of these young people will continue pursuing acting training in college and in their careers. The Drama for Healthy Living program presents plays about alcohol and substance abuse prevention and about relationship violence prevention. The plays are performed for all middle and high schools in the Charlotte-Mecklenburg School system.

The Children's Theatre of Cincinnati
Performance Venue: Fifth & Sycamore Streets, Cincinnati OH 45202
Administration Office: 2106 Florence Avenue, Cincinnati, OH 45206
Phone: (513) 569-8080
Fax: (513) 569-8084
Website: www.thechildrenstheatre.com

In 1924, the Junior League of Cincinnati developed a plan to introduce tri-state area children to the magic of theatre. Their plan evolved into the Children's Theatre, which incorporated in 1947. The theatre introduces young audiences in Ohio, Kentucky and Indiana to the performing arts through professional, fully staged productions that appeal to parents and educators, while teaching morals and values. Each season, they present three one-hour children's productions aimed at children ages 4 and up. Weekday performances are held for local school students, while weekend shows are for the public. Programs include the S.T.A.R. and Little S.T.A.R. programs. Presented in collaboration with the Northern Kentucky University Theatre Department, these summer programs offer professional classes and enrichment in musical theatre for 9 to 17 year olds. Also offered are ArtReach workshops which bring a professional teaching artist directly into the classroom and expands students' appreciation for music, drama and theater through lessons that are aligned with the curriculum.

Childsplay
PO Box 517, Tempe, AZ 85280
Phone: (480) 350-8101
E-mail: info@childsplayaz.org
Website: www.childsplayaz.com

Founded in 1977, Childsplay is a nonprofit, award-winning professional theatre company for young audiences and families. The program reaches young people through school field trips and school tours. Extensive support materials are given to teachers. These materials outline the plot of the play, discuss its context, suggest ways to prepare students for the theatrical experience and offer ideas for using the play for curriculum-related activities both before and after the production. They also offer teaching residencies at area schools. A typical company residency can last from three to five days, while an individual artist can visit a school for one day, one week or one month. The aim is to teach acting skills, which encourage students to use the body, voice and imagination to discover, create and communicate—skills that can be applied to any academic area.

Christian Community Theater
1545 Pioneer Way, El Cajon, CA 92020
Phone: (619) 588-0206
Fax: (619) 588-4384
Website: www.cyt.org

Christian Youth Theater (CYT) is a children's theater program offering after-school theater arts education for students ages 6 to 18. Since its founding in San Diego, California, in 1981, CYT has grown to be the largest youth theater program in the nation with programs across the country, providing training to thousands of students each year.

Every session (fall, winter and spring) CYT offers theater arts classes for children as an after-school activity. Each local branch conducts 3 ten-week sessions throughout the school year, teaching drama, voice, dance and a broad spectrum of specialty theatrical workshops as weekly two-hour classes. Enrolled students have the opportunity to work behind the scenes, or audition and perform on stage in a Broadway-style musical performed for the community. CYT has programs in Anderson, SC; Atlanta; Chicago; Denver; Kansas City; Phoenix; Richmond; San Diego; Spokane; Tucson and Vancouver.

City at Peace: Los Angeles
2210 Lincoln Blvd., Venice, CA 90291
Phone: (310) 313-6094
Fax: (310) 291-9455
E-mail: lianne@cpnational.org
Website: www.cpnational.org/la

City at Peace was launched in Los Angeles through the initiative of a local network of concerned parents, educators, artists, celebrities, business professionals and community organizers and is a chapter of the national organization headquartered in New York. They have served teenagers from over 60 schools and all walks of life from throughout Los Angeles County. City at Peace combines diversity, conflict resolution, leadership, social change and the arts in a replicable youth-led program. Participants also spend much of the year researching, designing, executing, and evaluating community action projects that address their concerns about issues affecting other young people and the communities in which they live.

City Hearts
PO Box 1314, Topanga, CA 90290
Phone: (310) 455-2898
E-mail: info@cityhearts.org
Website: www.cityhearts.org

City Hearts is a nonprofit organization which has offered free visual and per-forming arts classes to children in Los Angeles for over 20 years. The sched-ule serves more than 500 children per week, ages 5 to 18, with free after-school and weekend classes in theater, dance, music, photography, circus arts and Shakespeare. Their Summer Camp of the Arts reaches 200 students ages 5 to 10. See a detailed report in chapter 7.

CityKids
57 Leonard Street, New York, NY 10013
Phone: (212) 925-3320
Fax: (212) 925-0128
E-mail: information@citykids.com
Website: www.citykids.com

CityKids, working with 650 teens each year, aims to be youth-driven, youth-relevant, and evidence based, and to have multidimensional perspectives and effective programs.

The CityKids Repertory Company (Rep) is the performing arts project that takes ideas and issues from all of CityKids' programs and transforms them into original, youth-led, issue-based drama, music, song and dance performances. Rep performs at venues ranging from local schools and community centers to Madison Square Garden and the White House. The CityKids BridgeBuilder Initiative (BBI) grew out of young people's reaction to the events of 9/11. They wanted to create a safe space like CityKids at their schools where they could set the agenda and talk with peers and adults rather than being "talked at" by adults. Since its inception, BBI has grown into one of CityKids' core programs, offering CityKids' arts-based leadership training approach in 10 public high schools across New York City.

CLIMB Theatre
6415 Carmen Avenue E., Inver Grove Heights, MN 55076
Phone: (800) 767-9660
Fax: (651) 453-9274
E-mail: mail@climb.org
Website: www.climb.org

CLIMB (Creative Learning Ideas for Mind and Body) Theatre was founded in 1975 as a nonprofit theatre for persons with mental and physical disabilities. By 1980, CLIMB had extended these drama classes to children without dis-abilities. CLIMB produces original plays and classes for grades K-12 on topics like bullying prevention, environmental protection, acceptance of differences, substance abuse prevention, respect, the environment, violence prevention, self-control, and friendship. Last year it performed over 1,000 plays and taught over 5,000 classes reaching over 330,000 young people.

Columbus Children's Theatre

512 North Park Street, Columbus, OH 43215
Administration Office: 372 W. Nationwide Blvd., Columbus, OH 43215
Phone: (614) 224-6673
E-mail: CCTboxoffice@sbcglobal.net
Website: www.colschildrenstheatre.org

Founded in 1963 as the Columbus Junior Theatre of the Arts, the Columbus Children's Theatre (CCT) is dedicated to educating and involving greater Columbus area young people of all races, backgrounds and potential in all facets of the theatre arts. CCT touches the lives of over 100,000 children each year through its three major programs: the Children's Theatre Series, a season of live theatre performed for family audiences; the Theatre Academy, classes in acting, singing, college prep (auditioning, movement, monologues), dancing and stage combat; and the Professional Touring Company, which has worked since 1972 with local schools to reach their theatre/arts benchmarks. Many of the Professional Touring Company productions are interactive and use audience participation. The company reaches students in 65 of Ohio's 88 counties.

Concord Youth Theatre

358 Baker Avenue, PO Box 652, Concord, MA 01742
Phone: (978) 371-1482
Fax: (978) 371-1540
E-mail: info@concordyouththeatre.org
Website: www.concordyouththeatre.org

Concord Youth Theatre (CYT) founded in 1976 as Act/Tunes, is committed to making high-quality live theatre accessible, relevant, and memorable for young people and their families. Through performance company productions, theatre arts classes, summer workshops, and guest artist performances, CYT brings live theatre to hundreds of participants and audience members each season. CYT offers many classes for ages 5 to 12, including broadway dance, improv, storytelling, voice, and musical theatre. CYT also has two performance companies. Mainstage Performance Company is a traditional mainstage company that offers young people the opportunity to participate in a live theatre performance. "Not So Mainstage" Performance Company is a new CYT production company that offers the same educational and creative opportunities but has a rehearsal and performance schedule that is slightly less rigorous.

Cornerstone Theatre: Community Collaborations

708 Traction Avenue, Los Angeles, CA 90013
Phone: (213) 613-1700
Fax: (213) 613-1714

Website: www.wallacefoundation.org/KnowledgeCenter/Conerstone
Collaborations.htm

Cornerstone founded Community Collaborations in 1986 to serve youth ages
6 to 21. Using a 3 to 4 month-long residency format, Cornerstone collaborates
with a community host organization to lead young residents from creation to
production. Those who want to join the program must commit to rehearsing
5 to 7 days a week after an initial 3-day training session. Participants can study
any aspect of theater, including acting, directing, producing or set design.

Council of Fort Worth and Tarrant County: Neighborhood Arts Program
505 Main Street, Suite 200, Fort Worth, TX 76102
Phone: (817) 870-2564
Fax: (817) 335-6508
Website: www.cominguptaller.org/profile/pr18multi.htm

The Neighborhood Arts Program was founded in 1991 to serve kids ages 5 to
18. The predominantly Mexican-American Northside and the African-American Eastside low-income neighborhoods of Fort Worth are home to two of
the city's flourishing and culturally rich arts programs: the Arts Council of Fort
Worth and Tarrant County's multidisciplinary Ballet Folklorico Azteca and
Jubilee Theatre. Ballet Folklorico Azteca stages Mexican folk dance performances based on weekly year-round classes. Jubilee Theatre participants, meeting once a week after school, create original musicals and adaptations of classics.
Other dance classes and the Mondo Drum Ensemble also are offered.

Creative Arts Team: Youth Theatre Program
101 West 31st Street, Sixth Floor, New York, NY 10001
Phone: (212) 652-2800
Fax: (212) 652-2809
Website: www1.cuny.edu/portal_ur/content/academic_affairs/cat/programs/
youth_theatre.html

Since its founding in 1995, the Creative Arts Team (CAT) Youth Theatre has
presented original shows, all devised or written by the company and performed
at a wide variety of events including conferences and festivals in Chicago and
London and for the United Nations. The Creative Arts Team Youth Theatre
companies are divided into two age groups: middle school and high school.
Each company consists of members from the five boroughs of New York City,
who meet weekly after school from September through May to explore their
ideas and creativity and to build their skills through theatre games and exercises,
improvisations and scene work, rehearsal, critical reflection and group discussion. Issues explored in the middle school program are peer/family pressure,

self-esteem, violence prevention, cultural tolerance, substance abuse, and literacy skills. Issues explored in the high school program include health and wellness, HIV/AIDS education, violence prevention, antiharassment, prejudice and racism, self-esteem, peer/family pressure, substance abuse, family conflict, and anger management.

Crescent City Lights Youth Theater
305 Baronne Street, Suite 302, New Orleans, LA 70112
Phone: (504) 598-3800
Fax: (504) 598-3808
Website: www.summerstages.org

Crescent City Lights Youth Theater has provided professional theater experiences for young people—ages 7 to 17—in the Greater New Orleans area since its founding in 1993. The theater has staged 24 musicals and more than 600 young people have participated in the school year classes and summer productions. As of October 2006, it was looking for suitable space to hold classes in New Orleans. Hurricane Katrina severely damaged all of the facilities which the theater had used in prior years. As new spaces are renovated, the theater will revive classes. Despite the damage from Hurricane Katrina, the group continues to produce theatre. They will perform *The Dream* on Royal Street in January 2007. The program is tuition based. Tuition for cast members is $325.

Crossroads Theatre for Youth
PO Box 1715, Pago Pago, American Samoa 96799
Phone: (684) 699-5313
Fax: (684) 699-5318
E-mail: info@ctyweb.org
Website: www.ctyweb.org

Crossroads Theatre for Youth (CTY) is a nonprofit, faith-based organization established in 2002. CTY was created by young people who decided to respond to social ills that plagued their community. With a 3-year grant from the U.S Administration for Native Americans, CTY aims to educate and create awareness of youth and social issues by developing original work and performing theatre and drama education programs that make a lasting positive difference in the lives of children, families and educators in American Samoa. In less than 2 years, CTY has played to more that 15,000 children and family members in American Samoa.

Drama Divas
2781 24th Street, San Francisco, CA 94110
Phone: (415) 641-7657
Website: www.cominguptaller.org/profile/pr34theater.htm

Drama Divas was founded in 1991 and primarily serves kids ages 15–21. For 3 to 6 hours every week, a group of 15–20 gay and lesbian youth, most of whom are Latino, meet at Brava!, a nonprofit arts organization, to talk, write and act. Once a year, the participants put on a performance at Brava!'s theater. Performances are based on real-life experiences and deal with such issues as relationships, gender, class, family and race. The youth learn not only about acting, but also about lighting, stage design and theater direction and production.

Elizabeth Peabody House: The Theatre Cooperative
277 Broadway, Somerville, MA 02145
Phone: (617) 623-5510
Fax: (617) 623-5515
E-mail: info@elizabethpeabodyhouse.org
Website: www.elizabethpeabodyhouse.org/en/?page=main/programs/theater

Elizabeth Peabody House (EPH) was founded in 1896 in Boston as a memorial to Elizabeth Palmer Peabody, whose dedication to children led to the founding of the first kindergarten system in America. EPH provides educational, social and recreational programs for immigrants and community residents, including citizenship classes and social work services. The house is a center for cultural events, educational groups, and sports activities. The Theatre Cooperative allows children ages 9 to 12 to express themselves through theater games, scene study and monologues. The children also have the opportunity to write and develop their own stories and perform original works in front of an audience. There are three 10-week sessions available at the cost of $50 per session.

ENACT
80 Eighth Avenue, Suite 1102, New York, NY 10011
Phone: (212) 741-6591
Fax: (212) 741-6594
E-mail: info@enact.org
Website: www.enact.org

ENACT is a nonprofit teaching organization that empowers New York City students of all ages and skill levels by helping them understand and manage their own emotional growth through creative drama techniques. The ENACT team, made up of teaching artists—all professional actors with numerous stage, screen and television credits—educators, social workers, and drama therapists work collaboratively with teachers and administrators at schools all over the city to show students how to identify and remove the barriers that prevent them from learning. ENACT is an innovative drama-in-education company which teaches children and young adults how to use the basic techniques of creative drama to identify healthier options for expressing their feelings and opinions, and for dealing, in a positive way, with their own anger and fears. Since its founding in 1987, ENACT has worked with more than 100,000 students in schools within all 10 New York City Department of Education (DOE) school regions, and in all five boroughs of the city.

52nd Street Project
500 W. 52nd Street, Second Floor, New York, NY 10019
Phone: (212) 333-5252
E-mail: info@52project.org
Website: www.52project.org

The 52nd Street Project, founded in 1981 by actor/playwright Willie Reale, is dedicated to the creation and production of new plays for, and often by, kids between the ages of nine and 18 who reside in the Hell's Kitchen neighborhood in New York City. The project creates over 80 new plays and serves over 115 children every year. Past artist-volunteers include Billy Crudup, Edie Falco, Malcolm Gets, Spalding Gray, Dana Ivey, Susan Kim, Henry Krieger, Robert Sean Leonard, Natasha Lyonne, Roma Maffia, Jesse L. Martin, James McDaniel, Paul McCrane, Frances McDormand, James Naughton, Oliver Platt, Martha Plimpton, Theresa Rebeck, Jose Rivera, Lili Taylor, Pam Tyson, Wendy Wasserstein, Frank Wood and hundreds of others. The project has 6 playwriting/acting programs: Playmaking, Replay, One on One's, Two on Two's, Playback, and the Teen Project. All programs are free to the kids of the neighborhood and all of the project's productions are free to the general public.

Fort Lauderdale Children's Theatre
516 NE 13th Street, Fort Lauderdale, FL 33304
Phone: (954) 763-6882
E-mail: info@FLCTStar.org
Website: www.flct.org

The Fort Lauderdale Children's Theatre (FLCT) is a nonprofit, developmental center for the theatre arts founded in 1952 for the purpose of providing programs and services to youth and adults. FLCT classes are based on creative dramatics principles designed to provide formal theatre training and to develop self-esteem, discipline, and creativity for children, youth, adults, and senior citizens. They offer ongoing classes in drama and music theatre at two Broward County locations. Classes are offered for preschool to high school children and include costume, props, scenery, character development, performance, playwriting, improv, monologue work and text analysis.

Free Arts Minnesota
400 First Avenue North, Suite 518, Minneapolis, MN 55401
Phone: (612) 824-ARTS (2787)
Website: www.freeartsminnesota.org

Free Arts Minnesota began as a project of the Junior League of Minneapolis and is dedicated to bringing the healing powers of artistic expression into the lives of abused, neglected and at-risk children and their families in residential treatment centers, battered women's shelters, and therapeutic preschools. Believing that artistic expression is a successful way to externalize emotions and gain self-confidence, Free Arts uses drama, writing, music, painting, sculpting, and photography to increase children's self-esteem and build character by unlocking the imagination.

Free Street Programs

1419 W. Blackhawk, Chicago, IL 60622
Phone: (773) 772-7248
E-mail: gogogo@freestreet.org
Website: www.freestreet.org

Free Street began employing teens in jobs training summer theater creation and performance ensembles in 1991. Today, over 50 teens are employed at Free Street through After School Matters, a City of Chicago initiative, to create 3 original theater pieces and perform free shows for children at 45 Chicago Park District daycamps throughout the city. Free Street offers 5 different workshops: arts literacy residencies in public schools, where artists teach focused creativity, ensemble cooperation, and writing in elementary schools; act/write workshops, that teach, in partnership with Columbia College's Fiction Writing Department, sixth, seventh and eighth graders a creative process that leads to the publication of a book; free art classes, that offer visual art and creative writing for 5 to 11 year olds; free hip-hop classes, that teach rhythmic speaking and free-flowing writing to 8 to 11 year olds and teens; and free theater classes, which introduce the MadJoy acting process to teens.

Gestic Theatre Company

Minneapolis, MN
Phone: (612) 724-4514
E-mail: info@gtcdrama.com
Website: www.gestictheatre.com

Since 1995 the Gestic Theatre Company (GTC) Dramatic Dialogues has offered a series of innovative, interactive, theatrical programs on issues of importance to students. These programs allow students to talk back, engaging them directly in lively dialogues about date rape, diversity, or substance abuse. Students express their views not only to the performers, but also to each other. GTC offers 4 programs: diversity, sexual assault, substance abuse, and multi-issue. IssueActive Workshops take the process of Intervention Theatre further than is possible in a 90-minute performance. In these workshops the participants themselves determine the content. Through role-playing, participants collectively analyze these experiences and actively test new approaches to solving the problems revealed in the process. Students gain a deeper understanding of the issues that affect them and an appreciation of their own role in creating solutions.

The Helen Hayes Youth Theatre
PO Box 395, New City, NY 10956
Phone: (845) 826-2049
E-mail: helenhayesyt@aol.com
Website: www.helenhayesyouththeatre.com

The Helen Hayes Youth Theatre offers year-round theater classes and performance opportunities for young actors ages 5 to 18 from all levels of theater experience. The programs take place in Nyack, as well as in Westchester County, New York. Its mission is to provide rigorous training in the theater arts while also offering training in life skills such as public speaking, improved focus, social skills, self-confidence and team building under the watchful eye of a staff of highly committed theater professionals. Programs include Summer Stock and 101 Dalmatians. Summer Stock is for young performers ages 8 to 15. During this intensive 2-week program, each day is spent rehearsing a show in order to perform a one-hour long, full stage production including choreography, vocal direction, staging and character development as well as costumes, lights and scenic design. All levels of performance are welcome. Each session runs for two weeks with performances on the final Friday and Saturday evening. Tuition is $700 for the program. The 101 Dalmatians program is for 5 to 7 year olds. This half-day program consists of song, dance, games and crafts with the goal of presenting a 20-minute presentation (in costume) on the Saturday following the final class.

Honolulu Theatre for Youth
229 Queen Emma Square, Honolulu HI 96813
Phone: (808) 839-9885
E-mail: htymail@gmail.com
Website: www.htyweb.org

Every year Honolulu Theatre for Youth's (HTY) professional company presents a full season of plays for children from preschool to high school age. HTY presents plays at several theatres in Honolulu and neighboring islands. For more than 20 years, HTY drama specialists have worked with teachers to help extend student achievement in a range of subjects, from language arts to social studies to science, even math, in ways that significantly involve and engage every student. After school and weekend drama programs are also offered. Currently, the theatre is reassessing all programs, such as Taco, Imagine, the Pacific Young Playwrights and Stage One and Stage Two. No programs are planned for the 2006-2007 school year, but the theatre hopes to offer programs for 2007-2008.

InterAct Story Theatre

204 Stonegate Drive, Silver Spring, MD 20905
Phone: (301) 879-9305
Website: www.interactstory.com

Since their inception in 1981, InterAct has remained constant with their mission: to help students and teachers unlock and maximize their creative potential. Creative Kids is InterAct's after-school theatre program, a series of literature-based drama classes. In each class, a teaching artist leads a group of students to explore and enact a specially selected children's book. Classes can be scheduled midday, after school, or during a summer camp. The program is available in Washington, D.C., Baltimore, Northern Virginia, and surrounding areas only. InterAct also offers programs for elementary, middle, and high school aged kids in a variety of subjects, including acting, music, dance, team building, tolerance, and parent-child relationships.

The Laguna Playhouse

606 Laguna Canyon Road, Laguna Beach, CA 92651
Phone: (949) 497-ARTS
Website: www.lagunaplayhouse.com

The Laguna Playhouse Youth Theatre offers plays primarily aimed at children of elementary and middle school age. These may be existing plays or musicals based upon well-known, popular books or stories, but sometimes they may be new stage adaptations. The productions are directed and designed by theatre professionals and fully mounted with the playhouse's technical resources. The cast and staff for each production are drawn principally from the Youth Conservatory Program which offers talented youngsters a small-enrollment, high-level program of instruction in theatre skills, taught by theatre professionals. The curriculum encompasses acting, theatre production and dramatic literature. The Youth Conservatory is divided into four levels: Conservatory 1 and 2 (for ages 10–13, intermediate and advanced) and Repertory 1 and 2 (for ages 14–18, intermediate and advanced). Nonacting assignments include stage management, lighting and sound operation, box office and house management, props-construction and stagehand work.

Lexington Youth Theatre

Lexington, NC 27292
E-mail: LYTactingbug@aol.com
Website: www.lexingtonyouththeatre.com

Founded in 1985, the Lexington Youth Theatre (LYT) is a nonprofit community organization dedicated to the presentation of live theater performances by and for Davidson County's young people. The group is unique in choosing a cast made up entirely of students from kindergarten through 12th grade for each of its performances. Not only the cast, but also backstage crews and technical assistants are school-age children.

In addition to learning lines, music and stage movements, LYT actors must keep up with schoolwork and other commitments. For this reason, rehearsals are generally scheduled for weekday afternoons between 4 and 6 P.M. Study areas are provided for students while they wait for their scenes or musical numbers to be rehearsed. The group provides an avenue for exploration of many art forms including literature, music, dance and visual design. For more technically minded students, the inner workings of the theater provide a specialized environment for mechanical and electronic exploration through stagecraft, special effects, lighting and sound design.

Los Angeles Shakespeare Festival: Will Power to Youth
1238 W. First Street, Los Angeles, CA 90026
Phone: (213) 481-2273
Fax: (213) 975-9833
E-mail: ben@shakespearefestivalla.org
Website: www.shakespearefestivalla.org/wpy

The L.A. Shakespeare Festival offers multiple programs. Will Power to Youth is an employment program that hires 20 to 30 young people each 7-week session. Participants work with professional artists and human relations facilitators to create an adaptation of a Shakespeare play that reflects their thoughts and feelings about Shakespeare's themes. Will to Lead is a youth leadership and development program offered to Will Power to Youth alumni as well as members of the larger community. The program includes academic tutoring, theatre classes, counseling, and field trips. Will to Work places motivated young people into highly structured internships with the Shakespeare Festival, as well as in positions at other theatres in the local area. Will Power to Schools is an accredited in-service teacher training process that reinvigorates the teaching and learning of Shakespeare in the schools. Youth Arts Professionals Institute gives artists who create collaborative work with youth the opportunity to examine their practice as both teachers and artists. Participating artists gain skills in conflict resolution and community building as well as designing and leading workshops.

Marsh Youth Theatre
1062 Valencia Street, San Francisco, CA 94110
Phone: (415) 641-0235
Fax: (415) 643-9070
E-mail: myt@themarsh.org
Website: www.themarsh.org/myt.html

Marsh Youth Theatre (MYT), founded in 1989, provides youth ages 4 to 15 with a high-quality theater arts experience, integrating music, dance, drama, stage-craft and performance into one holistic program. Open to all young performers without audition and regardless of financial limitations, MYT exposes children to the world of multicultural arts by working with a diverse group of professional performing faculty. MYT's classes and performances take place in the Marsh's 3,000-square-foot dance/performance studio and theater. Classes, usually 8-weeks long, are offered for kids 5 to 12. Topics include hip-hop dance, storytelling, ensemble work, and movement. There is also a class for home-schooled kids only, called Children's Natural Wonders, which explores visual and performance art. MainStage Performance Ensemble is a program for fifth through ninth graders who are ready to engage in and commit to the challenges and rewards of a full-scale theater performance workshop.

The Masque Youth Theatre and School
14 Fourth Street SW, Rochester, MN 55902
Phone: (507) 287-0704
E-mail: go2masque@aol.com
Website: www.masque.org

At the Masque Youth Theatre and School, students perform in shows, teach classes, serve on the play selection committee, hold two positions on the Masque Board of Directors, serve as assistant directors and stage managers on productions, and at times even write and direct shows. They are also involved in lighting and sound control, building sets, and constructing costumes. Since its beginning, the Masque has maintained three troupes: the Masque Storytellers, the Masque Mimes, and the Masque Puppeteers. These troupes meet every Tuesday for an hour and a half, year-round, calling extra rehearsals if necessary. The troupes tour all over southeastern Minnesota. The Masque offers classes for ages 5 to 18. Classes for younger students focus on creative play through movement, puppetry, mask and creative dramatics. Classes for older students focus on mime, movement, improv, and acting.

Michigan Youth Theater
2122 Houser, Holly, MI 48442
Website: www.michiganyouththeater.org

Founded in January 2000, the Michigan Youth Theater is a nonprofit, youth-centered performing arts organization whose mission is to develop leadership, teamwork, and communications skills in youth ages 12 to 19 through theater production experiences while providing professional-quality, classics-based live theater experiences and education. Michigan Youth Theater is currently trying to start a traveling troupe. It is looking for interested 12–19 year olds who are willing to learn the skills to make a great crew. They will build the team with interested members who have participated in previous productions and workshops. Performances will be scheduled at libraries, schools, and community venues.

Milwaukee Repertory Theatre: TEENWORKS
108 E. Wells Street, Milwaukee, WI 53202
Phone: (414) 224-1761
Fax: (414) 224-9097
Website: www.cominguptaller.org/profile/pr137theater.htm

In 6 weeks of daily summer meetings, teens in the TEENWORKS program learn basic theater techniques and develop an original theater piece on a socially relevant issue. Working with a variety of Milwaukee Repertory professionals, including artists, administrators and craftspeople, teens polish their theater pieces and perform at the Stiemke Theater or the Powerhouse Theater. When the new school year begins, the group writes newsletters and prepares for future summer sessions by participating in biweekly theater workshops. Teens also have the opportunity to assist in the daily operations of the Milwaukee Repertory Theater as general work assistants.

Missoula Children's Theatre
200 N. Adams Street, Missoula, MT 59802
Phone: (406) 728-1911
Fax: (406) 721-0637
Website: www.mctinc.org

The mission of the Missoula Children's Theatre (MCT) is the development of life skills in children through participation in the performing arts. MCT provides a week-long residency "starring" 50–60 local students in a full-scale musical. MCT has been touring for more than 30 years, visiting nearly 1,100 communities annually in all 50 states, 4 Canadian provinces and overseas. Their team of two professional tour actor/directors arrives in a town with scenery, costumes, props, make-up and basic lighting, everything it takes to put on a play—except, a cast. This week-long residency begins with an open-group audition and culminates in two public performances. Children in grades K–12 are cast and rehearsed throughout the week, learning lines, songs and choreography to perform as an ensemble in producing a full-length musical. All shows are original adaptations of children's stories and fairytales.

Missouri River Youth Theatre
Phone: (660) 882-6076
E-mail: mrytheatre@yahoo.com
Website: www.mryt.org

Established in April of 2003, the Missouri River Youth Theatre (MRYT) aims to provide wholesome alternatives for self-expression and productivity by teaching the basics in theatre and exposing youth to acting and multifaceted aspects of theatrical production, All those under the age of 18 are welcome to come and be a part of the workshops and to try out for productions. Children must be old enough to get on and off stage happily and unaccompanied before they are enrolled in workshops or come to auditions. MRYT will work with community youth groups who contact them in advance to plan a production as an educational experience for their group.

Mosaic Youth Theatre of Detroit
610 Antoinette Street, Detroit, MI 48202
Phone: (313) 872-6910
Fax: (313) 872-6920
Website: www.mosaicdetroit.org

Mosaic, founded in 1992, now serves over 750 area youths each year. The Youth Ensemble is the core program, providing nine months of free intensive training in acting, vocal music and technical theatre. Ensemble members work with their directors and professional actors, writers, musicians and designers. Rehearsing after school and on weekends, the students are involved in every element of production, which includes writing the play, composing the music, and designing and building the set. Each year a full season of plays and concerts are presented to local audiences More than 100 young people, ages 12–18, are chosen for the ensemble through auditions held annually in October. The Mosaic Intermediate Training Program is designed as an intensive seven-month training program, modeled on the main Ensemble Program, where 11–16 year olds can acquire the necessary skills and develop the professionalism and maturity that are a prerequisite for Mosaic's main Ensemble Program. The most accomplished and experienced young artists participate in the Next Stage Company. These actors, singers and technicians are a professional company of paid artists, who begin their "next stage" as theatre professionals touring throughout metropolitan Detroit.

Motor City Youth Theatre
27555 Grantland, Livonia, MI 48150
Phone: (313) 535-8962
Website: www.mcyt.org

Motor City Youth Theatre trains a youth population ages five through 18, many of whose recreational needs are not often met through sports alone. They offer all children, not just the wealthy or the gifted, a place where they can improve their speaking, reading, dance, music artistic, and life skills while expressing themselves and improving their self-concept of knowledge and theatre. Motor

City Youth Theatre has worked in schools, churches, halls and even in a coffee shop. Motor City Youth Theatre offers workshops that are normally 5-weeks long and cost $25. Classes include acting, dance, character development, diction, and improv.

The Music Theatre Workshop

7359 N. Greenview Avenue, Chicago, IL 60626
Phone: (773) 973-7266
Fax: (773) 973-7077
E-mail: mtw@mtwchicago.org
Website: www.mtwchicago.org

Since 1984, the Music Theatre Workshop (MTW) has been a nonprofit performing arts organization serving at-risk youth in the Chicago region. Original shows created by the youth themselves explore historical and cultural understanding, diversity, and human relations, along with the problems of substance abuse, dysfunctional families, teen parenting, guns and gangs, and the causes, experiences, and effects of violence.

In playwriting/performance workshops participants working as a group to research, structure and write a short to full-length musical play. MTW has used this process with diverse groups of young people at the Cook County Juvenile Temporary Detention Center, the Field Museum, the University of Chicago Children's Hospital, and Chicago parks and schools.

New England Youth Theatre

PO Box 6394, Brattleboro, VT 05302
Phone: (802) 246-NEYT (6398)
Website: www.neyt.org

Founded in 1998, the New England Youth Theatre (NEYT) offers quality theatre training and performances to neighboring communities in Vermont, New Hampshire and Massachusetts, operating year-round and producing eight to ten plays and/or musicals per season. Spring brings student-directed and original works. NEYT alumni return to direct and perform in June. Summer brings performances by the Circus, Melodrama, Theatre Adventure and Shakespeare camps. NEYT offers several classes for ages 5 to 16 including movement, fundamentals of acting, improv, creating a character, musical theatre, playwriting and audition techniques.

The New Voice Ensemble

39 Conestoga Road, Malvern, PA 19355
Phone: (610) 647-1900
Website: www.peopleslight.org/2005-2006/24c-ed-NV.html

Begun in 1990, the New Voice Ensemble offers an intensive, year-round program originally focused on collaboration between People's Light artists and young people from the city of Chester. New Voice's mission is to make pieces that explore community and civic issues through theatre. In a world that is increasingly and intensely divided on a range of social concerns, it wants to encourage artists and students to gain new understanding of these issues through a process of dialogue, reflection and artistic exploration.

Oddfellows Playhouse Youth Theater

128 Washington Street, Middletown, CT 06457
Phone: (860) 347-6143
E-mail: oddfellows@wesleyan.edu
Website: www.oddfellows.org

Founded in 1975 by a small group of Wesleyan University students as a theater arts organization designed to include children from all backgrounds, Oddfellows Playhouse Youth Theater annually serves approximately 2,500 young people, ages 6 to 20, in a broad spectrum of theater arts activities. Oddfellows' core program consists of 3 eight-week terms from September to May of tuition-based performing arts classes and mainstage and mini-productions. A Neighborhood Troupes program offers free after-school weekly performing arts classes throughout the school year for 175 at-risk youth from Middletown and Portland's lowest income areas. A five-week summer Children's Circus teaches circus skills to over 200 Middletown youngsters, leading to a spectacular outdoor public performance. "Kids on the Block" is a disability awareness program for all fourth graders in Middletown and surrounding schools. Central to the Playhouse program is addressing racial, ethnic, and cultural isolation.

Open Doors

New York, NY
Phone: (212) 221-0885 ext. 202
Website: www.tdf.org

Open Doors is a theatre arts mentoring program for high school students founded in 1998 by the late playwright Wendy Wasserstein. Dedicated theatre professionals each mentor a group of eight underserved high school students, who have had no exposure to the theatre, for an entire school year. They attend six Broadway and/or off–Broadway productions, followed by lively, 90-minute post-performance discussions. The students keep a journal to document, and expand and reflect on their experiences.

Open Stages—The Urban Ensemble

150 W. 65th Street, New York, NY 10023
Phone: (212) 362-7600

Fax: (212) 873-0761
Website: www.cominguptaller.org/profile/pr125theater.htm

The Urban Ensemble provides a series of multigenerational theater workshops on cultural and social differences. The workshops are designed to engage New York residents whose interests normally are not met by mainstream cultural institutions: public housing residents, teen parents, juvenile delinquents and homeless families. About one-half of the participants are youth, ages 16–21. The program uses theater to explore issues of violence, safety and identity. Students from New York University's Tisch School and AmeriCorps volunteers facilitate weekly, 3-hour workshops that include writing exercises, theater games, photography and discussions.

Pennsylvania Youth Theatre

25 W. Third Street, Bethlehem, PA 18015
Phone: (610) 332-1400
Fax: (610) 332-1405
E-mail: office@123pyt.org
Website: www.123pyt.org

Founded in 1985 with the mission of educating, entertaining, and enriching the lives of young people and their families through theatre, Pennsylvania Youth Theatre's (PYT) Performing Arts School maintains a comprehensive after-school performing arts curriculum, which includes creative drama, acting, dance and voice instruction. It offers 55 performing arts classes, attended yearly by over 400 students ages 4 through 18. PYT's summer program is enjoyed by approximately 200 young people each summer, and includes a musical theatre day camp, an acting intensive program for teens, and weeklong introductory classes. The literature-based Mainstage productions are professionally staged shows that feature children in primary roles and are cast age appropriately, thus kids play kids and grown-ups play grown-ups. This enables PYT students to work alongside professional adult actors. The Pegasus Project serves community children and theatergoers who have a wide range of physical challenges. Children with physical, emotional, and cognitive challenges receive full scholarships.

Performing for Los Angeles Youth

601 W. Temple Street, Los Angeles, CA 90012
Phone: (213) 972-7587
Website: www.CenterTheatreGroup.org

Founded in 1971, Performing for Los Angeles Youth (PLAY) reaches over 35,000 students each year through a comprehensive arts education and theatre creation initiative. Programs include the Young Artist Theatre Series, in which students attend performances and master classes and workshops with professional theatre artists; and the Young Audiences Program, which introduces kids to theatre. Prior to attending a performance, teachers receive printed journals and teaching instruction in order to familiarize them with themes and elements specific to the show. Ready, Set, PLAY is an after-school program which introduces elementary school kids to basic performance skills including acting, movement, voice, improvisation, storytelling and design. Over 22 sessions, kids adapt a book into a play and design, construct and perform their creation. In the "Speak to Me" Artist Residency high school students spend a year developing and presenting an original play. Artist-mentors lead students through the processes of set, lighting, costume, sound, acting and dramaturgy.

Periwinkle National Theatre

456 Broadway, Suite 3, Monticello, NY 12701
Phone: (800) 888-8271
Fax: (845) 794-0304
E-mail: contact@periwinkle.org
Website: www.periwinkle.org

Founded in 1963, Periwinkle National Theatre is the country's oldest nonprofit educational touring theatre company. Periwinkle's work was one of the forerunners in the arts in education movement in America. It has performed in 38 states, Guam, Canada, the Virgin Islands and Egypt. Periwinkle creates theatre on social issues such as drug prevention, bullying, violence, alcoholism, abduction prevention, literacy, social skills, and self-esteem. In addition to writing and performing in-school workshops, there is an after-school workshop that places an increased emphasis on costume, scenery, and prop design. Students collaborate with teaching artists to create an original theatrical production in which they become playwrights, actors, designers, directors, and publicists.

Phantom Projects Educational Theatre Group

PO Box 250, La Mirada, CA 90637
Phone: (562) 902-0119
E-mail: phantomprojects@prodigy.net
Website: www.phantomprojects.com

Phantom Projects Educational Theatre Group produces theatre specifically for teen audiences. Mixing adult and teen performers, it brings professional quality shows to the 1,251-seat La Mirada Theatre for the Performing Arts. Phantom Projects believes that teens teaching teens has the most impact when presenting a "message-based" show. Therefore, all touring shows feature all-teen casts with not only a willingness to perform a character while on stage, but also a willingness to come out after the show and tell their own stories, about their own lives, and about their own mistakes and triumphs. Phantom Projects plays focus on teen pregnancy prevention, prejudice and tolerance, drug and alcohol prevention, self-image, and other social and personal issues.

Pied Piper Theatre
9419 Battle Street, Manassa, VA 20110
Phone: (703) 330-2787
E-mail: info@center-for-the-arts.com
Website: www.center-for-the-arts.com/pied_piper_Theatre.htm

Pied Piper Theatre is an immersion theater arts experience for young people, integrating all aspects of theater production and offering students the opportunity to learn under the supervision of a professional director, choreographer, music director, costume designer and set and lighting designer. Students, who audition for each production, act, sing and dance while others are trained in the technical aspects of theater, such as learning to apply make-up, build sets, and run the light board and sound equipment. Older students may serve as assistant directors and producers. Student musicians provide orchestral accompaniment for the productions.

Pittsburgh Playback Theatre: Hosanna House
2770 Fernwald Road, Pittsburgh, PA 15217
Phone: (412) 521-0444
E-mail: roni@pittsburghplaybacktheatre.org
Website: www.pittsburghplaybacktheatre.org

Pittsburgh Playback Theatre was founded in 1986. Its traveling theater troupe visits various sites, including Hosanna House in Wilkensburg, Pennsylvania, where professional actors are in their fourth year of engaging neighborhood teenagers as playwrights and actors. The interactive theater process allows participants to dramatize issues such as peer pressure, drug and alcohol abuse, dysfunctional families and sexuality. The kids meet once a week for 2 to 3 hours, become storytellers and learn to do "playback" by acting out each other's stories. Training is followed by preparation of a performance for schools and community groups.

Play by Play
Phone: (212) 221-0885 ext. 202
Website: www.tdf.org

Play by Play is New York City's only theatre newsletter written by and for high school students. It is issued quarterly and is distributed free of charge to students, teachers and the theatre community. The circulation is currently at 35,000 and reaches 144 high schools.

Playhouse on the Square

51 S. Cooper, Memphis, TN 38104
Phone: (901) 728-5631
E-mail: info@playhouseonthesquare.org
Website: www.playhouseonthesquare.org

Founded in 1985, Playhouse on the Square's Theatre for Youth Program now serves close to 25,000 young people every year in Memphis, Shelby County, and beyond, from preschoolers to young adults, either as audience members or as active participants. The Summer Youth Theatre Conservatory is open to any student interested in theatre regardless of experience. All of the courses are taught by professional artists. Classes are offered for kids ages 5 to 17 and focus on acting, movement, voice, music and dance. The After School Acting Program (ASAP) has grown to include sites throughout Memphis and the surrounding area, including Mississippi and Arkansas. ASAP is for children ages 7 to 12. Instruction in the elements of acting, improvisation, movement, music, and design are taught through a Style of Theatre.

Project Self-Discovery

899 Logan, Suite 207, Denver, CO 80203
Phone: (303) 830-8500
Fax: (303) 830-8420
E-mail: cleodance@aol.com
Website: www.cleoparkerdance.org/cleo_2000/html/programs_psd.cfm

Project Self-Discovery, in operation since 1992 and a subsidiary program of Cleo Parker Robinson Dance, has taken an active role in developing community-wide plans to provide pro-social alternatives to drugs, crime and violence for youths throughout the Denver metropolitan area.

All activities are designed to encourage participants to recognize their own self-worth and growth potential while actively practicing respect for the values of others. Thus, it is a project of "self-discovery." This model program provides high-risk students with the arts as an alternative to substance abuse and peer pressure.

The Rainbow Company Youth Theatre

821 Las Vegas Blvd. N., Las Vegas, NV 89101
Phone: (702) 229-6553
Fax: (702) 382-5199
Website: www.nevada.edu/~treed/rainbow

The Rainbow Company is a youth theatre group operating under the City of Las Vegas Cultural Affairs Division. At the core of Rainbow Company is its Ensemble, a group of 40 dedicated children, ages 10 to 18 who are selected by open audition. The Rainbow Company is dedicated to creating quality children's theatre productions for the youth of Nevada and is currently enjoying its 30th season. There are a variety of classes in all aspects of theatre for students ages 4 to high school and classes are offered year-round. The Arts Connection Kamp at Reed Whipple offers a full-day arts camp for several weeks during the summer. For the past 13 years the Rainbow Company tour show has appeared in elementary schools across southern Nevada.

RAP
Phone: (212) 221-0885 ext. 202
Website:www.tdf.org

RAP (Residency Arts Project) is an intensive playwriting program that brings the craft of live playmaking to young people who have little or no exposure to theatre. The teaching artist conducts a series of ten to 16 workshops per semester, uses professional productions as models, and gives students an opportunity to make artistic choices and experience the joy of creative expression.

Red Eagle Soaring Native American Theatre Group
Young Theatre Program
PO Box 22378, Seattle, WA 98122
Phone: (206) 447-8860
Fax: (206) 628-0839
E-mail: resoaring@earthlink.net
Website: http://home.earthlink.net/~resoaring

The nonprofit, all-volunteer Red Eagle Soaring Native American Theatre Group was founded in 1990. It offers drama workshops and performance projects for Native youth in the Seattle area and meets weekly at the Jefferson Community Center on Beacon Hill. It produced *Story Circles*, an HIV/AIDS prevention play for youth audiences, and performed several showcases of Native American talent entitled "Celebration of the First People." Their mission is to empower American Indian and Alaska Native youth through contemporary and traditional performing arts.

Riverside Youth Theatre
24200 Shady Ridge Circle, Moreno Valley, CA 92557
Phone: (951) 756-4240
E-mail: RiversideYouthTheatre@msn.com
Website: www.riversideyouththeatre.org

Riverside Youth Theatre (RYT) was formed in 2000 to provide more theatre opportunities for youth in a growing city. Their mission is to provide training for youth in the theatre arts in a fun, family-friendly environment and offer many classes for ages 5 to 20. Some classes include elementary and teen dance, group voice, music fundamentals and stage combat. Classes last 9 to 12 weeks and cost of $90–$120 per session. RYT mainly produces musicals with child performers. The 2006-2007 season includes *Broadway Meets the Movies*, *High School Musical*, *Seussical the Musical*, and *King of the Jungle*. Parents are often asked to help out backstage.

San Diego Junior Theatre
1650 El Prado, Suite 208, San Diego, CA 92101
Phone: (619) 239-1311
Fax: (619) 239-5048
E-mail: info@juniortheatre.com
Website: www.juniortheatre.com

San Diego Junior Theatre (SDJT) originally began as a community program of San Diego's Old Globe Theatre, but now operates as an independent, nonprofit organization. It is known to be the oldest, still operating children's theatre program in the country. In the past 58 years, SDJT has entertained over one million audience members. Classes and camps are held in three San Diego locations offering instruction in acting, improv, dance, singing and playwriting. San Diego Junior Theatre education outreach programs are open to all grade levels (pre-K through 12) for students ages 4 to 18. Education programs are customized for individual schools depending on the goals of the teachers, administrators, and/or the PTA/PTO organization requesting the program. These programs can be incorporated into the school day or can be after-school programs. In addition, SDJT offers Theatre-in-the-Park workshops before and after students attend school-day performances of the mainstage productions in Balboa Park.

The San Francisco Shakespeare Festival: Midnight Shakespeare
PO Box 460937, San Francisco, CA 94146
Phone: (800) 978-PLAY
Fax: (415) 865-4433
E-mail: sfshakes@sfshakes.org
Website: www.sfshakes.org

Midnight Shakespeare partners with community organizations like the East Bay Conservation Corps, the South Side Community Center of San Jose, and San Francisco Recreation and Parks, targeting underserved neighborhoods. Students in the 10-week program discover and examine the world of Shakespeare and perform an abridged Shakespeare play using their own life experiences to create fully developed characters. In addition to Midnight Shakespeare, the festival holds the annual Bay Area Shakespeare Camp Program for children ages

7 to 18. Each two-week session presents a series of structured, performance-oriented workshops under the guidance of trained Shakespeare Festival staff. Each camp finishes with a mini performance of a Shakespeare play.

Santa Barbara Youth Theatre

PO Box 40142, Santa Barbara, CA 93140
Phone: (805) 969-2565
Fax: (805) 692-5043
E-mail: info@sbyouththeatre.org
Website: www.sbyouththeatre.org

The Santa Barbara Youth Theatre (SBYT) offers a summer (musical) and winter (drama) program. During the six-week summer program students learn songs, dance routines and character development as well as a special dramaturgy lesson in the history of the production. There are several afternoon classes for specific instruction in the art of makeup and vocal training with guest artists. The winter program is approximately four weeks. Recent performances include *Footloose*, *Dracula*, *The Diviners*, *West Side Story*, *The Miracle Worker*, and *The Crucible*.

The Santa Fe Teen Arts Center: Warehouse 21

Warehouse 21, 1614 Paseo de Peralta, Santa Fe, NM 87501
Phone: (505) 989-4423
Fax: (505) 989-1583
E-mail: ana@warehouse21.org
Website: www.warehouse21.org

Founded in 1997, the Santa Fe Teen Arts Center, Warehouse 21 (W21) is Santa Fe's nationally acclaimed center for youth entertainment, entrepreneurialism and artistic production for individuals under the age of 21. Programs have served over 38,000 teenagers, young adults and adults from all socioeconomic and cultural backgrounds. W21 occupies a 3,500-square-foot, city-owned facility consisting of a 75-seat performance/workshop space, a recording studio, a darkroom, a silkscreen studio and four offices suited for youth training in administration, publishing, promotion, artistic production and media technology. Last year, a total of 2,700 teens and young adults under 21 were involved.

Seattle Children's Theatre

201 Thomas Street, Seattle, WA 98109
Phone: (206) 443-0807
Fax: (206) 443-0442
E-mail: info@sct.org
Website: www.sct.org

Founded in 1975, Seattle Children's Theatre (SCT) performs for approximately 250,000 children, parents, and teachers annually. Among its programs are Education Outreach, which includes Dramashops, Specialty Workshops, and Residencies custom designed to fit a school curriculum or based on one of SCT's Mainstage shows; Drama School, with school-year and summer classes and summer season productions which provide young people participatory theatre education and theatre arts training by professional artists; Deaf Youth Drama Program, which includes residencies, festivals, and a National Model program that offer a comfortable environment where deaf and hard-of-hearing children can learn about theatre and literature in their native language (American Sign Language), while building self-esteem and interpersonal skills.

Second Youth Family Theatre
PO Box 26186, Austin, TX 78755
Phone: (512) 386-8292
E-mail: info@secondyouth.com
Website: www.secondyouth.com

Second Youth is a nonprofit corporation that produces family-oriented theater productions and arts education programs for the residents of Austin, Texas, and surrounding communities. Since 1991, Second Youth programs have been seen by thousands of adults and children alike. Since September 2000, Second Youth Educational Outreach Programs have served over 5,000 students and educators in public schools, libraries and community centers. Their Theatre Arts Workshop is a summer youth theater program for 6 to 16 year olds exploring all aspects of theater. The workshop culminates in performances for friends, family, and the Austin community. During each program session the young people work as an ensemble, adapting classic children's literature to the stage. Some topic areas of the program are adaptation of literature, play/monologue writing, theater games/improvisation, dance/movement, voice, and prop/costume building.

Shakespeare & Young Company
70 Kemble Street, Lenox, MA 01240
Phone: (413) 637-1199
Fax: (413) 637-4274
E-mail: general@shakespeare.org
Website: www.shakespeare.org

Shakespeare & Young Company has offered spring and summer sessions to students ages 16–20 since 1990. Training can include acting, voice and movement work, text analysis, stage combat, dance, and clown. Spring session classes are held on the evenings and weekends and culminate in a public performance. The summer session offers an expanded schedule.

Smart Moves Players Theatre Arts Ensemble
508-A Charles Street, Easton, PA 18042
Phone: (610) 252-6983
Fax: (610) 253-6041
Website: www.cominguptaller.org/profile/pr29danthea.htm

Smart Moves was founded in 1992 and serves kids ages 9 to 18. What started as an educational program to prevent children and youth from participating in high-risk behavior has grown into a performance group of youth that tours schools, civic organizations and conferences. The Smart Moves Players Theater Arts Ensemble includes the all-female dance group, Sisters with Soul; the Smart Moves Touring Ensemble, a theater group; and a full troupe of 74 youth who write, choreograph, stage and perform at least three productions a year. The performances are adapted from literature and original work and feature soliloquies, music and dance.

Solano Youth Theatre
720 Main Street, Suisun City, CA 94585
Phone: (707) 863-7841
Fax: (707) 427-2400
E-mail: syt@solano.edu
Website: www.solanoyouththeatre.com

Solano Youth Theatre (SYT) is the youth division of Solano College's conservatory theatre training program. Surrounded by dedicated educators and industry professionals, young people from Solano County participate in productions, workshops and classes. Programming is designed to strengthen communication skills, promote team building, supplement teachers' classroom efforts and promote theatre arts. Over 600 students perform annually in one of SYT's two theatres for over 2,000 audience members. From beginning students to seasoned performers, SYT offers programming for students with a wide range of experience. Young performers receive instruction from accredited theatre facility and receive academic credit regardless of age. All shows feature professional-level sets, lighting, and costumes. All interested students are cast, 6 to 19 years old, regardless of experience, up to enrollment limits. Classes include audition prep, improv, voice, movement, storytelling, stage combat and playwriting.

SouthEast Effective Development: Rainier Valley Youth Theater
3515 S. Alaska Street, Seattle, WA 98118
Phone: (206) 725-7169
E-mail: rvyt@seedseattle.org
Website: www.seedseattle.org/arts/rvyt

Rainier Valley Youth Theatre (RVYT) is a multicultural, community-based youth theatre serving youth ages 7 to 21. Programs include the Young Playwright Festival, which begins with an intensive residency at local middle and high schools, with professional playwright educators teaching students this creative form of writing. After the residencies, the program culminates with the Young Playwrights Festival, featuring staged readings of selected student plays read by professional actors. The selected plays are also published in book form and distributed to libraries and schools. RVYT has facilitated the writing of over 300 student plays and published over 70 original plays by youth. Summer Arts and Culture Camp is offered for kids ages 6 to 9, with performing arts every morning and visual arts every afternoon. SummerSTAGE offers professional theatre training for youth ages 12 to 21 years old, who work as cast and crew members while training with some of Seattle's finest theatre and performing artists.

The Spartanburg Youth Theatre

385 S. Spring Street, Spartanburg, SC 29306
Phone: (864) 583-4891
E-mail: youththeatre@spartanarts.org
Website: www.sparklenet.com/youththeatre

The Spartanburg Youth Theatre presents four productions each October–May season, using young actors and actresses, with three public performances and two days of school-time performances of each show. More than 12,000 Spartanburg County students attend the Youth Theatre annually. In addition, the Youth Theatre's professional staff teaches a variety of classes for students in grades K–12. They also offer a summer drama camp. In two-week sessions, classes include creative dramatics, scene work, theatre games, warm ups, movement, team building, technical theatre (set design, stage makeup, costumes, and lighting). The classes prepare an informal performance for the last day.

Spirit of Broadway Youth Theatre

24 Chestnut Street, Norwich, CT 06360
Phone: (860) 886-2378
Fax: (860) 859-2672
E-mail: info@spiritofbroadway.org
Website: www.spiritofbroadway.org

Founded in 1998, the Spirit of Broadway Youth Theatre (SBT) is committed to improving the quality of life for their community through innovative, award-winning, high-quality, professional productions and educational offerings. The Youth Theater Program will soon be renamed "SBT Tomorrow's Leaders" to reflect the conviction that the leaders of tomorrow—today's young people— need holistic, comprehensive, challenging, hands-on and broad-based educational opportunities that have direct and meaningful applications to their lives and the global community. Classes have immediate and measurable goals that can be built on, over time, in a sequential fashion. Their Summerwerx Summer Theater Program enrollment is by audition only. This raises the bar of excellence and achievement for the participants and for the program. Students who have completed several of the "Tomorrow's Leaders" classes, will have the skill advantages needed to find success in the summer program.

Stage Doors

Phone: (212) 221-0885 ext. 202
Website: www.tdf.org

Stage Doors is a project-based arts education program that served 3,100 middle and high school students in 34 schools in 2006 by providing them with an in-depth introduction to live theatre.

State Street Project

PO Box 967, Trenton, NJ 08605
Phone: (609) 392-0766
Fax: (609) 392-0318
E-mail: info@passagetheatre.org
Website: www.passagetheatre.org/education.html

Modeled on New York City's 52nd Street Project, the State Street Project, founded in 1995, provides children with the chance to write and perform plays under the guidance of an artist-mentor. It offers 5 programs. Playmaking, where children ages 8 to 14 participate in an intensive playwriting workshop, culminates in a weekend retreat where the children write a short, two-character play. These original plays are rehearsed by professional adult actors and are given a full production. Holiday Productions is a program that produces a play every December with music that celebrates the holidays. In the Two on Two program two kids work with an adult director on performing a play written for them by an adult playwright. The three weeks of rehearsal culminate in an outdoor performance complete with scenery, costumes, and sound design, attended by the students' families and neighborhood residents. In Show You Know a team of artists collaborates with classroom teachers to use the arts to enhance classroom learning. The program culminates with a multidisciplinary performance and visual arts installation where the students got to "show what they know" to audiences. Poetry Nation is a program where students work with poets and are then encouraged to perform their poetry in class. Their original works are published in a book distributed to readers around the city.

Stepping Stone Theatre for Youth Development

314 Landmark Center, 75 W. Fifth Street, St. Paul, MN 55102

Phone: (651) 225-9265
Fax: (651) 225-1225
E-mail: info@steppingstonetheatre.org
Website: www.steppingstonetheatre.org

Stepping Stone produces a full season of six shows at the Landmark Center in Saint Paul, Minnesota, commissioning local playwrights to write shows that are educational and entertaining for children and families. All performers are youth and children who work with some of the Twin Cities' best professional theatre artists to create performances that are musical, moving, and fun. Stepping Stone offers a series of classes taught by professional theatre artists in creative dramatics, music and movement, improvisation, character development, dance, mime, stage combat, singing, and acting. The classes are geared for children and youth ages 3 and a half to 16.

STOP-GAP Theater
2900 Bristol Street, Suite D-105, Costa Mesa, CA 92626
Phone: (714) 979-7061
Fax: (714) 979-7065
E-mail: get-info@stopgap.org
Website: www.stopgap.org

Now in its 28th year of operation, STOP-GAP uses theatre therapeutically and educationally to inspire positive change in individual lives. In order to do this, STOP-GAP performs specially devised plays (1,000 each year) and workshops (500 each year) in classrooms, educational centers, hospitals and shelters throughout Los Angeles and Orange County, reaching between 45,000 and 50,000 people annually. Through the interactive STOP-GAP method, audience members actively participate in exploring issues which include safety, prevention of date rape, substance abuse, diversity and prejudice, decision making, and alternatives to violence. Performances are done for children in grades 3 through 12 and in detention halls and for adults in senior citizen centers.

Success through Academic and Recreational Support
PO Drawer 2217, Fort Myers, FL 33902
Phone: (941) 332-6671
Fax: (941) 338-2289
Website: www.cominguptaller.org/profile/pr54multi.htm

The Success through Academic and Recreational Support (STARS) Program was started in 1989 to serve children ages 8 to 14. Youth are enrolled in a variety of classes, including modern dance, African folk dance, cultural and heritage arts and celebrations, poetry, creative writing and vocal arts. Tutorial programs in math, reading and computers are available. The classes run in 6 to 10 week segments throughout the year. The City of Fort Myers police claim a 28 percent drop in juvenile arrests since the inception of the STARS Program.

TADA! Youth Theatre

15 W. 28th Street, Third Floor, New York, NY 10001
Phone: (212) 252-1619
Fax: (212) 252-8763
E-mail: info@tadatheater.com
Website: www.tadatheater.com

Since its founding in 1984, TADA! has offered any New York City (NYC) child with an interest or talent in theater, the opportunity to partake in professionally directed productions, staged readings, in-school/after-school arts education programs, and classes. It offers a subsidized ticket program for main stage shows and arts education in a wide variety of schools in low-income communities in all five boroughs. TADA! also maintains a free training/youth development program for NYC kids ages 8 to 18 and offers teens the opportunity to critique, perform in and be audience members for a playwriting contest and reading series.

Teatro del Barrio

3630 Harry Hines, Dallas, TX 75219
Phone: (214) 526-4076
Fax: (214) 526-0114
Website: www.cominguptaller.org/profile/pr111theater.html

Teatro del Barrio, founded in 1992 and a collaboration between Junior Players and Dallas-area youth agencies, serves children ages 11–18. The program brings theater classes to youth in the city's gang prevention program, juvenile detention centers, Camp Fire Boys and Girls programs and in programs run by local social service agencies. Professional actors work with the teens one or two times a week for 12 weeks after school on acting, scriptwriting and rehearsing. The program takes place at up to 10 sites each session, with each site running three consecutive sessions a year. The actors receive support from a professional familiar with the issues and conflicts that can arise when working with at-risk youth.

Teen Resource Project

136 Suffolk Street, Holyoke, MA 01040
Phone: (413) 532-6350
Fax: (413) 532-0335
Website: www.cominguptaller.org/profile/pr59theatvisual.htm

Founded in 1988 and serving kids ages 13–19, the Teen Resource Project is a community, after-school and summer program of the Community Adolescent Resource and Education Center (CARE), which works in Holyoke, Massachusetts, to prevent substance abuse, AIDS, and teen pregnancy. In partnership with the University of Massachusetts at Amherst, Holyoke teens meet 5 days a week to create original theater pieces and use different visual arts media to build skills and explore issues relevant to their lives. The project's theater company, the New Visions Theater, performs in English and Spanish.

Theatre Development Fund

1501 Broadway 21st Floor, New York, NY 10036
E-mail:info@tdf.org
Website: www.tdf.org

Theatre Development Fund is the largest not-for-profit service organization for the performing arts in the country. It was founded in 1968. They have several programs aimed at youths including Open Doors, Stage Doors, and RAP—all included elsewhere in this appendix in more detail.

Theatre in Diversion

303 Court Street, Covington, KY 41011
Phone: (606) 292-6421
Fax: (606) 292-6611
Website: www.cominguptaller.org/profile/pr01theater.htm

Founded in 1993, Theatre in Diversion serves children ages 8 to 17. The program was originated by Peg Phillips, an actress who starred in the TV show *Northern Exposure*. Theatre in Diversion is designed to divert teen offenders from the formal court system, reduce delinquent behavior, increase positive peer interaction, enhance critical thinking abilities, bond youth to the community, develop in youth an appreciation for the arts and increase their understanding of the legal system through dramatic interpretation of concepts such as authority, justice and responsibility. Program goals are met by engaging youth in role-playing and improvisational theater techniques in classes conducted by professional actors over a 10-week period, culminating in a final production.

Theatre of Youth

203 Allen Street, Buffalo, NY 14201
Phone: (716) 884-4400
Fax: (716) 819-9653
E-mail: rbrunschmid@theatreofyouth.org
Website: www.theatreofyouth.org

Founded in 1972, Theatre of Youth (TOY) is a nonprofit, professional theatre company that produces plays especially for children. There is a full-time artistic team and business staff. TOY mounts five plays during the school year. Over 50,000 children from all over the Western New York area attend with their schools and families. TOY is the resident theatre company of the Allendale Theatre. TOY has study guides that are given to teachers before performances. In them are activities for the students to complete in order to be ready for the play they will see. After the production, there is a "talk back" session where actors answer questions from the students.

Triboro Youth Theatre
106 Robert Street, Attleboro, MA 02703
Phone: (508) 222-6624
E-mail: triboroyouththeatre@comcast.net
Website: www.triboroyouththeatre.org

Triboro Youth Theatre (TYT) was founded in 1996 and strives to provide cultural enrichment for young people through the performing arts. Participants range from four years old through seniors in high school, who study acting, musical training, speech, creative movement and dance. Students can also choose to participate in off-stage areas of theatrical production, including stage crew, set construction, costume design, publicity, and internships. Triboro Youth Theatre is a production-based group, and utilizes a "learn by doing" approach through collaboration with professional staff and artists. Everyone is accepted into TYT's productions. Auditions are held to determine cast assignments. Rehearsals run for 8 to 12 weeks and most students attend once or twice a week allowing for other activities and school work. TYT also has the Triboro Musical Theatre, which produces shows that feature local talent.

Triumvirate Pi Theatre
PO Box 1452, Culver City, CA 90232
E-mail: triumviratepi@earthlink.net
Website: www.tri-pi.org

Triumvirate Pi (Tri Pi) is a nonprofit project of Community Partners, which provides a range of services to assist individuals, organizations and institutions in effectively addressing the complex social, economic and policy issues facing the Southern California region. Tri Pi is dedicated to creating provocative live theatre that breaks down perceived barriers of race, gender, and disability for Los Angeles theatre artists and audiences.

The Unusual Suspects
10536 Culver Blvd., Suite B, Culver City, CA 90232
Phone: (310) 558-3190
Fax: (310) 558-3191

E-mail: sally@theunusualsuspects.org
Website: www.theunusualsuspects.org

The Unusual Suspects Theatre Company (USTC) is a nonprofit organization, founded in 1993 in the wake of the city's civil unrest, of professional artists who bring theatre arts to youth, ages 12–21, from the foster care and juvenile justice systems. The core program is a 12-week intensive workshop meeting twice each week for 2 to 3 hours each session with a ratio of one volunteer for every 2 to 3 participants. The volunteers are industry professionals, actors, dancers, fight choreographers, directors, writers, producers, set designers, costumer designers and lighting designers. In the course of the program, the youth learn theatre and writing techniques; then they write, produce and perform a play of their own for parents, friends, peers, staff and USTC supporters.

Urban Arts Training Program
225 Baronne Street, Suite 1712, New Orleans, LA 70112
Phone: (504) 529-2430
Fax: (504) 527-2430
Website: www.cominguptaller.org/profile/pr19multi.htm

The Urban Arts Training Program was founded in 1992 and focuses on teens ages 14–18 with instruction in five arts areas—visual arts, dance, music, theater and computer graphics. Students also work in small crews to create public art projects for community groups.

Vaudeville Youth Theatre Company
20280 N. 59th Avenue, Suite 115-304, Glendale, AZ 85308
Website: www.thevaudeville.com

The Vaudeville Youth Theatre has a variety of programs designed for beginner students all the way to the most advanced, offering a variety of workshops throughout the year as well as main stage productions. Classes and productions are open to the community for children ages 4 to 19. No prior experience is necessary and the students do not have to take a workshop to be eligible for the productions. Some classes offered are Acting 1–3, Acting for the Camera, Auditioning, Musical Theatre, Scene Study, Improv, and Voice and Diction. Private piano and private voice classes are also available. The Vaudeville Junior Camp (ages 4 to 6) has 2, two-week sessions. Each session covers make believe, role playing, puppetry, stage movement, listening skills, character development and many more activities that will help young performers grow. The Summer Performing Art Academy (ages 7 to 15) has 2, three-week summer sessions. Each session produces a Junior Broadway Production.

Venture Theatre: Reality Crew
43 S. Third Street, Philadelphia, PA 19106

Phone: (215) 923-5927
Website: www.cominguptaller.org/profile/pr196theater.htm

Reality Crew was founded in 1992 and focuses on kids ages 15–18. The Reality Crew program draws youth from around Philadelphia to take part in theater training, from performance to marketing. They meet 8 hours a week at the Balch Institute for Ethnic Studies. Theater professionals teach playwriting, acting, voice and speech, movement, directing, stage management, costume design and sound and lights. Corporate business partners provide business training, often using their own operations for field study. Staff counselors help teens begin to prepare for college entrance or for careers in theater, while a speech pathologist links their experiences on stage to job interview presentation skills. A "think tank" session on Saturdays is an outlet for the culturally diverse group of teens to meet and talk about what's on their minds.

The Virginia Avenue Project

3000 Olympic Blvd., Santa Monica, CA 90404
Phone: (310) 264-4224
Fax: (310) 264-4230
E-mail: info@virginiaavenueproject.org
Website: www.virginiaavenueproject.org

The Virginia Avenue Project is a free, after-school program that uses the performing arts in conjunction with long-term, one-on-one mentoring to help kids discover their potential. Most students who participate in the project live and attend school in the Pico Corridor, a culturally diverse community in east Santa Monica. The project serves over 75 kids each year through arts and academic programs. Over 100 professional artists volunteer their time each year and an audience of over 3,000 attends project performances annually. The project is detailed in chapter 6.

Working Classroom

212 Gold SW, Albuquerque, NM 87102
Phone: (505) 242-9267
E-mail: nanel@workingclassroom.org
Website: www.workingclassroom.org

Working Classroom theater program is based on collaboration, innovation and cultural and social transformation. It provides aspiring actors with tuition-free professional training, produces thought-provoking, innovatively staged works that resonate with young, culturally diverse audiences and pushes the boundaries of youth theater while supporting emerging playwrights, directors and actors from historically ignored communities.

Youth at Arts: Graffiti as Art and Texas Young Playwrights Program

1110 Barton Springs, Austin, TX 78704
Phone: (512) 397-1456
Fax: (512) 397-1451
Website: www.cominguptaller.org/profile/pr74theater.htm

The City of Austin's Youth at Arts programs, founded in 1989, give children an opportunity to learn about the arts and build self-esteem by developing their creative abilities. The programs include more than a dozen activities for youth ages 3 to 19 at locations all over the city. One program is Graffiti as Art, where participants work with well-respected muralists and graffiti artists gain a historical understanding of graffiti and create murals and other works at sites throughout the city. Another program is the Texas Young Playwrights Program, where with assistance from the University of Texas' Department of Theatre and Dance and the Capitol City Playhouse, students learn about scriptwriting. Each student develops a one-act play, which is produced and critiqued by theater professionals during the Texas Young Playwrights Festival. The programs range in duration from a single intensive week to 3 months, depending on the host site.

Youth Theatre at the U

240 S. 1500 East Room 206, Salt Lake City, UT 84112
Phone: (801) 581-6098
Fax: (801) 585-9863
Website: www.youththeatre.utah.edu

Youth Theatre has a unique relationship with the University of Utah. As an entity of the Department of Theatre, the organization's staff is comprised of university faculty, staff, and students, complimented by a mix of professional guest artists from the Salt Lake community and the national young people's theatre community. After-school classes explore the world of drama with students, ages 5 to 18. The Theatre School for Youth is a summer performing arts training program for young people ages 5 to 18. Comprised of Preteen (ages 8 to 12), Teen (ages 12–18), and Dramatic Discoveries sessions (ages 5 to 8), this program attracts nearly 350 students each summer from the Wasatch Front and across the nation. The Youth Theatre Conservatory (YTC) Program provides education and performance opportunities for advanced level students ages 9 to 18 throughout the year. In each session, YTC students are immersed in intensive theatre training and are taught by some of Utah's finest resident theatre professionals and practitioners.

Youth Theatre Interactions

PO Box 1187, Yonkers, NY 10702

Phone: (914) 963-3040
Fax: (914) 963-3041
E-mail: info@youth-theatre.org
Website: www.youth-theatre.org

Youth Theatre Interactions (YTI) has provided an after-school environment, free of drugs and crime, for the youth of Yonkers and other areas of Westchester County since 1971. Most classes at Youth Theatre Interactions are offered on a beginner, intermediate and advanced level. Presently, it conducts 24 classes per week for youth ages 8 to 19. YTI offers a wide range of dance, acting, singing, and visual arts classes. It also holds residencies in several Yonkers schools and after-school programs.

Youth Theatre Northwest
8805 SE 40th Street, PO Box 296, Mercer Island, WA 98040
Phone: (206) 232-4145
Website: www.youththeatre.org

Started in 1984, Youth Theatre Northwest (YTN) is a school and a theatre offering several classes and programs for kids ages 3 to 18. There are Early Childhood programs (for kids 3 to 5), classes designed to enhance self-confidence, social interaction, and creative expression. Preparatory level classes (for kids 5 to 7) allow students to learn and explore different theatre styles and develop skills in vocal work and stage movement. Each quarter they offer a different focus for each class so students will develop new skills. Current classes are in musical theatre and acting. Intermediate level classes (for kids 8 to 11) are focused specialty classes with an emphasis on individual and small group work. Classes in dance, tools for actors and play production are currently offered. Advanced level drama classes (12 and older) are designed for students who are committed and dedicated to more intensive and focused theatre training.

Ypsilanti Youth Theatre
120 N. Huron Street, Ypsilanti, MI 48197
Website: www.ypsiyouththeatre.org

Meeting at St. Luke's Episcopal Church, Ypsilanti Youth Theatre (YYT) is open to even those who have no previous experience. It is only essential that participants are interested in, and enthusiastic about, drama. The theatre group works as a guild by having area local youth in grades 3 to 12 collaborate and work with various local theatre professionals as well as learning from one another. YYT has three theatrical performances a year that have children as the actors. It also offers a winter workshop each year. Classes are geared toward grades 3 to 12 and include movement, stage combat, improv, and playwriting.

Chapter Notes

Chapter 1

1. Robert Moran, "A Violent Trend: Phila. Near the Top," *Philadelphia Inquirer*, June 13, 2006.
2. Ibid.
3. Ibid.
4. *Santa Barbara News-Press*, May 15, 2002.
5. Quoted in *Santa Barbara News-Press*, June 16, 2001.
6. *Santa Barbara News Press*, June 11, 2002.
7. *Santa Barbara News-Press*, June 15, 2002.

Chapter 2

1. Lee M. Manning and Leroy G. Baruth, *Students at Risk* (Boston: Allyn and Bacon, 1995), 23.
2. U.S. Department of Health and Human Services, *Youth Violence: A Report of the Surgeon General—Executive Summary*, (Rockville, MD: U.S. Department of Health and Human Services, 2001), vii.
3. *Los Angeles Times*, March 1, 2001.
4. Richard J. Lundman, *Prevention and Control of Juvenile Delinquency* (Oxford: Oxford University Press, 1995), 241.
5. Calvert R. Dodge, ed., *A Nation Without Prisons: Alternatives to Incarceration* (Lexington, MA: Lexington Books), 40.
6. Aaron Kipnis, *Angry Young Men: How Parents, Teachers, and Counselors Can Help "Bad Boys" Become Good Men* (San Francisco: Jossey-Bass, 1999), 5.
7. James Garbarino, *Lost Boys: Why Our Sons Turn Violent and How We Can Save Them* (New York: Free Press, 1999), 4.
8. Quoted in *Santa Barbara News-Press*, September 6, 2001.
9. *Los Angeles Times*, March 28, 2002.
10. Quoted in *Santa Barbara News-Press*, April 10, 2002.
11. Martha Burt et al., *Building Supportive Communities for At-Risk Adolescents: It Takes More than Services* (Washington, D.C.: American Psychological Association, 1998), 51.
12. *Los Angeles Times*, May 19, 2002.
13. Allan Creighton with Paul Kivel, *Helping Teens Stop Violence: A Practical Guide for Counselors, Educators, and Parents* (Alameda, CA: Hunter House, 1990), 58.
14. *Philadelphia Inquirer*, June 21, 2006.
15. Milbrey W. McLaughlin et al., *Urban Sanctuaries: Neighborhood Organizations in the Lives and Futures of Inner-City Youth* (San Francisco: Jossey-Bass, 1994), 11.
16. Kipnis, *Angry Young Men*, 16.
17. Valerie Polakow, *The Public Assault on America's Children: Poverty, Violence, and Juvenile Justice* (New York: Teachers College Press, 2000), 87.
18. Kipnis, *Angry Young Men*, 78.
19. George H. Wood, *A Time to Learn: Creating Community in America's High Schools* (New York: Penguin Putnam, 1998), 60.
20. *The Nation*, May 28, 2001.
21. Polakow, *The Public Assault on America's Children*, 162.
22. Garbarino, *Lost Boys*, 4.
23. *Santa Barbara News-Press*, April 25, 2001.
24. McLaughlin, *Urban Sanctuaries*, xiii.

25. *Los Angeles Times*, May 3, 2001.
26. Quoted in *Parade*, May 5, 2002.
27. *Los Angeles Times*, January 1, 2000.
28. *Santa Barbara News-Press*, October 10, 2002.
29. Kipnis, *Angry Young Men*, 13, 82.
30. Ibid., 83.
31. Patricia Sternberg, *Theatre for Conflict Resolution: In the Classroom and Beyond* (Portsmouth: Heinemann, 1998), xiii.
32. Raymond B. Flannery, *Preventing Youth Violence: A Guide for Parents, Teachers, and Counselors* (New York: Continuum, 1999), 36.
33. *Los Angeles Times*, March 8, 2002.
34. Polakow, *The Public Assault on America's Children*, 74.
35. Ibid., 157.
36. Patricia Timberg, "Theater for At Risk Students," *Teaching Theatre* 4, no. 1, (1992): 11–12.
37. Garbarino, *Lost Boys*, 10.
38. James Garbarino et al., *Children in Danger: Coping with the Consequences of Community Violence* (San Francisco: Jossey-Bass, 1992), 23.
39. Burt et al., *Building Supportive Communities*, 28.
40. U.S. Department of Health and Human Services, *Youth Violence: A Report of the Surgeon General* (Rockville, MD: U.S. Department of Health and Human Services, 2001), 11.
41. Ibid., 72.
42. Ibid., 77.
43. Coming Up Taller website, www.cominguptaller.org.
44. Manning and Baruth, *Students at Risk*, 92.
45. Kipnis, *Angry Young Men*, 165.
46. Interview with the author, November 25, 2000.
47. Lundman, *Prevention and Control of Juvenile Delinquency*, 245.
48. Quoted in *Santa Barbara News-Press*, November 12, 2000.
49. Interview with the author, November 25, 2000.
50. Ibid.
51. Ibid.
52. Quoted in *Los Angeles Times*, October 19, 2000.
53. U.S. Department of Health and Human Services, *Youth Violence: A Report of the Surgeon General—Executive Summary*, viii.
54. Sternberg, *Theatre for Conflict Resolution*, xvi.
55. *Santa Barbara News-Press*, February 28, 2000.
56. *Los Angeles Times*, March 23, 2001.
57. Ibid., October 2, 2000.
58. Quoted in *Santa Barbara News-Press*, October 19, 2000.

59. Ibid.
60. Quoted in *Los Angeles Times*, December 5, 2000.
61. Kipnis, *Angry Young Men*, 116.
62. *Los Angeles Times*, November 19, 2000.
63. *Santa Barbara News-Press*, July 17, 2002.
64. Ibid., July 21, 2002.
65. Quoted in *Los Angeles Times*, July 13, 2002.
66. Pedro Noguera, "Reducing and Preventing Youth Violence: An Analysis of Causes and an Assessment of Successful Programs," *In Motion Magazine*, 2001, www.inmotionmagazine.com/er.html.
67. Garbarino, *Lost Boys*, 210.
68. *Los Angeles Times*, June 9, 2002.
69. *Santa Barbara News-Press*, February 11, 2002.
70. Stephen O'Conner, *Orphan Trains: The Story of Charles Loring Brace and the Children He Saved and Failed* (Boston: Houghton Mifflin, 2001), 330.
71. Joseph T. Hallinan, *Going Up the River: Travels in a Prison Nation* (New York: Random House, 2001), 19.
72. Hallinan, *Going Up the River*, xiii.
73. Polakow, *The Public Assault on America's Children*, 158–159.
74. Interview with the author, November 25, 2000.
75. Lundman, *Prevention and Control of Juvenile Delinquency*, 245.
76. Ibid., 103.
77. Quoted in *Los Angeles Times*, January 18, 2001.
78. *Los Angeles Times*, February 18, 2001.
79. Ibid.
80. *Newsweek*, February 26, 2001.
81. Lundman, *Prevention and Control of Juvenile Delinquency*, 156.
82. Ibid., 156.
83. Ibid., 244.
84. *Santa Barbara News-Press*, September 6, 2001.
85. Ibid.
86. *Los Angeles Times*, April 24, 2002.
87. Interview with the author, November 25, 2000.
88. U.S. Department of Health and Human Services, *Youth Violence: A Report of the Surgeon General*, 106.
89. Quoted in *Los Angeles Times*, February 16, 2002.
90. Dodge, *A Nation Without Prisons*, 241.
91. U.S. Department of Health and Human Services, *Youth Violence: A Report of the Surgeon General—Executive Summary*, xiii.
92. Interview with the author, November 25, 2000.
93. U.S. Department of Health and Human

Services, *Youth Violence: A Report of the Surgeon General—Executive Summary*, x.

94. *Los Angeles Times*, November 14, 2000.
95. *Coming Up Taller*, 47.
96. U.S. Department of Health and Human Services, *Youth Violence: A Report of the Surgeon General*, 32–33.
97. Curtis, Branch, ed., *Adolescent Gangs: Old Issues, New Approaches* (Philadelphia: Brunner/Mazel, 1999), 217.
98. Martin Sanchez Jankowski, *Islands in the Street: Gangs and American Urban Society* (Berkeley: University of California Press, 1991), 29.
99. Ibid., 311–12.
100. Vance Packard, *Our Endangered Children: Growing Up in a Changing World* (Boston: Little, Brown, 1983), 78.
101. Jane Addams, *Twenty Years at Hull House* (New York: New American Library, 1960), 60.
102. Quoted in James C. Scott, *Domination and the Arts of Resistance: Hidden Transcripts* (New Haven: Yale University Press, 1990), 45.
103. Scott, *Domination and the Arts of Resistance*, xi.
104. Ibid., 14.
105. John Holt, *How Children Fail* (New York: Pitman, 1964), 123.
106. Creighton and Kivel, *Helping Teens Stop Violence*, 64.
107. Ruth Perlstein and Gloria Thrall, *Ready to Use Conflict Resolution Activities for Secondary Students* (Nyack, NY: Center for Applied Research in Education, 1996), 5.
108. Packard, *Our Endangered Children*, 12.
109. Interview with the author, September 18, 2006.

Chapter 3

1. Doug Paterson, "Manifesto for a People's Theatre," *Drama Review* 27 no. 4 (Winter 1983): 71.
2. Maxine Klein, *Theatre for the 98%* (Boston: South End Press, 1978), 7.
3. Susan Chandler Haedicke, "Dramaturgy in Community-Based Theatre," *Journal of Dramatic Theory and Criticism* 13, no. 1 (Fall 1998): 7.
4. Allen Davis, *Spearheads for Reform: The Social Settlements and the Progressive Movement, 1890–1914* (New York: Oxford University Press, 1967), 18.
5. Ibid., 47.
6. Constance D'Arcy Mackay, *The Little Theatre in the United States* (New York: Henry Holt, 1917), 115.
7. Shannon Jackson, *Lines of Activity: Performance, Historiography, Hull House Domesticity* (Ann Arbor: University of Michigan Press, 2000), 233.
8. Jane Addams, *Twenty Years at Hull House* (New York: New American Library, 1960), 118.
9. Ibid., 273.
10. Jane Addams, *The Spirit of Youth and the City Streets* (New York: Macmillan, 1910), 87.
11. Ibid., 69.
12. Quoted in George W. Fluharty, "The Elizabeth Peabody House in Boston: A History an Evaluation," (Diss., New York University, 1958): 54.
13. Ibid., 89.
14. Quoted in Elliot W. Eisner, *Educating for Artistic Vision* (New York: Macmillan, 1972), 29.
15. Roger L. Bedard and C. John Tolch, eds., *Spotlight on the Child: Studies in the History of American Children's Theatre* (New York: Greenwood, 1989), 23.
16. George Geahigan, "The Arts in Education: A Historical Perspective," in *The Arts, Education, and Aesthetic Knowing: Ninety-First Yearbook of the National Society for the Study of Education*, eds. Bennett Reimer and Ralph Smith, 2 (Chicago: University of Chicago Press, 1992).
17. John Dewey, *Art as Experience* (New York: Minton, Balch, 1934), 79.
18. Ibid., 77.
19. Nellie McCaslin, *Theatre for Children in the United States: A History* (Norman: University of Oklahoma Press, 1971), 6.
20. Alice Minnie Herts, *The Children's Educational Theatre* (New York: Harper and Brothers, 1911), 42.
21. Ibid., 27.
22. Ibid., 64.
23. Dorothy Chansky, "Thinking Makes it So: Views and Uses of Shakespeare at the American Fins-de-Siecle, 1900/2000," *Journal of the American Drama and Theatre* 13, no. 3 (Fall 2001): 11.
24. Quoted in McCaslin, *Theatre for Children*, 5.
25. McCaslin, *Theatre for Children*, 14–15.
26. Emma Sheridan Fry, *Educational Dramatics* (New York: Lloyd Adams Noble, 1913), viii.
27. Ibid., 41–42.
28. Alfred Arvold, *The Little Country Theatre* (New York: Macmillan, 1923), 15.
29. Mackay, *The Little Theatre in the United States*, iii and 1.
30. Clarence Arthur Perry, *The Work of the Little Theatres* (New York: Russell Sage Foundation, 1933), 9.
31. McCaslin, *Theatre for Children*, 30.
32. Bedard and Tolch, *Spotlight on the Child*, 40.

33. Quoted in Gavin M. Bolton, *Drama as Education: An Argument for Placing Drama at the Center of the Curriculum* (London: Longman Group, 1984), 188.

34. Christine Redington, *Can Theatre Teach? An Historical and Evaluative Analysis of Theatre in Education* (Oxford: Pergamon, 1983), 31.

35. Quoted in Bolton, *Drama as Education*, 55.

36. Peter Slade, *Child Drama* (New York: Philosophical Library, 1955), 344.

37. Slade, *Child Drama*, 342.

38. Brian Way, *Development Through Drama* (London: Longman, 1967), 1.

39. McCaslin, *Theatre for Children*, 129.

40. Isabel B. Burger, *Creative Play Acting: Learning Through Drama* (New York: A.S. Barnes, 1950), x.

41. McCaslin, *Theatre for Children*, 129.

42. Geahigan, "The Arts in Education," 9.

43. Ibid., 9.

44. McCaslin, *Creative Drama*, 82.

45. Quoted in Betty Wagner, *Dorothy Heathcote: Drama as a Learning Medium* (Washington, D.C.: National Education Association, 1976), 13.

46. Redington, *Can Theatre Teach?* 2.

47. Jeffrey D. Wilhelm and Brain Edmiston, *Imagining to Learn: Inquiry, Ethics, and Integration Through Drama* (Portsmouth, N.H. Heinemann, 1998), 67.

48. Redington, *Can Theatre Teach?* 48.

49. Emanuel Shipow, "A Comparative Study of the Integration of Theatre and Drama into Education: Moscow, London, Los Angeles," (Diss., UCLA, 1970), 174.

50. Ibid., 76.

51. Ibid., 302.

52. Ibid., 306.

53. Geahigan, "The Arts in Education," 2.

54. Bruce McConachie and Daniel Friedman, eds., *Theatre for Working-class Audiences in the United States, 1830–1980* (Westport, CT: Greenwood, 1985), 25–33.

55. McConachie and Friedman, *Theatre for Working-class Audiences*, 62–66.

56. Robert Gard and Gertrude Burley, *Community Theatre: Idea and Achievement* (Westport, CT: Greenwood, 1959), 10.

57. McConachie and Friedman, *Theatre for Working-class Audiences*, 101.

58. Steve Grolin, *The Fragile Bridge: Paterson Silk Strike, 1913* (Philadelphia: Temple University Press, 1993), 21.

59. Quoted in Grolin, *The Fragile Bridge*, 3.

60. Grolin, *The Fragile Bridge*, 61.

61. Ibid., 48.

62. Ibid., 134.

63. Quoted in Joyce L. Kornbluh, ed., *Rebel Voices: An IWW Anthology* (Ann Arbor: University of Michigan Press, 1964), 201.

64. Mabel Dodge Luhan, *Movers and Shakers* (Albuquerque: University of New Mexico Press, 1936), 188.

65. Quoted in Paul R. Cappucci, *William Carlos Williams' Poetic Response to the 1913 Paterson Silk Strike* (Lewiston: Edwin Mellon, 2002), 47.

66. Luhan, *Movers and Shakers*, 204.

67. Quoted in Robert A. Rosenstine, *Romantic Revolutionary: A Biography of John Reed* (New York: Vintage, 1975), 131.

68. Luhan, *Movers and Shakers*, 203.

69. John Dos Passos, *Midcentury* (Boston: Houghton Mifflin, 1961), 259.

70. Quoted in Grolin, *The Fragile Bridge*, 166.

71. Quoted in Kornbluh, *Rebel Voices*, 202.

72. Linda Nochlin, "The Paterson Strike Pageant of 1913," *Art in America* 62 (May-June 1974): 66.

73. Dos Passos, *Midcentury*, 259.

74. Quoted in Grolin, *The Fragile Bridge*, 167.

75. Wisner Payne Kinne, *George Pierce Baker and the American Theatre* (Cambridge: Harvard University Press, 1954), 140.

76. Thomas H. Dickinson, *The Insurgent Theatre* (New York: B.W. Huebsch, 1917), 109.

77. McConachie and Friedman, *Theatre for Working-class Audiences*, 94.

78. Archibald Henderson, ed., *Pioneering a People's Theatre* (Chapel Hill: University of North Carolina Press, 1945), 10.

79. Arvold, *The Little Country Theatre*, 61.

80. Robert Gard, *Grassroots Theater: A Search for Regional Arts in America* (Madison: University of Wisconsin Press, 1999), xviii.

81. Ibid., 59.

82. Ibid., 141.

83. Ibid., 43.

84. Ibid., 15–16.

85. Louise Burleigh, *The Community Theatre in Theory and Practice* (Boston: Little, Brown, 1917), xxxiv.

86. Ibid., xxxii.

87. Ibid., 100.

88. Dudley Cocke, Harry Newman, and Janet Salmons-Rue, eds., *From the Ground Up: Grassroots Theatre in Historical and Contemporary Perspective* (Ithaca, NY: Community Based Arts Project, 1993), 22.

89. Don B. Wilmeth and Tice L. Miller, eds., *Cambridge Guide to American Theatre* (New York: Cambridge University Press, 1993), 28.

90. Cocke et al. *From the Ground Up*, 22.

Chapter 4

1. Dudley Cocke, Harry Newman, and Janet Salmons-Rue, eds., *From the Ground Up: Grassroots Theatre in Historical and Contemporary Perspective* (Ithaca, NY: Community Based Arts Project, 1993), 46, 47.

2. Roger L. Bedard and C. John Tolch, eds., *Spotlight on the Child: Studies in the History of American Children's Theatre* (New York: Greenwood, 1989), 111.

3. Jay Williams, *Stage Left* (New York: Scribner's, 1974), 260.

4. Quoted in C.W.E. Bigsby, *A Critical Introduction to Twentieth Century American Drama, Volume 1, 1900–1940* (Cambridge: Cambridge University Press, 1982), 199.

5. Bruce McConachie and Daniel Friedman, eds., *Theatre for Working-Class Audiences in the United States, 1830–1980* (Westport, CT: Greenwood, 1985), 111.

6. Quoted in Graham Holderness, ed., *The Politics of Theatre and Drama* (Hong Kong: Macmillan, 1992), 103.

7. Quoted in John Willett, *The Theatre of Erwin Piscator: Half a Century of Politics in the Theatre* (New York: Holmes and Meier, 1979), 121.

8. Quoted in Sonja Kuftinec, "Educating the Creative Theatre Artist," *Theatre Topics* 11, no. 1 (March 1, 2001): 47.

9. Bertolt Brecht, *The Messingkauf Dialogues* (London: Eyre Methuen, 1965), 100.

10. Andrew E. Doe, "Brecht's Lehrstucke: Propaganda Failures," *Educational Theatre Journal* 14 (December 1962): 290.

11. Ibid., 290.

12. Bertolt Brecht, The Measures Taken *and Other Lehrstucke* (London: Eyre Methuen, 1977), 6.

13. Julian Beck, *The Life of the Theatre: The Relation of the Artist to the Struggle of the People* (San Francisco: City Lights Books, 1972), 6.

14. Quoted in Theodore Shank, *American Alternative Theatre* (New York: St. Martin's, 1988), 9.

15. Pierre Biner, *The Living Theatre* (New York: Horizon Press, 1972), 99.

16. Quoted in Shank, *American Alternative Theatre*, 10.

17. Bigsby, *A Critical Introduction to Twentieth Century American Drama*, 96.

18. Beck, *The Life of the Theatre*, 95.

19. Quoted in William French, *Maryat Lee's EcoTheatre: A Theater for the Twenty-First Century* (Morgantown: West Virginia University Press, 1998), 6.

20. Ibid., 120–24.

21. Maryat Lee, *Dope! A One Act Drama* (New York: Samuel French, 1953), 22.

22. Ibid., 5.

23. Quoted in French, *Maryat Lee's Eco-Theatre*, 34.

24. Ibid., 44.

25. Ibid., 143.

26. William French, "A Double-Threaded Life: Maryat Lee's EcoTheatre," *Drama Review* 27, no. 2 (Summer 1983): 27.

27. French, *Maryat Lee's EcoTheatre*, 120–21.

28. C.W.E. Bigsby, A Critical Introduction to *Twentieth Century American Drama: Volume 3, Beyond Broadway* (Cambridge: Cambridge University Press, 1985), 376.

29. Quoted in Bigsby, A Critical Introduction to *Twentieth Century American Drama: Volume 3*, 377.

30. Ibid., 394.

31. Thomas C. Dent, Richard Schechner, and Gilbert Moses, eds., *The Free Southern Theater by the Free Southern Theater* (Indianapolis: Bobbs-Merrill, 1969), 211.

32. John O'Neal, "Art and the Movement," *Southern Exposure* 9, no. 1 (Spring 1981): 80.

33. Quoted in Dent et al., *The Free Southern Theater*, 178.

34. Janelle Reinelt, *Crucibles of Crisis: Performing Social Change* (Ann Arbor: University of Michigan Press, 1996), 15.

35. Jan Cohen-Cruz, "A Hyphenated Field," *New Theatre Quarterly* 16, no. 4 (2000): 372.

36. Stefan Brecht, *Peter Schumann's Bread and Puppet Theatre* (London: Routledge, 1988), 741.

37. Don B. Wilmeth and Tice L. Miller, eds., *Cambridge Guide to American Theatre* (New York: Cambridge University Press, 1993), 84.

38. Karen Malpede Taylor, *People's Theatre in Amerika* (New York: Drama Book Specialists, 1972), 331.

39. Wilmeth and Miller, eds., *Cambridge Guide*, 412

40. Bigsby, *A Critical Introduction to Twentieth Century American Drama: Volume 3*, 336.

41. Shank, *American Alternative Theatre*, 60.

42. Ibid., 74.

43. Taylor, *People's Theatre*, 294.

44. McConachie and Friedman, *Theatre for Working-class Audiences*, 189.

45. Bigsby, *A Critical Introduction to Twentieth Century American Drama: Volume 3*, 363.

Chapter 5

1. Quoted in Alfred T. Hennelly, *Liberation Theology: A Documentary History* (Maryknoll, NY: Orbis, 1990), 432.

2. Ibid., 416.

3. Penny Lernoux, *Cry of the People* (New York: Penguin, 1982), 41.

4. Ernesto Cardenal, *The Gospel in Solentiname*, Vol. 1 Maryknoll, NY: Orbis, 1978), 48.

5. Philip Zwerling and Connie Martin, *Nicaragua: A New Kind of Revolution* (Westport, CT: Lawrence Hill, 1985), 46.

6. Paulo Freire, *Pedagogy of the Oppressed* (New York: Continuum, 1993), 33.

7. Ibid., 82.

8. Zwerling and Martin, *Nicaragua*, 67.

9. Zwerling, "Revolution in Nicaragua: An Eyewitness Report," 7.

10. Augusto Boal, *The Rainbow of Desire* (London: Routledge, 1995), 1.

11. Quoted in Edgar Quiles, "The Theatre of Augusto Boal," (Diss., Michigan State University, 1981), 15.

12. Augusto Boal, *Theatre of the Oppressed* (New York: Urizen, 1979), 165.

13. Augusto Boal, *Tecnicas Latinoamericanas De Teatro Popular: Una revolucion Copernicana al reves* (Buenos Aires: Ediciones Corregidor Saici y E. 1974), 135.

14. Boal, *Theatre*, 155.

15. Boal, *Rainbow*, 71.

16. Boal, *Theatre*, 46.

17. Ibid., 39.

18. Quoted in John Willett, ed., *Brecht on Theatre: The Development of An Aesthetic* (New York: Hill and Wang, 1964), 78.

19. Augusto Boal, *Hamlet and the Baker's Son: My Life in Theatre and Politics* (London: Routledge, 2001), 200.

20. Boal, *Rainbow*, 2–3.

21. Ibid., 40.

22. Quiles, "The Theatre of Augusto Boal," 68–75.

23. Boal, *Theatre*, 141.

24. Boal, *Hamlet*, 288–89.

25. Dorothy A. Goodwin, "An Investigation of the Efficacy of Creative Drama as a Method for Teaching Social Skills to Mentally Retarded Youths and Adults" (Diss., Bowling Green State University, 1984), 101.

26. Sonja Kuftinec, "(De)Constructing the American Cabin: Cornerstone Theatre and Transactions of Community" (Diss., Stanford University, 1996), 22.

27. Quoted in Kuftinec, "(De)Constructing," 215.

28. Ibid., 23.

29. *Los Angeles Times*, June 21, 2002.

30. Sonja Kuftinec, "Staging the City with the Good People of New Haven," *Theatre Journal* 53, no. 2 (May 2001): 220.

31. Sara Brady, "Welded to the Ladle," *Drama Review* 44, no. 3 (Fall 2000): 52.

32. Ibid., 60.

33. Ibid., 67.

34. Ibid., 70.

35. Project Zero website, http://pzweb.harvard.edu.

36. Quoted in David McArthur and Sally Ann Law, *The Arts and the Prosocial Impact Study: A Review of the Current Programs and Literature* (Santa Monica, CA: Rand, 1996), 2.

37. Museums Without Walls, *Arts in Focus: Los Angeles Countywide Arts Education Survey* (Los Angeles: Arts Education Task Force of Arts for L.A., 2001), 14.

38. Peter London, *Step Outside: Community-Based Art Education* (Portsmouth: Heinemann, 1994), 12.

39. Baz Kershaw, *The Politics of Performance: Radical Theatre as Cultural Intervention* (London: Routledge, 1992), 243.

40. Ibid., 2.

41. Ibid., 252.

42. Ibid., 253.

43. Cosby Warren Robertson, "The Theater as a Vehicle for Community Action," (Diss., Florida State University, 1972), 91.

44. Marian Liebmann, ed., *Arts Approaches to Conflict* (London: Jessica Kingsley, 1988), 89.

45. Quoted in David McArthur and Sally Ann Law, *The Arts and the Prosocial Impact Study: A Review of the Current Programs and Literature* (Santa Monica, CA: Rand, 1996), 22.

46. *Los Angeles Times*, March 9, 2001.

47. McArthur and Law, *The Arts and the Prosocial Impact Study*, ii.

48. Quoted in Anne Stone, David McArthur, Sally Ann Law, and Joy Moini. *The Arts and Prosocial Impact Study: Program Characteristics and Prosocial Effects* (Los Angeles: Rand, 1998), 1.

49. Quoted in Stone et al., *The Arts and Prosocial Impact*, v.

50. McArthur and Law, *The Arts and the Prosocial Impact Study*, iv.

51. Judith Humphreys Weitz, *Coming Up Taller: Arts and Humanities Programs for Children and Youth at Risk* (Washington, DC: President's Committee on the Arts, April 1996), 11.

52. R.A. Leis, "The Popular Theatre and Development in Latin America," *Educational Broadcasting International* 12, no. 1 (1979): 11.

53. Bonnie Simon and Michael Mullen, *STOP-GAP: Final Research Report* (Costa Mesa, CA: STOP-GAP, March 1993), 11.

54. Ibid., 14.

55. Ibid, 7.

56. Ibid, 16.

57. Robert E. Stake, "The Countenance of Educational Evaluation," *Teachers College Record* 68, no. 7 (April 1968): 529–38.

58. Ibid., 533.

Chapter 6

1. Virginia Avenue Project brochure.
2. Interview with the author, May 19, 2001.
3. *Three Minutes from Broadway: The Story of the 52nd Street Project*. Video. Directed by Lyn Greene. Derry, NH: Chip Taylor Communications, 1992.
4. Ibid.
5. Ibid.
6. Ibid.
7. Interview with the author, May 19, 2001.
8. Ibid.
9. Ibid.
10. Ibid.
11. Interview with the author, August 14, 2001.
12. Quoted in Anne Stone, David McArthur, Sally Ann Law, and Joy Moini. *The Arts and Prosocial Impact Study: An Examination of Best Practices* (Santa Monica, CA: Rand, 1997), 27.
13. Interview with the author, May 19, 2001.
14. Interview with the author, August 14, 2001.
15. Ibid.
16. Interview with the author, August 12, 2001.
17. Ibid.
18. Interview with the author, August 14, 2001.
19. Ibid.
20. Interview with the author, May 19, 2001.
21. Interview with the author, September 12, 2006.

Chapter 7

1. Letter to the author, May 15, 2001.
2. City Hearts brochure, undated, 1.
3. Interview with the author, February 4, 2002.
4. Ibid.
5. Ibid.
6. Interview with the author, March 8, 2002.
7. Ibid.
8. Ibid.
9. Interview with the author, June 17, 2001.
10. Interview with the author, September 25, 2006.
11. Rebekah Brown, interview with the author, September 17, 2006.
12. Ibid.

13. Ibid.
14. Interview with the author, September 21, 2006.
15. Ibid.
16. Interview with the author, September 18, 2006.
17. Interview with the author, September 25, 2006.

Chapter 8

1. Interview with the author, September 3, 2006.
2. Paul Griffin, *City at Peace Guidebook* (New York: City at Peace, 1998), 28.
3. Ibid., 31.
4. Ibid., 31.
5. Ibid., 3.
6. Ibid., 51.
7. Ibid., 57.
8. Interview with the author, December 17, 2001.
9. Interview with the author, September 3, 2006.
10. Interview with the author, September 13, 2006.
11. Interview with the author, September 16, 2006.

Chapter 9

1. Edward B. Fiske, *Champions of Change: The Impact of the Arts on Learning* (Washington, DC: President's Committee on the Arts and the Humanities, 2000), iv.
2. Ibid., viii.
3. Ibid., 2.
4. Ibid., xi.
5. Ibid., 3.
6. Ibid., 55.
7. Ibid., 4.
8. Coming Up Taller, website, www.cominguptaller.org.
9. Americans for the Arts, website, www.artsusa.org.
10. Ibid.
11. Museums Without Walls. *Arts in Focus: Los Angeles Countywide Arts Education Survey* (Los Angeles: Arts Education Task Force of Arts for L.A., 2001), 8.
12. *Los Angeles Times*, May 13, 2002.
13. Martha Burt, Gary Resnick, and Emily Novick, *Building Supportive Communities for At-Risk Adolescents: It Takes More Than Services* (Washington, DC: American Psychological Association, 1998), 59.
14. *Santa Barbara News-Press*, September 7, 2002.

15. Ibid.

16. Burt et al., *Building Supportive Communities*, 50.

17. *Santa Barbara News-Press*, October 10, 2000.

18. U.S. Department of Health and Human Services, *Youth Violence: A Report of the Surgeon General* (Rockville, MD: U.S. Department of Health and Human Services, 2001), 32–33.

19. Interview with the author, May 19, 2001.

20. Quoted in *Three Minutes from Broadway: The Story of the 52nd Street Project*. Video. Directed by Lyn Greene. Derry, NH: Chip Taylor Communications, 1992.

21. Bertolt Brecht, *The Messingkauf Dialogues* (London: Eyre Methuen, 1965), 107.

22. Richard Schechner, "Performers and Spectators Transported and Transformed," *Kenyon Review* 3, no. 4 (1981): 91–92.

23. Victor W. Turner, *From Ritual to Theatre: The Human Seriousness of Play* (New York: Performing Arts Journal Publications, 1982), 93.

24. Michael Nichols and Melvin Zax, *Catharsis in Psychotherapy* (New York: Gardner, 1977), 43.

25. Erving Goffman, *Presentation of Self in Everyday Life* (Scotland: University of Edinburgh, 1958), 72.

26. Quoted in Mady Schutzman and Jan Cohen-Cruz, eds., *Playing Boal: Theatre, Therapy, Activism* (London: Routledge, 1994), 90.

27. Jacob Moreno, *Mental Catharsis and the Psychodrama* (Beacon, NY: Beacon House, 1940), 220.

28. Ibid., 223.

29. Ibid., 209.

30. Ibid., 230.

31. Ibid., 240.

32. Ibid., 235.

33. Michael Nichols and Melvin Zax, *Catharsis in Psychotherapy* (New York: Gardner, 1977), 74.

34. Jacob Moreno, *The Theatre of Spontaneity* (New York: Beacon House, 1947), 4–5.

35. T.J. Scheff, *Catharsis in Healing, Ritual, and Drama* (Berkeley: University of California Press, 1979), 79.

36. Ibid., 13.

37. Ibid., 48.

38. T.J. Scheff, "Audience Awareness and Catharsis in Drama," *Psychoanalytic Review* 63, no. 4 (Winter 1976–1977): 552.

39. Scheff, *Catharsis*, 210.

40. Ibid., 14.

41. Ibid., 34.

42. Ibid., 50–51.

43. Scheff, "Audience Awareness," 539.

44. Interview with the author, September 1, 2006.

45. Scheff, *Catharsis*, 13.

46. Interview with the author, October 31, 2001.

47. Augusto Boal, *Games for Actors and Non-Actors* (London: Routledge, 1992), 28.

48. Ibid., 28.

49. Ibid., 35.

50. Augusto Boal, *The Rainbow of Desire* (London: Routledge, 1995), 4.

51. Ibid., 4.

52. Ibid., 5.

53. Ibid., 6.

54. Ibid., 6–7.

55. John Martin, *Introduction to the Dance* (Brooklyn: Dance Horizons, 1965), 5.

56. Gavin M. Bolton, *Drama as Education: An Argument for Placing Drama at the Centre of the Curriculum* (London: Longman, 1984), 205.

57. James Garbarino, *What Children Can Tell Us: Eliciting, Interpreting, and Evaluating Information from Children* (San Francisco: Jossey-Bass, 1989), 159.

58. Boal, *Theatre*, 155.

59. R.A. Leis, "The Popular Theatre and Development in Latin America," *Educational Broadcasting International* 12, no. 1 (1979): 12–13.

60. Michael Rohd, *Theatre for Community, Conflict & Dialogue* (Portsmouth, NH: Heinemann, 1998), 19.

61. Leis, "The Popular Theatre and Development in Latin America," 11.

62. Howard Gardner, *Frames of Mind: The Theory of Multiple Intelligences* (New York: Basic, 1983), 8.

63. Ibid., 119.

64. Ibid., 12.

65. Elliot W. Eisner, *Educating Artistic Vision* (New York: Macmillan, 1972), 201.

66. Richard Courtney, *Drama and Intelligence: A Cognitive Theory* (Montreal: McGill-Queen's University Press, 1990), 22.

67. Ibid., 179.

68. Ibid., 5.

69. Ibid., 9.

70. Ibid., 28.

71. Ibid., 178.

72. Joe Norris, "Drama as Research: Realizing the Potential of Drama in Education as a Research Methodology," *Youth Theatre Journal* 14 (2000), 41.

73. Nellie McCaslin, *Creative Drama in the Intermediate Grades* (New York: Longman, 1987), 1.

74. Dwight Conquergood, "Ethnography, Rhetoric, and Performance," *Quarterly Journal of Speech* 78 (1992): 92.

75. Allan Creighton with Paul Kivel, *Helping Teens Stop Violence: A Practical Guide for Counselors, Educators, and Parents* (Alameda, CA: Hunter House, 1990), 13.

76. Fatima Mernissi, *Dreams of Trespass: Tales of a Harem Girlhood* (Cambridge, Massachusetts: Perseus, 1994), 76.

77. Ibid., 105–11.

78. U.S. Department of Health and Human Services, *Youth Violence: A Report of the Surgeon General* (Rockville, MD: U.S. Department of Health and Human Services, 2001), 123.

79. City Hearts brochure, undated.

80. Paul Griffin, *City at Peace Guidebook* (New York: City at Peace, 1998), 2.

81. Interview with author, September 13, 2006.

82. Judith Humphreys Weitz, *Coming Up Taller: Arts and Humanities Programs for Children and Youth at Risk* (Washington, DC: President's Committee on the Arts, April 1996), 34.

83. *Three Minutes from Broadway.*

84. Anne Stone, David McArthur, Sally Ann Law, and Joy Moini. *The Arts and Prosocial Impact Study: Program Characteristics and Prosocial Effects* (Los Angeles: Rand, 1998), v.

85. John Holt, *How Children Fail* (New York: Pitman, 1964), 165.

86. David N. Perkins, *Smart Schools: From Training Memories to Educating Minds* (New York: Free Press, 1992), 32.

87. *Los Angeles Times*, August 8, 2001.

Bibliography

Addams, Jane. *The Spirit of Youth and the City Streets*. New York: Macmillan, 1910.

____. *Twenty Years at Hull House*. New York: New American Library, 1960.

Alexander, Jane. *Command Performance: An Actress in the Theater of Politics*. New York: Public Affairs, 2000.

Americans for the Arts website, www.artsusa.org.

Anderson, Robert. "The Muses of Chaos and Destruction of 'Arena Conta Zumbi.'" *Latin America Theatre Review* 29, no. 2 (1996): 15–28.

Artaud, Antonin. *The Theatre and Its Double*. New York: Grove Press, 1958.

Arvold, Alfred. *The Little Country Theater*. New York: Macmillan, 1923.

Bakhtin, Mikhail. *Rabelais and His World*. Cambridge, MA: M.O. Press, 1968.

Ballerini, Julia. "Photography as a Charitable Weapon: Poor Kids and Self-Representation." *Radical History Review* 69 (1997) 168–88.

Baxandall, Lee, and Stefan Morawski, eds. *Marx and Engels on Literature and Art*. St. Louis: Telos Press, 1973.

Beck, Julian. *The Life of the Theatre: The Relation of the Artist to the Struggle of the People*. San Francisco: City Lights Books, 1972.

Becker, Carol, ed. *The Subversive Imagination: Artists, Society, and Social Responsibility*. London: Routledge, 1994.

Bedard, Roger L., and C. John Tolch, eds. *Spotlight on the Child: Studies in the History of American Children's Theatre*. New York: Greenwood, 1989.

Beltran, Luis Ramiro. *Farewell to Aristotle: "Horizontal" Communication*. Published by the International Commission for the Study of Communications Problems and UNESCO. Undated.

Benner, Timothy. "Teaching Social Values and Skills With Theatre." Thesis, Emerson College, 1997.

Beyond Creating: The Place for Art in America's Schools. A report by the Getty Center for Education in the Arts, April 1985.

Bigsby, C.W.E. *A Critical Introduction to Twentieth-Century American Drama: Volume 1, 1900–1940*. Cambridge: Cambridge University Press, 1982.

____. *A Critical Introduction to Twentieth-Century American Drama: Volume 3, Beyond Broadway*. Cambridge: Cambridge University Press, 1985.

Biner, Pierre. *The Living Theatre*. New York: Horizon Press, 1972.

Black, Beverly. "Evaluating a Psychoeducational Sexual Assault Prevention Program Incorporating Theatrical Presentation, Peer Education, and Social Work." *Research on Social Work Practice* 10, no. 5 (September 2000).

Blair, Brent. Interview with author. February 24, 2001.

Bloom, Benjamin, ed. *Developing Talent in Young People*. New York: Ballantine, 1985.

Blumenthal, Eileen. *Joseph Chaikin: Exploring the Boundaries of Theatre*. New York: Cambridge University Press, 1984.

Boal, Augusto. *Games for Actors and Non-Actors*. London: Routledge, 1992.

____. *Hamlet and the Baker's Son: My Life in Theatre and Politics*. London: Routledge, 2001.

229

_____. *Legislative Theatre*. London: Routledge, 1998.

_____. *The Rainbow of Desire*. London: Routledge, 1995.

_____. *Tecnicas Latinoamericanas De Teatro Popular: Una revolucion Copernicana al reves*. Buenos Aires: Ediciones Corregidor Saici y E., 1974.

_____. *Theatre of the Oppressed*. New York: Urizen Books, 1979.

Bolton, Gavin M. *Drama as Education: An Argument for Placing Drama at the Centre of the Curriculum*. London: Longman, 1984.

_____.*Towards a Theory of Drama in Education*. London: Longman, 1979.

Booker, Keith M. *Techniques of Subversion in Modern Literature: Transgression, Abjection, and the Carnivalesque*. Gainesville: University of Florida, 1991.

Bowles, Norma, ed. *Cootie Shots: Theatrical Inoculations against Bigotry for Kids, Parents, and Teachers*. New York: Theatre Communications Group, 2001.

Brady, Sara. "Welded to the Ladle." *Drama Review* 44, no.3 (Fall 2000): 51–74.

Branch, Curtis, ed. *Adolescent Gangs: Old Issues, New Approaches*. Philadelphia: Brunner/Mazel, 1999.

Braunstein, Deborah, and Leslie Sellers. "Development Through Drama/Theatre in Education: Lessons from the Front." Thesis, Emerson College, 1998.

Brecht, Bertolt. The Measures Taken *and Other* Lehrstucke. London: Eyre Methuen, 1977.

_____. *The Messingkauf Dialogues*. London: Eyre Methuen, 1965.

Brecht, Stefan. *Peter Schumann's Bread and Puppet Theatre*. London: Routledge, 1988.

Breckinridge, Sophonisba, ed. *The Child in the City*. New York: Arno Press, 1970.

Brenson, Michael. *Visionaries and Outcasts: The NEA, Congress, and the Place of the Visual Artists in America*. New York: New Press, 2001.

Brino-Dean, Terry. "Real for Whom? The Drama League of America and Community-Based Theatre." Paper delivered to American Society for Theatre Research panel, November 16, 2001.

Brown, Rebekah B. Interview with author. April 15, 2002, and September 17, 2006.

Broyles-Gonzalez, Yolanda. *El Teatro Campesino: Theatre in the Chicano Movement*. Austin: University of Texas Press, 1994.

Brustein, Robert. *Revolution as Theatre: Notes on the New Radical Style*. New York: Liveright, 1971.

Burger, Isabel B. *Creative Play Acting: Learning Through Drama*. New York: A.S. Barnes, 1950.

Burleigh, Louise. *The Community Theatre in Theory and Practice*. Boston: Little, Brown, 1917.

Burnham, Linda Frye, and Steven Durland, eds. *The Citizen Artist: 20 Years of Art in the Public Arena*. Gardiner, NY: Critical Press, 1998.

Burt, Martha, Gary Resnick, and Emily Novick. *Building Supportive Communities for At-Risk Adolescents: It Takes More Than Services*. Washington, DC: American Psychological Association, 1998.

"Bush's Childproof Budget." Editorial, *Nation*. May 28, 2001.

Bushnell, Don, and Kathi Corbera Bushnell. *The Arts, Education, and the Urban Sub-Culture*. Washington, DC: U.S. Department of Health, Education, and Welfare, 1969.

Byam, L. Dale. *Community in Motion: Theatre for Development in Africa*. Westport, CT: Bergin & Garvey, 1999.

Calof, Stuart. Telephone interview with author. March 8, 2002, and September 21, 2006.

Cappucci, Paul R. *William Carlos Williams' Poetic Response to the 1913 Paterson Silk Strike*. Lewiston: Edwin Mellon, 2002.

Cardenal, Ernesto. *The Gospel in Solentiname*. Vol. 1. Maryknoll, NY: Orbis, 1978.

Carlson, Marvin. *Theories of the Theatre: A Historical and Critical Survey from the Greeks to the Present*. Ithaca: Cornell University Press, 1984.

Carroad, Diane L. "City at Peace: Inspiring Kids to Imitate and Improve Life." *Children Today* 22, no. 1 (January-February 1993): 18–22.

Case, Sue-Ellen, and Janelle Reinelt. *The Performance of Power: Theatrical Discourse and Politics*. Iowa City: University of Iowa Press, 1991.

Catterall, James. "The Fourth R: The Arts and Learning." *Teachers College Record* 96, no. 2 (Winter 1994), 299–328.

_____. "Involvement in the Arts and Success in Secondary School." *Americans for the Arts Monographs* 1, no 9. (November 1997).

Chansky, Dorothy. "'Thinking Makes It So': Views and Uses of Shakespeare at the American *Fins-de-Siecle*, 1900/2000." *Journal of American Drama and Theatre* 13, no.3 (Fall 2001).

Cisneros, Steve. Interview with author. May 10, 2001.

City Hearts brochure. Pasadena: Green Street Press, undated.

Clegg, D. "The Dilemma of Drama in Education." *Theatre Quarterly* 3 (January 1973): 31–42.

Coalition Against Gun Violence 8, no 1 (Spring 2002).

Cocke, Dudley, Harry Newman, and Janet Salmons-Rue, eds. *From the Ground Up: Grassroots Theatre in Historical and Contemporary Perspective*. Ithaca, NY: Community Based Arts Project, 1993.

Cohen-Cruz, Jan. "A Hyphenated Field." *New Theatre Quarterly* 16, no. 4 (2000): 364–78.

____, ed. *Radical Street Performance: An International Anthology*. London: Routledge, 1998.

____. "Theatre of the Oppressed Workshops with Women." *Drama Review* 127 (Fall 1990): 66–75.

____. "When the Gown Goes to Town: The Reciprocal Rewards of Fieldwork for Artists." *Theatre Topics* 11, no. 1 (March 2001): 55–62.

____. "Witnessing a Drama of the Soul." *High Performance*. 75 (1997): 15–19.

Colleran, Jeanne, and Jenny S. Spencer. *Staging Resistance: Essays on Political Theatre*. Ann Arbor: University of Michigan Press, 1998.

Coming Up Taller website, www.comingup taller.org.

Community Workshop on Economic Development (CWED). *From the Bottom Up: Building Communities from Within*. Chicago: CWED, 1992.

Conquergood, Dwight. "Ethnography, Rhetoric, and Performance." *Quarterly Journal of Speech* 78 (1992): 80–97.

____. *Homeboys and Hoods: Gang Communication and Cultural Space*. Hillsdale, NJ: Lawrence Erlbaum, 1993.

____. "Rethinking Ethnography: Towards a Critical Cultural Politics." *Communication Monographs* 58, no.2 (June 1991): 179–94.

Costis, Sophocles. Interview with author. February 4, 2002.

Courtney, Richard. *Drama and Feeling: An Aesthetic Theory*. Montreal: McGill-Queen's University Press, 1995.

____. *Drama and Intelligence: A Cognitive Theory*. Montreal: McGill-Queen's University Press, 1990.

Creighton, Allan, with Paul Kivel. *Helping Teens Stop Violence: A Practical Guide for Counselors, Educators, and Parents*. Alameda, CA: Hunter House, 1990.

Curran, Leigh. Interview with author, May 19, 2001, August 14, 2001, and September 12, 2006.

Davis, Allen F. *Spearheads for Reform: The Social Settlements and the Progressive Movement, 1890–1914*. New York: Oxford University Press, 1967.

Davis, Jed H., ed. *Theatre Education: Mandate for Tomorrow*. New Orleans: Anchorage Press, 1985.

Davis, Nancy. Interview with author, September 10, 1999, and September 3, 2006.

Dent, Thomas C., Richard Schechner, and Gilbert Moses, eds. *The Free Southern Theater by the Free Southern Theater*. Indianapolis: Bobbs-Merrill, 1969.

Dewey, John. *Art as Experience*. New York: Minton, Balch, 1934.

____. *Schools of To-Morrow*. New York: E.P. Dutton, 1915.

Dickinson, Thomas H. *The Insurgent Theatre*. New York: B.W. Huebsch, 1917.

Dodd, Nigel, and Winifred Hickson, eds. *Drama and Theatre in Education*. London: Heinemann, 1971.

Dodge, Calvert R., ed. *A Nation Without Prisons: Alternatives to Incarceration*. Lexington, MA: Lexington Books, 1975.

Doe, Andrew E. "Brecht's Lehrstucke: Propaganda Failures." *Educational Theatre Journal* 14 (December 1962): 289–96.

Donmoyer, Robert, and Raylene Kos, eds. *At-Risk Students: Portraits, Programs, and Practices*. Albany: State University of New York Press, 1993.

Doran, Justin. Interview with the author, February 4, 2002, and September 18, 2006.

Dos Passos, John. *Midcentury*. Boston: Houghton Mifflin, 1961.

DuBois, Page. "Ancient Tragedy and the Metaphor of Katharsis." *Theatre Journal* 54, no. 1 (March 2002) 19–22.

Earnest, Steve. "The Changing Character of the Collective in Lehrstucke by Brecht and Muller." *Theatre Symposium* 9 (2001): 30–37.

Eddy, Junius. *The Upside Down Curriculum*. Washington, DC: U.S. Department of Education, 1981.

Eisner, Elliot W. *The Art of Educational Evaluation: A Personal View*. London: Falmer Press, 1985.

____. *Educating Artistic Vision*. New York: Macmillan, 1972.

Elam, Harry J. *Taking It to the Streets: The Social Protest Theatre of Luis Valdez and Amiri Baraka*. Ann Arbor: University of Michigan Press, 1997.

Ellsworth, Elizabeth. *Teaching Positions: Difference, Pedagogy, and the Power of Address*. New York: Columbia University, 1997.

Emler, Nicholas, and Stephen Reicher. *Adolescence and Delinquency*. Oxford: Blackwell, 1993.

Epskamp, Kees P. *Theatre in Search of Social Change: The Relative Significance of Different Theatrical Approaches*. The Hague: Center for the Study of Education in Developing Countries, 1989.

Erven, Eugene Van. *The Playful Revolution: Theatre and Liberation in Asia*. Bloomington: University of Indiana Press, 1992.

Feldman, Edmund Burke. *Becoming Human through Art: The Aesthetic Experience in the School*. Englewood Cliffs, NJ: Prentice-Hall, 1970.

Finlay-Johnson, Harriet. *The Dramatic Method of Teaching*. Boston: Ginn, 1912.

Bibliography

Fiske, Edward B. *Champions of Change: The Impact of the Arts on Learning.* Washington, DC: President's Committee on the Arts and the Humanities, 2000.

Flannery, Raymond B. *Preventing Youth Violence: A Guide for Parents, Teachers, and Counselors.* New York: Continuum, 1999.

Florence, Namulundah. *bell hook's Engaged Pedagogy: A Transgressive Education for Critical Consciousness.* Westport, CT: Bergin & Garvey, 1998.

Flowers, Jeff. Interview with the author. December 17, 2001, and September 16, 2006.

Fluharty, George W. "The Elizabeth Peabody House in Boston: A History and Evaluation." Diss., New York University, 1958.

Fox, Jonathan, ed. *The Essential Moreno: Writings on Psychodrama, Group Method, and Spontaneity by J.L. Moreno, M.D.* New York: Springer, 1987.

Fraden, Rena. *Imagining Medea: Rhodessa Jones and Theater for Incarcerated Women.* Chapel Hill: University of North Carolina Press, 2001.

Freire, Paulo. *Pedagogy of Hope: Reliving Pedagogy of the Oppressed.* New York: Continuum, 1996.

_____. *Pedagogy of the Oppressed.* New York: Continuum, 1993.

French, William. "A Double-Threaded Life: Maryat Lee's EcoTheatre." *Drama Review* 27, no. 2 (Summer 1983): 15–25.

_____. *Maryat Lee's EcoTheatre: A Theater for the Twenty-First Century.* Morgantown: West Virginia University Press, 1998.

Frohnmayer, John. *Leaving Town Alive: Confessions of an Art Warrior.* New York: Houghton Mifflin, 1993.

Fry, Emma Sheridan. *Educational Dramatics.* New York: Lloyd Adams Noble, 1913.

Garbarino, James, *Lost Boys: Why Our Sons Turn Violent and How We Can Save Them.* New York: Free Press, 1999.

Garbarino, James, Nancy Dubrow, Kathleen Kostelny, and Carole Pardo. *Children in Danger: Coping with the Consequences of Community Violence.* San Francisco: Jossey-Bass, 1992.

Garbarino, James, Frances M. Stott, and Faculty of Erikson Institute. *What Children Can Tell Us: Eliciting, Interpreting, and Evaluating Information from Children.* San Francisco: Jossey-Bass, 1989.

Gard, Robert. *Grassroots Theater: A Search for Regional Arts in America.* Madison: University of Wisconsin Press, 1999.

Gard, Robert, and Gertrude S. Burley. *Community Theatre: Idea and Achievement.* Westport, CT: Greenwood, 1959.

Gardner, Howard. *Art, Mind, and Brain: A Cognitive Approach to Creativity.* New York: Basic, 1982.

_____. *Frames of Mind: The Theory of Multiple Intelligences.* New York: Basic, 1983.

_____. *The Unschooled Mind: How Children Think and How Schools Should Teach.* New York: Basic, 1991.

Geahigan, George. "The Arts in Education: A Historical Perspective." In *The Arts, Education, and Aesthetic Knowing: Ninety-First Yearbook of the National Society for the Study of Education,* edited by Bennett Reimer and Ralph A. Smith. Chicago: University of Chicago Press, 1992.

Gilligan, James. *Violence: Our Deadly Epidemic and Its Causes.* New York: Putnam, 1996.

Goffman, Erving. *Presentation of Self in Everyday Life.* Scotland: University of Edinburgh, 1958.

Goldstein, Ezra. "Writing from the Edge." *Teaching Theatre* 6, no. 3, (1995).

Goleman, Daniel. *Emotional Intelligence: Why It Can Matter More than I.Q.* New York: Bantam, 1995.

Golin, Steve. *The Fragile Bridge: Paterson Silk Strike 1913.* Philadelphia: Temple University Press, 1988.

Goodwin, Dorothy A. "An Investigation of the Efficacy of Creative Drama as a Method for Teaching Social Skills to Mentally Retarded Youths and Adults." Diss., Bowling Green State University, 1984.

Grady, Sharon. *Drama and Diversity: A Pluralistic Perspective for Educational Drama.* Portsmouth, NH: Heinemann, 2001.

Griffin, Paul. *City at Peace Guidebook.* New York: City at Peace, 1998.

_____. Interview with the author, October 11, 2000, and September 13, 2006.

Green, Shawn. "Boal and Beyond: Strategies for Creating Community Dialogue." *Theatre* 31, no. 3 (Fall 2001): 47–54.

Gutierrez, Gustavo. *A Theology of Liberation: History, Politics, and Salvation.* Maryknoll, NY: Orbis, 1973.

Haedicke, Susan Chandler. "Dramaturgy in Community-Based Theatre." *Journal of Dramatic Theory and Criticism* 13, no. 1 (Fall 1998): 125–32.

Hallinan, Joseph T. *Going up the River: Travels in a Prison Nation.* New York: Random House, 2001.

Hallowell, Edward M. *Connect.* New York: Pantheon, 1999.

Haney, Craig, Curtis Banks, and Philip Zimbardo. "Interpersonal Dynamics in a Simulated Prison." *International Journal of Criminology and Penology* 1 (1973): 69–97.

Heath, Shirley Brice, and Milbrey McLaughlin, eds. *Identity and Inner-City Youth: Beyond*

Ethnicity and Gender. New York: Teachers College Press, 1993.

Henderson, Archibald, ed. *Pioneering a People's Theatre.* Chapel Hill: University of North Carolina Press, 1945.

Hennelly, Alfred T. *Liberation Theology: A Documentary History.* New York: Maryknoll, NY: Orbis, 1990.

Heritage, Paul. "The Courage to be Happy." *Drama Review* 38, no. 3 (Fall 1994): 25.

Herts, Alice Minnie. *The Children's Educational Theatre.* New York: Harper and Brothers, 1911.

Hetland, Lois, and Ellen Winner. "The Arts and Academic Achievement: What the Evidence Shows." *Arts Education Policy Review* 102, no. 5 (May 2001): 3.

Hodgson, John, ed. *The Uses of Drama: Sources Giving a Background to Acting as a Social and Educational Force.* London: Eyre Methuen, 1972.

Holderness, Graham, ed. *The Politics of Theatre and Drama.* Hong Kong: Macmillan, 1992.

Holt, John. *How Children Fail.* New York: Pitman, 1964.

_____. *How Children Learn.* New York: Pitman, 1967.

Holzman, Lois, ed. *Performing Psychology: A Postmodern Culture of the Mind.* London: Routledge, 1999.

hooks, bell. *Teaching to Transgress: Education as the Practice of Freedom.* New York: Routledge, 1994.

Hughes, Langston. *Scottsboro Limited; Four Poems and a Play in Verse.* New York: Golden Stair Press, 1932.

Huizinga, Johan. *Homo Ludens: A Study of the Play Element in Culture.* New York: Harper and Row, 1970.

Jackson, Shannon. "Civic Play-Housekeeping: Gender, Theatre, and American Reform." *Theatre Journal* 48 (October 1996): 337–61.

_____. *Lines of Activity: Performance, Historiography, Hull-House Domesticity.* Ann Arbor: University of Michigan Press, 2000.

Jackson, Tony, ed. *Learning Through Theatre: Essays and Casebooks on Theatre in Education.* Manchester: Manchester University Press, 1980.

_____. *Learning Through Theatre: New Perspectives on Theatre in Education.* London: Routledge, 1993.

Jankowski, Martin Sanchez. *Islands in the Street: Gangs and American Urban Society.* Berkeley: University of California Press, 1991.

Jason, Sherry. Interview with the author, March 19, 2001.

_____. Letter to the author, May 15, 2001.

Jennings, Sue. *Theatre, Ritual and Transformation: The Senoi Temiars.* London: Routledge, 1995.

Jimerson, Shane. "City@ Peace Community Mediation Program Evaluation: Final Report." Unpublished, Santa Barbara, CA, 2000.

Johnson, Liz, and Cecily O'Neill. *Dorothy Heathcote: Collected Writings on Education and Drama.* Evanston, IL: Northwestern University Press, 1984.

Johnston, Chris. *House of Games: Making Theatre from Everyday Life.* New York: Routledge, 1998.

Jones, Phil. *Drama as Therapy: Theatre as Living.* London: Routledge, 1996.

Joseph, May. "Experiments in a Theatre of the Oppressed." *Movement Research Performance Journal* (Fall-Winter 1997-1998): 5–6.

Kaagan, Stephen S. *Aesthetic Persuasion: Pressing the Cause of Arts Education in American Schools.* Malibu: Getty Center for Education in the Arts, 1991.

Kanellos, Nicolas. *A History of Hispanic Theatre in the United States: Origins to 1940.* Austin: University of Texas Press, 1990.

Kay, Jane Holtz. "Artists as Social Reformers." *Art in America* (January-February 1969): 44–47.

Kelly, Angela Duffy. "A Study of the Efficacy of the Creative Process Found in the Arts as a Treatment Modality with at Risk Teens for the Prevention and Intervention of Self Destructive Behaviors." Diss., Fielding Institute (Santa Barbara, CA), 2001.

Kershaw, Baz. *The Politics of Performance: Radical Theatre as Cultural Intervention.* London: Routledge, 1992.

Kidd, Ross. "Liberation or Domestication: Popular Theatre and Non-formal Education in Africa." *Educational Broadcasting International* 12, no. 1 (1979): 3–9.

_____. *The Popular Performing Arts, Non-formal Education, and Social Change in the Third World: A Bibliography and a Review Essay.* The Hague: Centre for the Study of Education in Developing Countries, 1982.

Kinne, Wisner Payne. *George Pierce Baker and the American Theatre.* Cambridge: Harvard University Press, 1954.

Kipnis, Aaron. *Angry Young Men: How Parents, Teachers, and Counselors Can Help "Bad Boys" Become Good Men.* San Francisco: Jossey-Bass, 1999.

_____. Interview with author, November 25, 2000, and September 18, 2006.

Klein, Maxine. *Theatre for the 98%.* Boston: South End Press, 1978.

Kozol, Jonathan. *Children of the Revolution: A Yankee Teacher in the Cuban Schools.* New York: Delacorte, 1978.

Kornbluh, Joyce L., ed. *Rebel Voices: An IWW Anthology.* Ann Arbor: University of Michigan Press, 1964.

Kuftinec, Sonja. "A Cornerstone for Rethinking Community Theatre." *Theatre Topics* 6, no. 1 (1996): 91–104.

_____. "(De)Constructing the American Cabin: Cornerstone Theatre and Transactions of Community." Diss., Stanford University, 1996.

_____. "Educating the Creative Theatre Artist" *Theatre Topics* 11, no. 1, (March 1, 2001): 43–53.

_____. "Staging the City with the Good People of New Haven." *Theatre Journal*, 53, no. 2, (May 2001): 197–222.

Lacey, Stephen, and Brian Woolland. "Educational Drama and Radical Theatre Practice." *New Theatre Quarterly* 8, no. 29 (1992): 81–91.

Lavender, Andy. "Theatrical Utopia." *New Statesman and Society* 8, no. 336 (January 20, 1995): 32.

Lee, Maryat. *Dope! A One Act Drama.* New York: Samuel French, 1953.

Leis, R.A. "The Popular Theatre and Development in Latin America." *Educational Broadcasting International* 12, no. 1 (1979): 10–13.

Liebmann, Marian, ed. *Arts Approaches to Conflict.* London: Jessica Kingsley, 1988.

Lerner, Ruby. "Reclaiming People's Theatre." *Southern Exposure* 14, no. 3–4 (1986): 9–10.

Lerner, Sharon. "Class Dismissed." *Utne Reader* 98 (March-April 2000): 26–27.

Lernoux, Penny. *Cry of the People.* New York: Penguin, 1982.

Lewy, Robin Gayle. "An Approach to Community Action through Drama in the United States Inspired by Third World Techniques." Thesis, University of Nebraska, 1985.

London, Peter. *Step Outside: Community-Based Art Education.* Portsmouth: Heinemann, 1994.

Luhan, Mabel Dodge. *Movers and Shakers.* Albuquerque: University of New Mexico Press, 1936.

Lundman, Richard J. *Prevention and Control of Juvenile Delinquency.* Oxford: Oxford University Press, 1995.

Lynch, Edward. *Liberation Theology and Christian Democracy.* New York: Praeger, 1991.

Mackay, Constance D'Arcy. *The Little Theatre in the United States.* New York: Henry Holt, 1917.

Mamet, David. *3 Uses of the Knife: On the Nature and Purposes of Drama.* New York: Columbia University Press, 1998.

Manning, Lee M., and Leroy G. Baruth. *Students at Risk.* Boston: Allyn and Bacon, 1995.

Martin, John. *Introduction to the Dance.* Brooklyn: Dance Horizons, 1965.

Martin-Baro, Ignacio. *Writings for a Liberation Psychology.* Cambridge: Harvard University Press, 1994.

Maruishi, Mark E. *The Use of Psychological Testing for Treatment Planning and Outcomes Assessment.* Mahwah, NJ: Lawrence Erlbaum, 1999.

Mastrosimone, William. "Bang, Bang, You're Dead." Unpublished, 1999.

McArthur, David, and Sally Ann Law. *The Arts and the Prosocial Impact Study: A Review of the Current Programs and Literature.* Santa Monica, CA: Rand, 1996.

McCaslin, Nellie. *Creative Drama in the Intermediate Grades.* New York: Longman, 1987.

_____. *Historical Guide to Children's Theatre in America.* New York: Greenwood, 1987.

_____. *Theatre for Children in the United States: A History.* Norman: University of Oklahoma Press, 1971.

McConachie, Bruce. "Approaching the 'Structure of Feeling' in Grassroots Theatre." *Theatre Topics* 8, no. 1 (1998): 33–53.

_____. Interview with the author, March 2001.

_____, and Daniel Friedman, eds. *Theatre for Working-Class Audiences in the United States, 1830-1980.* Westport, CT: Greenwood, 1985.

McGrath, John. "The Theory and Practice of Political Theory." *Theatre Quarterly* 9, no. 35 (Autumn 1979): 43–54.

McLaren, Peter. *Che Guevara, Paulo Freire, and the Pedagogy of Revolution.* Lanham: Rowman and Littlefield, 2000.

_____. *Critical Pedagogy and Predatory Culture: Oppositional Politics in a Postmodern Era.* London: Routledge, 1995.

McLaughlin, Milbrey W., Merita A. Irby, and Juliet Langman. *Urban Sanctuaries: Neighborhood Organizations in the Lives and Futures of Inner-City Youth.* San Francisco: Jossey-Bass, 1994.

Mecca, Andrew, Neil Smelser, and John Vasconcellos, eds. *The Social Importance of Self-Esteem.* Berkeley: University of California Press, 1989.

Mernissi, Fatima. *Dreams of Trespass: Tales of a Harem Girlhood.* Cambridge, MA: Perseus, 1994.

Merten, Donna M. *Research Methods in Education and Psychology: Integrating Diversity with Quantitative and Qualitative Approaches.* Thousand Oaks, CA: SAGE, 1998.

Mienczakowski, Jim. "The Theatre of Ethnography: The Reconstruction of Ethnography into Theatre with Emancipatory Potential." *Qualitative Inquiry* 1, no. 3 (1995): 360–75.

Mitchell, Richard W. "Community Based Theatre: A Viable and Vibrant Alternative." *The Dramatist* 2, no. 4 (March-April 2000).

Moreno, Jacob. *Mental Catharsis and the Psychodrama.* Beacon, NY: Beacon House, 1940.

_____. *Psychodrama*, Vol. 1, 4th ed. Ambler, PA: Beacon House, 1985.

_____. *The Theatre of Spontaneity*. New York: Beacon House, 1947.

Mormino, Lee D. "Impacts of Live Theater on Youth Audiences and Intention Development on Issues Concerning Substance Abuse." Thesis, Loyola University (Chicago), 1995.

Museums Without Walls. Arts in Focus: Los Angeles Countywide Arts Education Survey. Los Angeles: Arts Education Task Force of Arts for L.A., 2001.

National Council for Community and Justice website, www.nccj.org.

Nichols, Michael, and Melvin Zax. *Catharsis in Psychotherapy*. New York: Gardner, 1977.

Nochlin, Linda. "The Paterson Strike Pageant of 1913." *Art in America* 62 (May-June 1974): 64–68.

Noguera, Pedro. "Reducing and Preventing Youth Violence: An Analysis of Causes and an Assessment of Successful Programs." In *Motion Magazine*, 2001. www.inmotionmaga zine.com/er.html.

Norris, Joe. "Drama as Research: Realizing the Potential of Drama in Education as a Research Methodology." *Youth Theatre Journal* 14 (2000), 40–51.

O'Brien, Michael, and Craig Little. *Reimaging America: The Arts of Social Change*. Philadelphia: New Society, 1990.

O'Connor, Stephen. *Orphan Trains: The Story of Charles Loring Brace and the Children He Saved and Failed*. Boston: Houghton Mifflin, 2001.

O'Neal, John. "Art and the Movement." *Southern Exposure* 9, no. 1 (Spring 1981): 80–83.

_____. "Motion of the Ocean." *Drama Review* 12, no. 4 (Summer 1968): 70–77.

Orenstein, Claudia. *Festive Revolutions: The Politics of Popular Theatre and the San Francisco Mime Troupe*. Jackson: University of Michigan Press, 1998.

Otty, Nick. "Theatre of the Oppressed: Cultural Action for Freedom." *Contemporary Theatre Review* 3, no. 1 (1995): 87–100.

Overton, Grace Sloan. *Drama in Education: Theory and Technique*. New York: Century, 1926.

Owens, Timothy J., Sheldon Stryker, and Noreen Goodman, eds. *Extending Self-Esteem Theory and Research*. Cambridge: Cambridge University Press, 2001.

Packard, Vance. *Our Endangered Children: Growing Up in a Changing World*. Boston: Little, Brown, 1983.

Pasolli, Robert. *A Book on the Open Theatre*. New York: Bobbs-Merrill, 1970.

Paterson, Doug. "The Embodiment of Embodied Pedagogy: Using Boal Techniques with At-Risk Teens." Unpublished.

_____. "Manifesto for a People's Theatre."

Drama Review 27, no. 4 (Winter 1983): 70–73.

Perkins, David N. *The Intelligent Eye: Learning to Think by Looking at Art*. Santa Monica: Getty Center for Education in the Arts, 1994.

_____. *Smart Schools: From Training Memories to Educating Minds*. New York: Free Press, 1992.

Perlstein, Ruth, and Gloria Thrall. *Ready to Use Conflict Resolution Activities for Secondary Students*. Nyack, NY: Center for Applied Research in Education, 1996.

Perry, Clarence Arthur. *The Work of the Little Theatres*. New York: Russell Sage Foundation, 1933.

Pogrebin, Letty Cottin. "Do Americans Hate Children?" *Ms*. 12 (November 1983): 47–50, 126–27.

Polakow, Valerie. *The Public Assault on America's Children: Poverty, Violence, and Juvenile Injustice*. New York: Teachers College Press, 2000.

Quiles, Edgar. "The Theatre of Augusto Boal." Diss., Michigan State University, 1981.

Read, Herbert. *Education through Art*. New York: Pantheon, 1958.

Redington, Christine. *Can Theatre Teach? An Historical and Evaluative Analysis of Theatre in Education*. Oxford: Pergamon Press, 1983.

Reed, A. "The Underclass as Myth and Symbol." *Radical America* 24 (1992): 24–40.

Reinelt, Janelle. *Crucibles of Crisis: Performing Social Change*. Ann Arbor: University of Michigan Press, 1996.

Robertson, Cosby Warren. "The Theater as a Vehicle for Community Action." Diss., Florida State University, 1972.

Robinson, Ken, ed. *Exploring Theatre and Education*. London: Heinemann, 1980.

Rohd, Michael. Interview with the author, November 29, 2000.

_____. *Theatre for Community, Conflict & Dialogue*. Portsmouth, NH: Heinemann, 1998.

Rolland, Romain. *The People's Theater*. New York: Henry Holt, 1918.

Roman, Melvin. *On the Power and Necessity of Art*. Pennsylvania: Pennsylvania State University, 1969.

Rosenstone, Robert A. *Romantic Revolutionary: A Biography of John Reed*. New York: Vintage, 1975.

Sainer, Arthur. *The New Radical Theatre Notebook*. New York: Applause, 1997.

Salas, Jo. "Culture and Community: Playback Theatre." *Drama Review* 27, no. 2 (Summer 1983):15–25.

Saldana, Johnny. "Playwriting with Data: Ethnographic Performance Texts." *Youth Theatre Journal* 13 (1999): 60–73.

Samuel, Raphael, Ewan MacColl, and Stuart Cosgrove. *Theatre of the Left, 1880–1935: Work-*

Bibliography

ers' Theatre Movements in Britain and America. London: Routledge, 1985.

Santana, Jose. Interview with the author, September 13, 1999; April 17, 2001; May 22, 2001; and July 2, 2002.

____. "The Secret." Diss. (video portion), Pacifica Graduate Institute, 2002.

Schechner, Richard. Environmental Theater. New York: Hawthorne, 1973.

____. "Performers and Spectators Transported and Transformed." Kenyon Review 3, no. 4 (1981): 83–113.

Schechner, Richard, and Willa Appel, eds. By Means of Performance. Cambridge: Cambridge University Press, 1990.

Schechner, Richard, Willa Appel, and Mady Schutzman, eds. Ritual, Play and Performance: Readings in the Social Sciences/Theatre. New York: Seabury, 1976.

Scheff, T.J. "Audience Awareness and Catharsis in Drama." The Psychoanalytic Review 63, no. 4 (Winter 1976–1977): 529–54.

____. Catharsis in Healing, Ritual, and Drama. Berkeley: University of California Press, 1979.

____. Interview with author, September 19, 2001; October 31, 2001; and September 1, 2006.

Schutzman, Mady. "Activism, Therapy, or Nostalgia?" Drama Review 127 (Fall 1990): 77–87.

Schutzman, Mady, and Jan Cohen-Cruz, eds. Playing Boal: Theatre, Therapy, Activism. London: Routledge, 1994.

Scott, James C. Domination and the Arts of Resistance: Hidden Transcripts. New Haven: Yale University Press, 1990.

Sennett, Richard, and Jonathan Cobb. The Hidden Injuries of Class. New York: Knopf, 1972.

Shank, Theodore. American Alternative Theatre. New York: St. Martin's, 1988.

Shipow, Emanuel, "A Comparative Study of the Integration of Theatre and Drama into Education: Moscow, London, Los Angeles." Diss., UCLA, 1970.

Shulman, Harry Manual. Juvenile Delinquency in American Society. New York: Harper and Row, 1961.

Simon, Bonnie, and Michael Mullen. STOP-GAP: Final Research Report. Costa Mesa, CA: STOP-GAP, March 1993.

Simos, Jack. Social Growth through Play Production. New York: Association Press, 1957.

Singleton, Royce A., and Bruce Straits. Approaches to Social Research. Oxford: Oxford University Press, 1999.

Slade, Peter. Child Drama. New York: Philosophical Library, 1955.

____. Child Drama and Its Value in Education. Galloway Gazette Press (Kent, UK), 1965.

____. Experience of Spontaneity. London: Longmans, 1968.

Spencer, Russ. "The Rites of Rage." Salt Journal 1, no. 1 (November-December 1997): 16–21.

Spolin, Viola. Improvisation for the Theater. Evanston: Northwestern University Press, 1963.

Stake, Robert E. "The Countenance of Educational Evaluation." Teachers College Record 68, no. 7 (April 1968): 523–57.

Sternberg, Patricia. Theatre for Conflict Resolution: In the Classroom and Beyond. Portsmouth: Heinemann, 1998.

Stone, Anne, David McArthur, Sally Ann Law, and Joy Moini. The Arts and Prosocial Impact Study: An Examination of Best Practices. Santa Monica, CA: Rand, 1997.

____. The Arts and Prosocial Impact Study: Program Characteristics and Prosocial Effects. Los Angeles: Rand, 1998.

Szanto, George H. Theater & Propaganda. Austin: University of Texas Press, 1978.

Taylor, Karen Malpede. People's Theatre in Amerika. New York: Drama Book Specialists, 1972.

Taylor, Philip. The Drama Classroom: Action, Reflection, Transformation. London: Routledge, 2000.

____, ed. Researching Drama and Arts Education: Paradigms and Possibilities. London: Falmer Press, 1996.

Taylor, Ronald. Aesthetics and Politics. London: NLB, 1977.

Three Minutes from Broadway: The Story of the 52nd Street Project. Video. Directed by Lyn Greene. Derry, NH: Chip Taylor Communications, 1992.

Timberg, Patricia Cullen. "Theatre for at Risk Students." Teaching Theatre 4, no. 1, (1992): 11–15.

Turner, Victor W. From Ritual to Theatre: The Human Seriousness of Play. New York: Performing Arts Journal Publications, 1982.

Upward Bound Program, U.S. Department of Education website, www.ed.gov/programs/trioupbound

U.S. Department of Health and Human Services. Youth Violence: A Report of the Surgeon General. Rockville, MD: U.S. Department of Health and Human Services, 2001.

U.S. Department of Health and Human Services: Youth Violence: A Report of the Surgeon General—Executive Summary. Rockville, MD: U.S. Department of Health and Human Services, 2001.

Versenyi, Adam. Theatre in Latin America: Religion, Politics, and Culture from Cortes to the 1980s. Cambridge: Cambridge University Press, 1993.

Wagner, Betty. Dorothy Heathcote: Drama as a

Learning Medium. Washington, DC: National Education Association, 1976.

Way, Brian. *Development through Drama.* London: Longman, 1967.

Weaver, Anthony John. "An Experience of Educational Theatre in Community Development in Nicaragua." *Community Development Journal* 1, no. 5, (January 1970).

Weigler, Will. *Strategies for Playbuilding: Helping Groups Translate Issues into Theatre.* Portsmouth, NH: Heinemann, 2001.

Weinberg, Mark S. "Community Based Theatre: A Participatory Model for Social Transformation." *Theatre Symposium* 8 (2000): 22–33.

Weisman, Philip. *Creativity in the Theater: A Psychoanalytic Study.* New York: Basic, 1965.

Weitz, Judith Humphreys. *Coming Up Taller: Arts and Humanities Programs for Children and Youth at Risk.* Washington, DC: President's Committee on the Arts, April 1996.

Werner, Emmy E., and Ruth S. Smith. *Overcoming the Odds: High Risk Children from Birth to Adulthood.* Ithaca: Cornell University Press, 1992.

Wilhelm, Jeffrey D., and Brian Edmiston. *Imagining to Learn: Inquiry, Ethics, and Integration Though Drama.* Portsmouth, N.H.: Heinemann, 1998.

Willett, John, ed. *Brecht on Theatre: The Development of an Aesthetic.* New York: Hill and Wang, 1964.

_____. *The Theatre of Erwin Piscator: Half a Century of Politics in the Theatre.* New York: Holmes and Meier Publishers, 1979.

Williams, Jay. *Stage Left.* New York: Charles Scribner's Sons, 1974.

Williams, Loisetta. "Effectiveness of Family Life Education Through Teen Theatre." Master's thesis. San Diego: San Diego State University, 1989.

Wilmeth, Don B., and Tice L. Miller, eds. *Cambridge Guide to American Theatre.* New York: Cambridge University Press, 1993.

Wood, George H. *A Time to Learn: Creating Community in America's High Schools.* New York: Dutton, 1998.

Wypijewski, JoAnn. "The Wonder Years." *The Nation.* May 20, 2002, 24–29.

Zelizer, Viviana A. *Pricing the Priceless Child: The Changing Social Value of Children.* New York: Basic Books, Inc., 1985.

Zimbardo, Philip K. "The Stanford Prison Experiment." *Writing and Reading Across the Curriculum.* Laurence Behrens and Leonard Rosen, eds. New York: Addison Wesley, Longman, 2000, 363–376.

Zwerling, Philip. "Revolution in Nicaragua: An Eyewitness Report." Sermon delivered September 7, 1980 at the First Unitarian Church of Los Angeles.

_____, and Connie Martin. *Nicaragua: A New Kind of Revolution.* Westport, Connecticut: Lawrence Hill and Co., 1985.

Index

www.ingramcontent.com/pod-product-compliance
Lightning Source LLC
Chambersburg PA
CBHW020242290326
41929CB00045B/1526